Contents at a glance

THE IET LIBRARY
2 SAVOY PLACE
LONDON WC2R 0BL
UK

This book is due for return on or before the last date shown below.

Micr
App

Scot Hil
Ted Pat

T
2 SAVOY

35(
+44 (0)20 7344
SHELF 68
LOC KC

Gresswell Ltd., London, N.21   Cat. No. 1208

DG 02242/71

35096

Published with the authorization of Microsoft Corporation by:
O'Reilly Media, Inc.
1005 Gravenstein Highway North
Sebastopol, California 95472

Copyright © 2013 by Scot Hillier Technical Solutions, LLC and Ted Pattison Group, Inc.
All rights reserved. No part of the contents of this book may be reproduced or transmitted in any form or by any means without the written permission of the publisher.

ISBN: 978-0-7356-7498-1

1 2 3 4 5 6 7 8 9 LSI 8 7 6 5 4 3

Printed and bound in the United States of America.

Microsoft Press books are available through booksellers and distributors worldwide. If you need support related to this book, email Microsoft Press Book Support at *mspinput@microsoft.com*. Please tell us what you think of this book at *http://www.microsoft.com/learning/booksurvey.*

Microsoft and the trademarks listed at *http://www.microsoft.com/about/legal/en/us/IntellectualProperty/ Trademarks/EN-US.aspx* are trademarks of the Microsoft group of companies. All other marks are property of their respective owners.

The example companies, organizations, products, domain names, email addresses, logos, people, places, and events depicted herein are fictitious. No association with any real company, organization, product, domain name, email address, logo, person, place, or event is intended or should be inferred.

This book expresses the author's views and opinions. The information contained in this book is provided without any express, statutory, or implied warranties. Neither the authors, O'Reilly Media, Inc., Microsoft Corporation, nor its resellers, or distributors will be held liable for any damages caused or alleged to be caused either directly or indirectly by this book.

Acquisitions and Development Editor: Kenyon Brown

Production Editor: Rachel Steely

Editorial Production: Dianne Russell, Octal Publishing, Inc.

Technical Reviewer: Wayne Ewington

Copyeditor: Bob Russell, Octal Publishing, Inc.

Indexer: Bob Pfahler

Cover Design: Twist Creative

Cover Composition: Zyg Group, LLC

Illustrator: Rebecca Demarest

Contents

What do you think of this book? We want to hear from you!

Microsoft is interested in hearing your feedback so we can continually improve our
books and learning resources for you. To participate in a brief online survey, please visit:

microsoft.com/learning/booksurvey

Chapter 4   Developing SharePoint apps   137

What do you think of this book? We want to hear from you!

Microsoft is interested in hearing your feedback so we can continually improve our
books and learning resources for you. To participate in a brief online survey, please visit:

microsoft.com/learning/booksurvey

Introduction

With the release of SharePoint 2013, Microsoft has dramatically changed the rules for SharePoint developers. The introduction of the new app development model is intended to essentially eliminate the development of full-trust and sandboxed solutions for SharePoint. Although both of these solution types are still available in SharePoint 2013, the message from Microsoft is clear: all new SharePoint development should be done by using the app model.

We cover the reasons for this seismic shift in detail in Chapter 1, so we won't repeat them here. However, the SharePoint community will probably be left with many questions about the future even after understanding Microsoft's logic. Certainly, the most important questions revolve around whether organizations will actually accept the primacy of the app model. Most SharePoint installations are on-premises farms with significant investment in custom full-trust solutions. These solutions take the form of Web Parts, workflows, application pages, event handlers, and so on that perform significant custom processing. Clearly, organizations cannot abandon these investments overnight. On the other hand, no one can deny the momentum pressuring organizations to move more functionality into the cloud where the full-trust model simply does not work effectively.

For developers, the situation is both intriguing and concerning. Many SharePoint developers—the authors of this book included—have spent a decade mastering the intricacies of the full-trust model. Now, we find ourselves faced with the reality that a portion of this knowledge might be in jeopardy. Even though all the expertise surrounding SharePoint infrastructure, architecture, and declarative processing is still useful, the app model forbids the use of the server-side object model, which has been the "bread and butter" of SharePoint developers for more than ten years.

On the positive side, the app model opens up new and exciting possibilities for development. Cloud-based apps allow for scenarios that were difficult or impossible to create in previous versions of SharePoint. Developers now have client-side access to every major workload in SharePoint through the client-side object model and REST, which means that SharePoint 2013 fits perfectly into cloud-based and cross-platform development models. Additionally, SharePoint developers now have access to a marketplace to sell their applications to Microsoft Office 365 users.

Although this book can't answer all of the adoption questions the community will face, it can certainly help you to get started in app development. There are many new skills for you to learn including advanced JavaScript patterns, OAuth security, and cloud-based development models. If you are like the hundreds of Microsoft employees and partners we have already taught, you'll find yourself reacting with a mix of excitement, joy, denial, and frustration. We look forward to working through it with you and the rest of the SharePoint community.

Who this book is for

This book is written for experienced SharePoint developers who are proficient with Microsoft Visual Studio 2012, the Microsoft .NET 4.0 framework, and who understand the fundamentals of the Share-Point object model. The code samples in this book are written in JavaScript and C# and are intended to represent the spectrum of possible app solutions. The primary audience for the book is SharePoint architects and developers who are looking to master the new app model in SharePoint 2013.

Organization of this book

This book is organized into four chapters:

Chapter 1, "Introducing SharePoint apps," covers the new app model in detail. This chapter presents the historical context that justifies the app model and the fundamental development process.

Chapter 2, "Client-side programming," first provides a JavaScript and jQuery primer for SharePoint developers with an emphasis on professional patterns. The second half of the chapter presents the fundamentals of the client-side object model and REST APIs for SharePoint 2013.

Chapter 3, "App security," presents the security concepts necessary to successfully develop apps. This chapter explains the concept of the app principal and presents the details behind the OAuth security model.

Chapter 4, "Developing SharePoint apps," presents professional patterns for app development such as Model-View-ViewModel (MVVM) and Model-View-Controller (MVC). Within these patterns, the chapter shows the basics of creating apps with various workloads, such as search, Business Connectivity Services (BCS), and the social capabilities.

Prerelease software

To help you become familiar with SharePoint 2013 as early as possible, this book was written by using examples that work with SharePoint 2013 Preview. Consequently, the final version might include new features, and features discussed in this book might change or disappear altogether. You can refer to the "Capabilities and features in SharePoint 2013" topic on TechNet at *technet.microsoft.com/en-us/ sharepoint/fp142374.aspx* for the most up-to-date list of changes to the product. Be aware, however, that you might also notice some differences between the "Release to Manufacture" (RTM) version of the product and the descriptions and screen shots that are provided in this book.

 More Info You can find information about the Exchange Server 2013 Preview at *technet. microsoft.com/en-us/library/bb124558(v=exchg.150).aspx*. You can find more information about the Lync 2013 Preview at *lync.microsoft.com/en-us/Pages/Lync-2013-Preview.aspx*.

Code samples

You can download the companion code samples from the book 's catalog page at:

http://go.microsoft.com/FWLink/?Linkid=274914

Copy and unzip the files in the root of the C: drive. If you copy and unzip the files in another folder, you might get an error message because the total file paths are too long.

Support & feedback

The following sections provide information on errata, book support, feedback, and contact information.

Errata

We've made every effort to ensure the accuracy of this book and its companion content. Any errors that have been reported since this book was published are listed on our Microsoft Press site at oreilly. com:

http://go.microsoft.com/FWLink/?Linkid=274913

If you find an error that is not already listed, you can report it to us through the same page.

If you need additional support, send an email to Microsoft Press Book Support at *mspinput@ microsoft.com.*

Please note that product support for Microsoft software is not offered through the addresses above.

We want to hear from you

At Microsoft Press, your satisfaction is our top priority, and your feedback our most valuable asset. Please tell us what you think of this book at:

http://www.microsoft.com/learning/booksurvey

The survey is short, and we read every one of your comments and ideas. Thanks in advance for your input!

Stay in touch

Let's keep the conversation going! We're on Twitter: *http://twitter.com/MicrosoftPress.*

## CHAPTER 1

Introducing SharePoint apps

Let's begin with a bit of history so that you can understand why and how the Microsoft SharePoint app model came about. It was back with SharePoint 2007 that Microsoft first invested to transform SharePoint technologies into a true development platform by introducing features and farm solutions. With the release of SharePoint 2010, Microsoft extended the options available to developers by introducing sandboxed-solution deployment as an alternative to farm-solution deployment. With SharePoint 2013, Microsoft has now added a third option for SharePoint developer with the introduction of SharePoint apps.

When developing for SharePoint 2013, you must learn how to decide between using a farm solution, a sandboxed solution, or a SharePoint app. To make this decision in an informed manner, you must learn what's different about developing SharePoint apps. As you will see in this chapter, SharePoint app development has several important strengths and a few noteworthy constraints when compared to the "old school" approach of developing SharePoint solutions for SharePoint 2010.

As you begin to get your head around what the new SharePoint app model is all about, it's helpful to understand one of Microsoft's key motivations behind it. SharePoint 2007 and SharePoint 2010 have gained large-scale adoption worldwide and have generated billions of dollars in revenue primarily due to companies and organizations that have installed SharePoint on their own hardware in an *on-premises farm*. And, whereas previous versions of SharePoint have been very successful products with respect to all these on-premises farms, Microsoft's success and adoption rate in hosted environments such as Microsoft Office 365 have been far more modest.

The release of SharePoint 2013 represents a significant shift in Microsoft's strategy for evolving the product. Microsoft's focus is now concerned with improving how SharePoint works in the cloud, especially with Office 365. Microsoft's primary investment in SharePoint 2013 has been to add features and functionality that work equally well in the cloud as they do in on-premises farms.

Understanding the new SharePoint app model

The move from SharePoint solutions development to SharePoint app development represents a significant change in development technique and perspective. However, Microsoft is not making this change just for the sake of making a change; there are very valid technical reasons that warrant such a drastic shift in the future of the SharePoint development platform.

To fully understand Microsoft's motivation for beginning to transition away from SharePoint solutions to the new SharePoint app model, you must first understand the problems and pain points of SharePoint solutions development. Therefore, this section will begin by describing the limitations and constraints imposed by SharePoint solution development. After that, the discussion turns to the design goals and architecture of the new SharePoint app model and addresses how this architecture improves upon the limitations and constraints imposed by SharePoint solution development.

Understanding SharePoint solution challenges

The first problem with SharePoint solutions development is that most of the custom code written by developers runs within the SharePoint host environment. For example, managed code deployed in a farm solution runs within the main SharePoint worker process (*w3wp.exe*). Managed code deployed by using a sandboxed solution runs within the SharePoint sandboxed worker process (*SPUCWorkerProcess.exe*).

There are two primary reasons why Microsoft wants to get rid of custom code that runs within the SharePoint environment. The first reason has to do with increasing the stability of SharePoint farms. This one should be pretty obvious. Eliminating any type of custom code that runs within the SharePoint environment results in lower risk, fewer problems, and greater stability for the hosting farm.

The second reason has to do with the ability to upgrade an on-premises farm to newer versions of SharePoint. SharePoint solutions are often developed with full trust and perform complex operations. These solutions are often tightly bound to a particular feature set, which means that they might not move gracefully to the next version of SharePoint. Fearing a complete rewrite of dozens of solutions, many customers delay upgrading their SharePoint farms.

Microsoft has witnessed many of their biggest SharePoint customers postponing the upgrade of their production on-premises farms for months and sometimes years until they have had time to update their SharePoint solution code and test it against the new version of Microsoft.SharePoint.dll. Because this is a problem that negatively affects SharePoint sales revenue, you can bet it was pretty high on the priority list of problems to fix when Microsoft began to design SharePoint 2013.

Another significant problem with SharePoint solution development has to do with security and permissions. The root problem is that code always runs under the identity and with the permissions of a specific user. As an example, think about the common scenario in which a site administrator activates a feature from a SharePoint solution that has a feature receiver. There is a security issue in that a SharePoint solution with a feature receiver is able to execute code that can do anything that the site administrator can do. There really isn't a practical way to constrain the SharePoint solution code so that it runs with a lesser set of permissions than the user that has activated the feature.

Most SharePoint professionals are under the impression that code inside a sandboxed solution is constrained from being able to perform attacks. This is only partially true. The sandbox protects the farm and other site collections within the farm, but it does not really protect the content of the site collections in which a sandboxed solution is activated. For example, there isn't any type of enforcement to prohibit the feature activation code in a sandboxed solution from deleting every item and every document in the current site collection.

Another issue with sandboxed solutions is that there's no ability to perform impersonation. Therefore, custom code in a sandboxed solution always runs as the current user. This can be very limiting when the current user is a low-privileged user such as a contributor or a visitor. There is no way to elevate privileges so that your code can do more than the current user.

Farm solutions, on the other hand, allow for impersonation. This means a developer can elevate privileges so that farm solution code can perform actions even when the current user does not possess the required permissions. However, this simply replaces one problem with another.

A farm solution developer can call *SPSecurity.RunWithElevatedPrivileges*, which allows custom code to impersonate the all-powerful SHAREPOINT\SYSTEM account. When code runs under this identity, it executes with no security constraints whatsoever. The code can then essentially do whatever it wants on a farm-wide basis. This type of impersonation represents the Pandora's Box of the SharePoint development platform because a farm solution could perform an attack on any part of a farm in which it's deployed, and it must be trusted not to do so. As you can imagine, this can cause anxiety with SharePoint farm administrators who are much fonder of security enforcement than they are of trust.

In a nutshell, the security problems with SharePoint solutions stem from the fact that you cannot effectively configure permissions for a specific SharePoint solution. This limitation cannot be overcome, because the SharePoint solution development model provides no way to establish the identity of SharePoint solution code independent of user identity. Because there is no ability to establish the identity of code from a SharePoint solution, there is no way to configure permissions for it.

The last important pain point of SharePoint solution development centers around installation and upgrade. The installation of farm solutions is problematic because it requires a farm administrator, and it often requires restarting Internet Information Services (IIS) on all the front-end web servers, causing an interruption in service. Although the deployment of a SharePoint solution doesn't involve these problems, it raises other concerns. Business users often have trouble with the process of finding and uploading sandboxed solutions in order to activate them. Furthermore, a business user has very little to indicate whether or not to trust a sandboxed solution before activating it and giving its code access to all the content within the current site collection.

Of all the issues surrounding SharePoint solution development, nothing is more prone to error and less understood than the support for upgrading code from one version of a SharePoint solution to another. Even though Microsoft added support for feature upgrade and assembly version redirection in SharePoint 2010, almost no one is using it. The required steps and the underlying semantics of the feature upgrade process have proved to be too tricky for most developers to deal with. Furthermore, the vast majority of professional SharePoint developers have made the decision never to change the assembly version number of the assembly dynamic-link library (DLL) deployed with a SharePoint solution. That's because creating and managing the required assembly redirection entries across a growing set of *web.config* files is just too painful and error prone.

You have just read about the most significant pain points with respect to SharePoint solution development. Here is a summary of these points.

- Custom code running inside the SharePoint host environment poses risks and compromises scalability.

- Custom code with dependencies on in-process DLLs causes problems when migrating from one version of SharePoint to the next.

- A permissions model for custom code based entirely on the identity of the current user is inflexible.

- User impersonation solves the too-little-permissions problem but replaces it with the too-many-permissions problem, which is even worse.

- SharePoint solutions lack effective support and easily understood semantics for distribution, installation, and upgrade.

Understanding SharePoint app model design goals

The SharePoint app model was designed from the ground up to remedy the problems with Share-Point solutions that were discussed in the previous section. This means that the architecture of the SharePoint app model is very different from that of SharePoint solutions, which represent SharePoint's original development platform. This new architecture was built based on the following design goals.

- Apps must be supported in Office 365 and in on-premises farms.

- App code never runs within the SharePoint host environment.

- App code programs against SharePoint sites by using web service entry points to minimize version-specific dependencies.

- App code is authenticated and runs under a distinct identity.

- App permissions can be configured independently of user permissions.

- Apps are deployed by using a publishing scheme based on app catalogs.

- Apps that are published in a catalog are easier to discover, install, and upgrade.

You have now seen the design goals for the new SharePoint app model, and you understand the motivating factors behind them. This should provide you with greater insight and a better appreciation as to why Microsoft designed the SharePoint app model the way it did. Now, it's time to dive into the details of the SharePoint app model and its underlying architecture.

Understanding SharePoint app model architecture

Microsoft designed the SharePoint app model to work in the Office 365 environment as well as within on-premises farms. However, developing for Office 365 introduces a few important new concepts that will be unfamiliar to many experienced SharePoint developers. One of the new concepts that is essential to the development of SharePoint apps is a *SharePoint tenancy*.

A SharePoint tenancy is a set of site collections that are configured and administrated as a unit. When a new customer establishes an Office 365 account to host its SharePoint sites, the Office 365 environment creates a new tenancy. The customer's business users that access the tenancy are known (not surprisingly) as *tenants*.

When the Office 365 environment creates a new tenancy for a customer, it creates an administrative site collection which is accessible to users who have been configured to play the role of a *tenant administrator*. A tenant administrator can create additional site collections and configure the set of services that are available to all the sites running within the tenancy.

The concept of tenancies was first introduced in SharePoint 2010 to support hosting environments such as Office 365. Although the creation and use of tenancies is essential to the Office 365 environment, their use has not been widely adopted in on-premises farms. This is primarily due to the fact that SharePoint farm administrators can create site collections and configure the services available to users within the scope of a web application.

The architecture of the SharePoint app model requires that apps are always installed and run within the context of a specific tenancy. This can be a bit confusing for scenarios in which you want to install SharePoint apps in an on-premises farm that doesn't involve the explicit creation of tenancies. However, SharePoint 2013 is able to support installing and running SharePoint apps in on-premises farms by transparently creating a farm-wide tenancy behind the scenes that is known as the *default tenancy*.

Working with app service applications

SharePoint 2013 relies on two service applications to manage the environment that supports SharePoint apps. The first service application is the App Management Service, which is new to SharePoint 2013. The second service application is the Site Subscriptions Settings Service, which was introduced in SharePoint 2010. A high-level view of a SharePoint 2013 farm running these two service applications is shown in Figure 1-1.

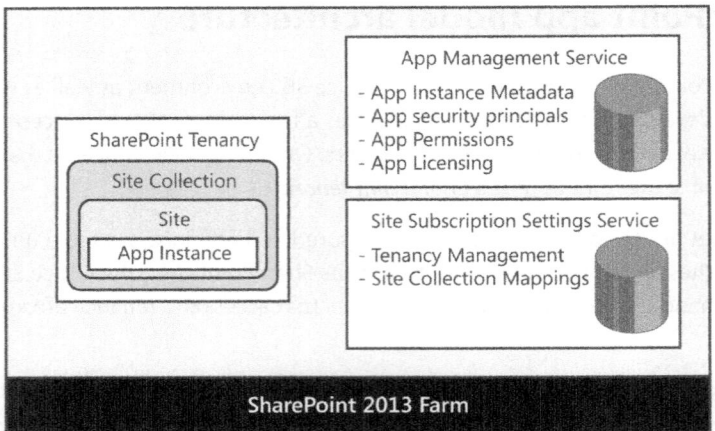

FIGURE 1-1 A SharePoint Farm that supports apps requires an instance of the App Management Service and the Site Subscription service to be running.

The App Management Service has its own database that is used to store the configuration details for apps as they are installed and configured. The App Management Service is also responsible for tracking other types of app-specific configuration data that deals with app security principals, app permissions, and app licensing.

The Site Subscription Settings Service takes on the responsibility of managing tenancies. Each time a new tenancy is created, this service adds configuration data for it in its own database. The Site Subscription Settings Service is particularly important to the SharePoint app model due to the requirement that SharePoint apps must always be installed and run within the context of a specific tenancy.

When you are working within the Office 365 environment, you never have to worry about creating or configuring these two service applications, because they are entirely managed behind the scenes. However, things are different when you want to configure support for SharePoint apps in an on-premises farm. In particular, you must explicitly create an instance of both the App Management Service and the Site Subscription Settings Service.

Creating an instance of App Management Service is easier because it can be done by hand via the Central Administration or by using the Farm Creation Wizard. Creating an instance of Site Subscription Settings Service is a bit trickier because it must be done by using Windows PowerShell. However, when you create an instance of the Site Subscription Settings Service by using Windows PowerShell, it automatically creates the default tenancy which then makes it possible to install SharePoint apps in sites throughout the farm.

Building an environment for SharePoint app development

If you plan on developing SharePoint apps that will be used within private networks such as a corporate LAN, it makes sense to build out a development environment with a local SharePoint 2013 farm. Critical Path Training provides a free download in PDF format called the *SharePoint Server 2013 Virtual Machine Setup Guide*, which provides you with step-by-step instructions to install all the software you need to create a development environment with a local SharePoint 2013 farm. You can download the guide from *http://criticalpathtraining.com/Members*.

Understanding app installation scopes

A SharePoint app must be installed before it can be made available to users. When you install a SharePoint app, you must install it within the context of a target web. Once the app has been installed, users can then launch the app and begin to use it. The site from which an app has been launched is known as the *host web*.

There are two different scopes in which you can install and configure a SharePoint app. The scenario that is easier to understand is when an app is installed at *site scope*. In this scenario, the app is installed and launched within the scope of the same SharePoint site. In this scenario, the host web will always be the same site where the app has been installed.

SharePoint apps can also be installed and configured at *tenancy scope*. In this scenario, an app is installed in a special type of SharePoint site known as an *app catalog site*. Once the app has been installed in an app catalog site, the app can then be configured so that users can launch it from other sites. In this scenario, the host web will not be the same site where the app has been installed.

The ability to install and configure apps at tenancy scope is especially valuable for scenarios in which a single app is going to be used by many different users across multiple sites within an Office 365 tenancy or an on-premises farm. A single administrative user can configure app permissions and manage licensing in one place, which prevents the need to install and configure the app on a site-by-site basis. The topic of installing apps will be revisited in greater detail at the end of this chapter.

This book discusses many different scenarios in which SharePoint apps behave the same way, regardless of whether they have been installed in an Office 365 tenancy or in an on-premises farm. Therefore, the book frequently uses the generic term *SharePoint host environment* when talking about scenarios that work the same across either environment.

Understanding app code isolation

When you develop a SharePoint app, you obviously need to write custom code to implement your business logic, and that code must run some place other than on the web servers in the hosting SharePoint farm. The SharePoint app model provides you with two places to run your custom code. First, a SharePoint app can contain client-side code that runs inside the browser on the user's computer. Second, a SharePoint app can contain server-side code that runs in an external website that is implemented and deployed as part of the app itself.

There are many different ways in which you can design and implement a SharePoint app. For example, you could create a SharePoint app that contains only client-side resources such as web pages and client-side JavaScript code that are served up by the SharePoint host environment. This type of app is known as a *SharePoint-hosted app* because it is contained entirely within the app web. You could write a SharePoint-hosted app that uses Microsoft Silverlight, Microsoft VBScript, Flash, or whatever client-side technology you prefer.

Now, imagine that you want to create a second SharePoint app in which you want to write server-side code in a language such as C#. This type of SharePoint app will require its own external website so that your server-side code has a place to execute outside of the SharePoint host environment. In SharePoint 2013 terminology, a SharePoint app with its own external website is known as a *cloud-hosted app*, and the external website is known as the *remote web*. The diagram in Figure 1-2 shows the key architectural difference between a SharePoint-hosted app and a cloud-hosted app.

From the diagram in Figure 1-2, you can see that both SharePoint-hosted apps and cloud-hosted apps have a start page that represents the app's primary entry point. With a SharePoint-hosted app, the app's start page is served up by the SharePoint host; however, with a cloud-hosted app, the start page is served up from the remote web. Therefore, the SharePoint host environment must track the remote web URL for each cloud-hosted app that has been installed so that it can redirect users to the app's start page.

There is infrastructure in the SharePoint host environment that creates a client-side JavaScript component known as an *app launcher* that is used to redirect the user from a page served up by the SharePoint host environment over to the remote web.

When you decide to develop a cloud-hosted SharePoint app, you must often take on the responsibility of hosting the app's remote web. However, this responsibility of creating and deploying a remote web along with a SharePoint app also comes with a degree of flexibility. You can implement the remote web associated with a SharePoint app by using any existing web-based development platform.

For example, the remote web for a cloud-hosted SharePoint app could be implemented by using a non-Microsoft platform such as Java, LAMP, or PHP. However, the easiest and the most common approach for SharePoint developers is to design and implement the remote web for cloud-hosted apps by using ASP.NET web forms or MVC4. Chapter 4, "Developing SharePoint Apps," discusses several patterns that use these technologies.

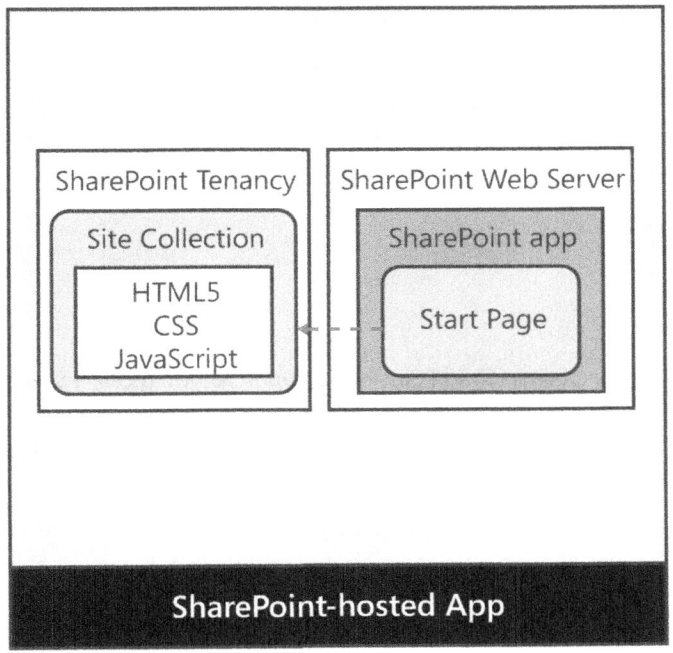

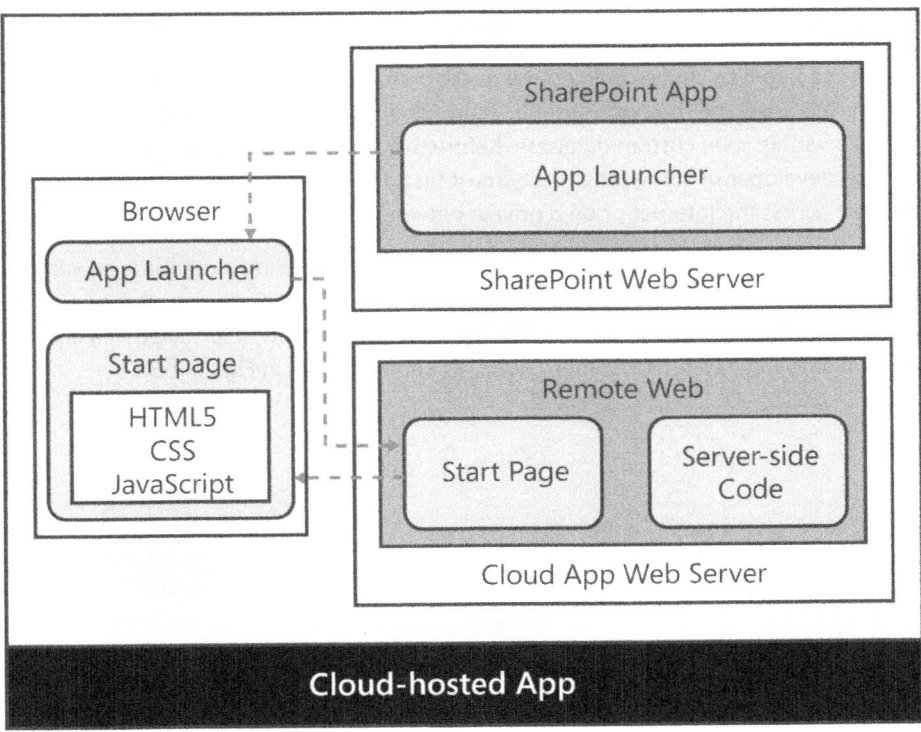

FIGURE 1-2 A cloud-hosted app differs from a SharePoint-hosted app in that it has an associated remote web, which must be deployed on a separate infrastructure from the SharePoint farm.

Understanding app hosting models

Thus far, this chapter has discussed how a SharePoint app can be categorized as either a SharePoint-hosted app or a cloud-hosted app. However, the SharePoint app model actually defines three app hosting models, not just two. Any time you create a new SharePoint app project in Microsoft Visual Studio 2012 you must pick from one of the following three app hosting models.

- SharePoint-hosted
- Provider-hosted
- Autohosted

This chapter has already explained SharePoint-hosted apps. As you recall, a SharePoint-hosted app is simply an app that adds its start page and all its other resources into the SharePoint host environment during installation. Now, it's time to explain the differences between the other two app hosting models.

A provider-hosted app and an autohosted app are just two variations of the hosting model for a cloud-hosted app. Both types of apps have an associated remote web that is capable of hosting the app's start page and any other resources the app requires. Furthermore, both provider-hosted apps and autohosted apps can and often will host their own custom databases to store app-specific data. The difference between these two different app hosting models involves how the remote web and its associated database are created when an app is deployed and installed.

It makes sense to begin by first examining the hosting model for a provider-hosted app. Imagine a scenario in which a developer has just finished testing and debugging a provider-hosted app that has a remote web with its own custom database. Before the app can be installed in a SharePoint host environment, the developer or some other party must first deploy the website for the remote web to make it accessible across the Internet or on a private network.

The custom database used by the remote web must also be created on a database server and made accessible to the remote web as part of the deployment process. Once the remote web and its custom database are up and running, the provider-hosted app can then be installed in a SharePoint tenancy and made available to the customer's users, as demonstrated in Figure 1-3.

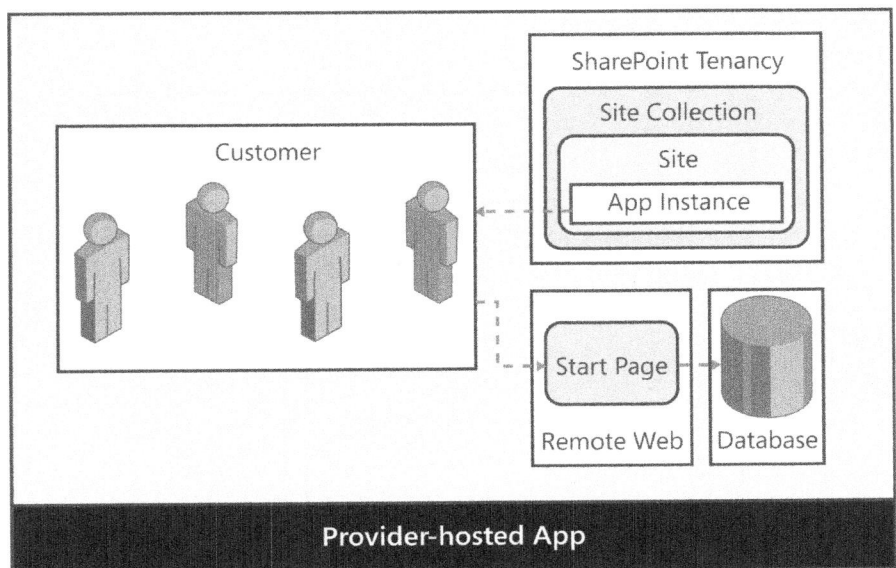

FIGURE 1-3 Provider-hosted apps are deployed in their own infrastructure including any required databases.

Once a provider-hosted app has been deployed, the company that developed the app usually assumes the responsibility for its ongoing maintenance. For example, if a company develops a provider-hosted app and deploys its remote web on one or more of its local web servers, it must ensure that those web servers remain healthy and accessible. If it deploys the remote app for its provider-hosted in a hosting environment such as Windows Azure, it must pay a monthly fee for the hosting services. Furthermore, it will be responsible for backing up the app's database and then restoring it if data becomes lost or corrupt.

Keep in mind that a provider-hosted app can be installed in more than one SharePoint site. Furthermore, a provider-hosted app can be installed in many different SharePoint sites that span across multiple customers and multiple SharePoint host environments. This is a common scenario which is known as *multi-tenancy*. What is critical to acknowledge is that multi-tenancy introduces several noteworthy design issues and deployment concerns. Let's look at an example.

Think about a scenario involving multi-tenancy in which a provider-hosted app has been installed by many different customers and the number of users is continually growing larger. All these users will be accessing the same remote web through a single entry point, which is the app's start page, as shown in Figure 1-4.

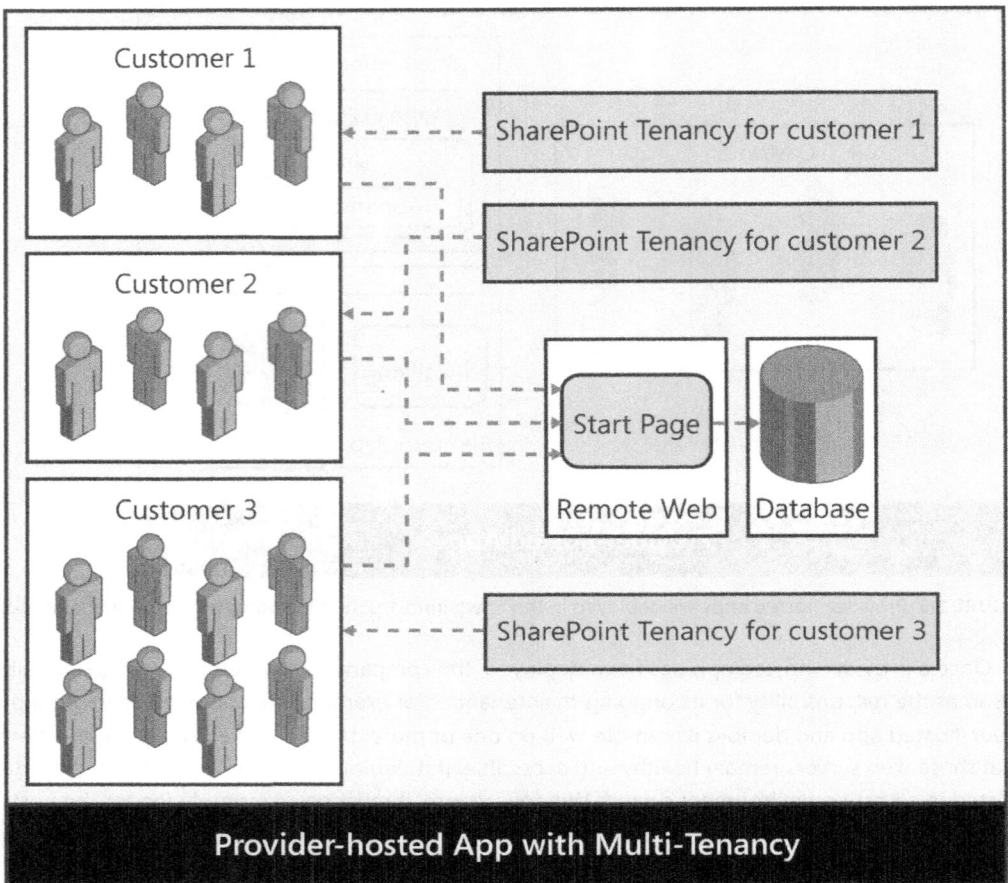

FIGURE 1-4 A provider-hosted app in a multi-tenant environment must be designed to scale and to isolate data on a customer-by-customer basis.

As you can imagine, a provider-hosted app in this type of multitenant scenario must have a way to scale up as the number of users increases. Furthermore, this type of app should generally be designed to isolate the data for each customer to keep it separate from the data belonging to other customers—you would never want one customer accessing another customer's data. Depending on the customers' industry, there could even be government regulations or privacy concerns that prevent the app from storing data for different customers within the same set of tables or even within the same database.

The important takeaway is that multi-tenancy introduces complexity. The development of a provider-hosted app that will be used in a multi-tenant scenario typically requires a design that isolates data on a customer-by-customer basis. As you can imagine, this increases both the time and the cost associated with developing a provider-hosted app.

Now that you have seen some of the inherit design issues that arise due to multi-tenancy, you will be able to more fully appreciate the benefits of the hosting model for autohosted apps. Autohosted apps offer value because they prevent the developer from having to worry about many of the issues involved with app deployment, scalability, and data isolation.

The first thing to understand about autohosted apps is that they are only supported in the Office 365 environment. Although this constraint might change in future releases, with SharePoint 2013 you cannot install an autohosted app in an on-premises farm. The reason for this is that the hosting model for autohosted apps is based on a private infrastructure that integrates the Office 365 environment with Windows Azure and its ability to provision websites and databases on demand.

The central idea behind the hosting model for autohosted apps is that the Office 365 environment can deploy the remote web on demand when an app is installed. You can also configure an autohosted app so that it creates its own private database during app installation. Once again, the Office 365 environment and its integration with Windows Azure is able to create a SQL Azure database on demand and then make it accessible to the remote web.

Autohosted apps offer value over provider-hosted apps because the Office 365 environment transparently handles the deployment of the remote web and potentially the creation of a custom database, as well. Autohosted apps also transfer the ongoing cost of ownership of the remote web and its database from the developer over to the customer who owns the Office 365 tenancy where the app has been installed. Therefore, the app developer doesn't have to worry about babysitting web servers, backing up databases, or coming up with a strategy scaling up the remote web as the number of users increases.

The benefits of an autohosted app over a provider-hosted app also extend into app design, which can serve to lower development costs. That's because each customer receives its own private database whenever installing an autohosted app, as illustrated in Figure 1-5. The benefit is that the developer isn't required to add complexity to the app's design and implementation to provide isolation because each customer's data is isolated automatically.

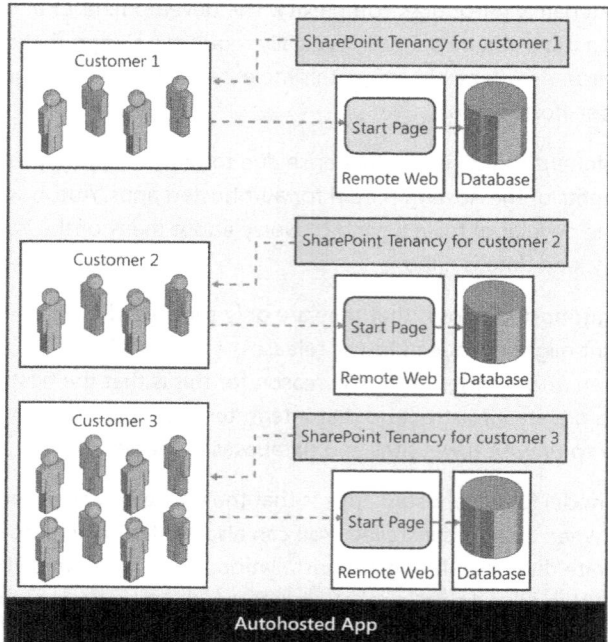

FIGURE 1-5 An autohosted app creates the required remote web and any databases automatically during deployment.

Reviewing the app manifest

Every SharePoint app requires an XML file called *AppManifest.xml*, which is known as the *app manifest*. The app manifest contains essential metadata for the app that is read and tracked by the SharePoint host environment when an app is installed. Listing 1-1 presents a simple example of what the app manifest looks like for a SharePoint-hosted app.

LISTING 1-1 An app manifest

```
<App xmlns=http://schemas.microsoft.com/sharepoint/2012/app/manifest
    Name="MySharePointApp"
    ProductID="{b93e8f64-4d14-4c72-be47-3b89f7f5fdf6}"
    Version="1.0.0.0"
    SharePointMinVersion="15.0.0.0" >

  <Properties>
    <Title>My SharePoint App</Title>
    <StartPage>~appWebUrl/Pages/Default.aspx?{StandardTokens}</StartPage>
  </Properties>
```

```
    <AppPrincipal>
      <Internal />
    </AppPrincipal>

  </App>
```

The app manifest contains a top-level <App> element which requires a set of attributes such as *Name*, *ProductID*, and *Version*. Within the <App> element there is an inner <Properties> element that contains important child elements such as <Title> and <StartPage>. The <Title> element contains human-readable text that is displayed to the user in the app launcher. The <StartPage> element contains the URL that the SharePoint host environment uses in the app launcher to redirect the user to the app's start page.

Listing 1-1 shows the minimal amount of metadata required in an app manifest; however, the app manifest for most real-world apps will contain a good deal more. The app manifest often contains addition metadata to configure other essential aspects of an app, such as app-level events, authentication, permissions, and the SharePoint services that an app requires from the SharePoint host environment. Table 1-1 lists the most common elements you might be required to add to an app manifest.

TABLE 1-1 The elements used in the App Manifest file

Element	Purpose
Name	Creates the URL to the app web.
ProductID	Identifies the app.
Version	Indicates the specific version of the app.
SharePointMinVersion	Indicates the version of SharePoint.
Properties\Title	Provides text for the app launcher.
Properties\StartPage	Redirects the user to the app's start page.
Properties\SupportedLanguages	Indicates which languages are supported.
Properties\WebTemplate	Supplies a custom site template for the app web.
Properties\InstalledEventEndpoint	Executes custom code during installation.
Properties\UpgradedEventEndpoint	Executes custom code during upgrade.
Properties\UninstallingEventEndpoint	Executes custom code during uninstallation.
AppPrincipal\Internal	Indicates there is no need for external authentication. This is what is always used for SharePoint-hosted apps.
AppPrincipal\RemoteWebApplication	Indicates that the app is provider-hosted and requires external authentication.

Element	Purpose
AppPrincipal\AutoDeployedWebApplication	Indicates that the app is autohosted and requires external authentication.
AppPermissionRequests\AppPermissionRequest	Add permission requests that must be granted during app installation
AppPrerequisites\AppPrerequisite	Indicates what SharePoint services must be enabled in the SharePoint host environment for the app to work properly.
RemoteEndpoints\RemoteEndpoint	Configures allowable domains for cross-domain calls using the web proxy.

Using the app manifest designer in Visual Studio 2012

When you are working with the app manifest in a SharePoint app project, Visual Studio 2012 provides the visual designer shown in Figure 1-6. This visual designer eliminates the need to edit the XML in the *AppManifest.xml* file by hand. The designer provides drop-down lists that makes editing more convenient and adds a valuable degree of validation as you are selecting the app start page or configuring permission requests, feature prerequisites, and capability perquisites.

Although you should take advantage of the visual designer whenever you can to edit the app manifest, it is important to understand that it cannot make certain types of modifications that you might require. Therefore, you should also become accustomed to opening the *AppManifest.xml* file in code view and making changes to the XML within by hand. Fortunately, in times when you need to manually edit the *AppManifest.xml* file, Visual Studio 2012 is able to provide IntelliSense, based on the XML schema behind the app manifest.

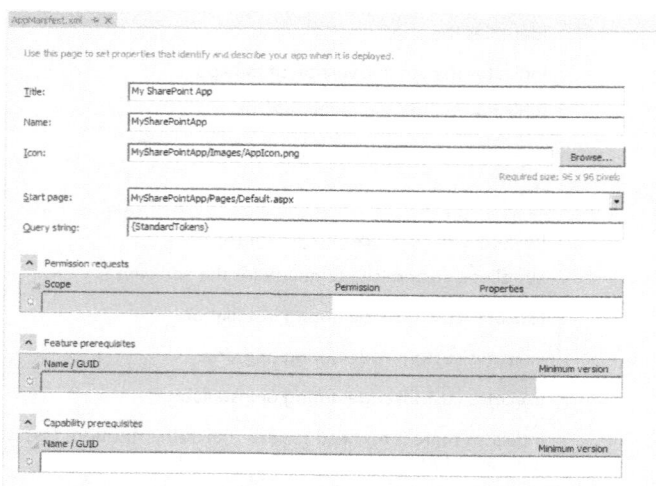

FIGURE 1-6 Visual Studio 2012 provides a visual editor to edit the app manifest.

Setting the start page URL

Every app has a start page whose URL must be configured by using the <StartPage> element within the app manifest. The SharePoint host environment uses this URL when creating app launchers that redirect the user to the app's start page. For a SharePoint-hosted app, the start page must be located in a child site known as the app web that will be discussed in more detail later in this chapter. For a cloud-hosted app, the start page will usually be located in the remote web.

When you are configuring the URL within the <StartPage> element for a SharePoint-hosted app you must use a dynamic token named ~appWebUrl, as demonstrated in the following:

```
~appWebUrl/Pages/Default.aspx
```

This use of the ~appWebUrl token is required because the actual URL to the app's start page will not be known until the app has been installed. The SharePoint host environment is able to recognize the ~appWebUrl token during app installation and it replaces it with the absolute URL to the app web.

In the case of a provider-hosted app whose start page exists within the remote web, the <StartPage> element can be configured with the actual URL that is used to access the start page where the remote web has been deployed, such as in the following:

```
https://RemoteWebServer.wingtip.com/MyAppsRemoteWeb/Pages/Default.aspx
```

When you are debugging provider-hosted apps and autohosted apps, you can use a convenient dynamic token named ~remoteAppUrl that eliminates the need to hardcode the path to the remote web during the development phase. For example, you can configure the <StartPage> element with the following value:

```
~remoteAppUrl/Pages/Default.aspx
```

The reason this works during debugging is due to some extra support in Visual Studio 2012. When you create a new SharePoint app project and select the option for a provider-hosted app or an autohosted app, Visual Studio 2012 automatically creates a second project for the remote web that is configured as the *Web Project*. Whenever you debug the Visual Studio solution containing these two projects, Visual Studio 2012 performs a substitution to replace ~remoteAppUrl with the current URL of the Web Project. After the substitution, the app manifest contains a start page URL that looks like this:

```
https://localhost:44300/Pages/Default.aspx
```

The key point is that Visual Studio 2012 replaces the ~remoteAppUrl token during a debugging session before the app manifest is installed into the SharePoint host environment. This provides you with a convenience in the debugging phase of a SharePoint app project.

Now, think about what happens after you have finished testing and debugging an app and its remote web. Visual Studio 2012 provides a *Publish* command with which you can build a final version of the *AppManifest.xml* file that will be distributed along with your app. In this case, what will Visual Studio 2012 do with the ~remoteAppUrl token? The answer is different depending on whether the app is an autohosted app or a provider-hosted app.

When you use the *Publish* command with an autohosted app, Visual Studio 2012 builds a final version of the *AppManifest.xml* in which the *~remoteAppUrl* token remains within the <StartPage> element. This is done because the actual URL to the remote web of an autohosted app will not be known until the app installation process has started and the Office 365 environment has created the remote web. You can see that the *~remoteAppUrl* token is replaced by Visual Studio 2012 in some scenarios and by the Office 365 environment in other scenarios.

When you use the *Publish* command with a provider-hosted app, the final version of the *AppManifest.xml* cannot contain the *~remoteAppUrl* token. You must know the URL to the remote web ahead of time. Therefore, when it is used with a provider-hosted app, the *Publish* command prompts you for several pieces of information including the actual URL where the remote web will be deployed.

When creating the URL for the <StartPage> element, it is a standard practice to include a query string that contains another dynamic token named *{StandardTokens}*, as demonstrated in the following example:

```
~remoteAppUrl/Pages/Default.aspx?{StandardTokens}
```

The *{StandardTokens}* token is never replaced by Visual Studio 2012. Instead, this dynamic token remains inside the final version of the app manifest that is installed in the SharePoint host environment. The SharePoint host environment performs a substitution on *{StandardTokens}* token whenever it creates the URL for an app launcher. This substitution involves replacing the *{StandardTokens}* token with a standard set of query string parameters that are frequently used in SharePoint app development such as the *SPHostUrl* parameter and the *SPLangauge* parameter, as shown in the following:

```
default.aspx?SPHostUrl=http%3A%2F%2Fwingtipserver&SPLanguage=en%2DUS
```

When you implement the code behind the start page of a SharePoint app, you can generally expect that the page will be passed the two query string parameters named *SPLanguage* and *SPHostUrl*, which are used to determine the language in use and the URL that points back to the host web. In some scenarios, the SharePoint host environment will add additional query string parameters.

Understanding the app web

Each time you install a SharePoint app, you must install it on a specific target site. A SharePoint app has the ability to add its own files to the SharePoint host environment during installation. For example, a SharePoint-hosted app must add a start page and will typically add other resources, as well, such as a CSS file and a JavaScript file to implement the app's user experience. The SharePoint host environment stores these files in the standard fashion by adding them to the content database associated with the site in which the app is being installed.

Beyond adding basic files such as a start page and a JavaScript file, a SharePoint app also has the ability to create other SharePoint-specific site elements in the SharePoint host during installation such as lists and document libraries. Let's look at an example.

Imagine that you want to create a simple SharePoint app to manage customers. During installation, the app can be designed to create a customer list using the standard Contacts list type along with a set of pages designed to provide a snazzy user experience for adding and finding customers. Your app could additionally be designed to create a document library upon installation so that the app can store customer contracts as Microsoft Word documents, whereby each Word document would reference a specific customer item in the customers list.

So, where does the SharePoint host environment store the content added by an app during installation? The answer is inside a special child site that the SharePoint host environment creates under the site where the app has been installed. This child site is known as the *app web*.

The app web is an essential part of the SharePoint app model because it represents the isolated storage that is owned by an installed instance of a SharePoint app. The app web provides a scope for the app's private implementation details. Note that an app by default has full permissions to read and write content within its own app web. However, SharePoint app has no other default permissions to access content from any other location in the SharePoint host environment. The app web is the only place where an app can access content without requesting permissions that then must be granted by a user.

There is a valuable aspect of the SharePoint app model that deals with uninstalling an app and ensuring that all the app-specific storage is deleted automatically. In particular, the SharePoint host environment will automatically delete the app web for an app whenever the app is uninstalled. This provides a set of cleanup semantics for SharePoint apps that is entirely missing from the development model for SharePoint solutions; when an app is uninstalled, it doesn't leave a bunch of junk behind.

Understanding the app web-hosting domain

Now, it's time to focus on the start page for a SharePoint-hosted app. As you have seen, the start page for a SharePoint-hosted app is added to the app web during installation. Consider a scenario in which you have installed a SharePoint app with the name of MyFirstApp in a SharePoint team site, which is accessible through the following URL:

```
https://intranet.wingtip.com.
```

During app installation, the SharePoint host environment creates the app web as a child site under the site where the app is being installed. The SharePoint host environment creates a relative URL for the app web based on the app's *Name* property. Therefore, in this example, the app web is created with a relative path of *MyFirstApp*. If the app's start page named default.aspx is located in the app web within the Pages folder, the relative path to the start page is MyFirstApp/Pages/default.aspx. Your intuition might tell you that the app's start page will be accessible through a URL that combines the URL of the host web together with the relative path to the app's start page, as in the following:

```
https://intranet.wingtip.com/MyFirstApp/Pages/default.aspx
```

However, this is not the case. The SharePoint host environment does not make the app web or any of its pages accessible through the same domain as the host web that is used to launch the app. Instead, the SharePoint host environment creates a new unique domain on the fly each time it creates a new app web as part of the app installation process. By doing so, the SharePoint host environment can isolate all the pages from an app web in its own private domain. The start page for a SharePoint-hosted app is made accessible through a URL that looks like this:

```
https://wingtiptenant-ee060af276f95a.apps.wingtip.com/MyFirstApp/Pages/Default.aspx
```

At this point, it should be clear why you are required to configure the <StartPage> element for a SharePoint-hosted app by using the ~appWebUrl token. The URL to the app web is not known until the SharePoint host environment creates the new domain for the app web during installation. After creating the domain for an app web, the SharePoint host environment can replace the ~appWebUrl token with an actual URL.

Let's examine the URL that is used to access the app web in greater detail. Consider the following URL, which is used to access an app web in an on-premises farm:

```
wingtiptenant-ee060af276f95a.apps.wingtip.com/MyFirstApp
```

The first part of the app web URL (wingtiptenant) is based on the name of the tenancy where the app has been installed. This value is configurable in an on-premises farm. In the Office 365 environment, the tenancy name is established when the customer creates a new account, and it cannot be changed afterward.

The second part of the app web URL (ee060af276f95a) is known as an APPUID. This is a unique 14-character identifier created by the SharePoint host environment when the app is installed. Remember that the APPUID is really an identifier for an installed instance of an app, as opposed to an identifier for the app itself.

The third part of the app web URL (apps.wingtip.com) is the app web hosting domain. You have the ability to configure this in an on-premises farm to whatever value you would like. Just ensure that you have also configured the proper DNS setting for this domain so that it resolves to an IP address pointing to the web server(s) of your on-premises farms. In Office 365 the app web-hosting domain is always sharepoint.com.

Now, ask yourself this fundamental question: why doesn't the SharePoint host environment serve up pages from the app web by using the same domain as the host web from which the app has been launched? The reasons why the SharePoint host environment serves up pages from the app web in their own isolated domain might not be obvious. There are two primary reasons why the SharePoint app model does this. Both of these reasons are related to security and the enforcement of permissions granted to an app.

The first reason for isolating an app web in its own private domain has to do with preventing direct JavaScript calls from pages in the app web back to the host web. This security protection of the SharePoint app model builds on the browser's built-in support for prohibiting cross-site scripting (XSS). Because JavaScript code running on pages from an app web originates from a different domain, this code cannot directly call back to the host web. More specifically, calls from JavaScript running on app web pages do not run with the same established user identity as JavaScript code-behind pages in the host web. Therefore, the JavaScript code running on app web pages doesn't automatically receive the same set of permissions as JavaScript code running on pages from the host web.

The second reason for creating an isolated domain for each app web has to do with processing of JavaScript callbacks that occur on the web server of the SharePoint host environment. Because the SharePoint host environment creates a new unique domain for each app web, it can determine exactly which app is calling when it sees a JavaScript callback originating from a page in an app web.

The key point is that the SharePoint host environment is able to use an internal mechanism to authenticate an app that uses JavaScript callbacks originating from its app web. As a result, the SharePoint host environment can enforce a security policy based on the permissions that have been granted to the app.

Remember that a SharePoint app has a default set of permissions by which it can access its app web but has no other permissions by default to access any other site. The ability of the SharePoint host environment to authenticate an app by inspecting the URL of incoming calls originating from the app web hosting domain is essential to enforcing this default permissions scheme.

Working with app user-interface entry points

Every SharePoint app requires a start page. As you know, the URL to the start pages is used within an app launcher to redirect the user from the host web to the start page. This type of entry into the user interface of the app is known as a *full immersion experience* because the app takes over the user interface of the browser with a full-page view.

The user interface guidelines of SharePoint app development require the app start page to provide a link back to the host web. This requirement exists so that a user can always return to the host web from which the app has been launched. When you are developing a SharePoint-hosted app, there is a standard master page used in app webs named *app.master* that automatically adds the required link back to the host web for you.

When developing a cloud-based app with the start page in the remote web, you cannot rely on a SharePoint master page to automatically provide the link on the start page which redirects the user back to the host web. Instead, you must use a technique that involves reading the *SPHostUrl* parameter which is passed to the start page in the query string. This is one of the key reasons why you always want to follow the practice of adding the *{StandardTokens}* token to the start page URL of a cloud-hosted app.

There are several different techniques that you can use in the code behind a start page in the remote web to read the *SPHostUrl* parameter value from the query string and use it to configure the required link back to the host web. For example, you can accomplish this task with server-side C# code or with client-side JavaScript code. In Chapter 4, you can see how to accomplish this task by using a client-side JavaScript component known as the chrome control.

In addition to the required start page, a SharePoint app can optionally provide two other types of entry points known as *app parts* and *UI custom actions*. Unlike the start page, you use app parts and UI custom actions to extend the user interface of the host web.

Building app parts

An app part is a user interface element that is surfaced on pages in the host web by using an IFrame. Once an app with an app part has been installed, a user can then add an app part to pages in the host web by using the same user interface experience that is used to add standard web parts.

You implement an app part in Visual Studio 2012 by using a *client web part*. This makes most developers ask, "What's the different between an app part and a client web part?" The best way to think about this is that the term "app part" is meant for SharePoint users, whereas the term "client web part" is used by developers to describe the implementation of an app part.

Despite having similar names, client web parts are very different from the standard web parts that are familiar to most SharePoint developers. In particular, a client web part cannot have any server-side code that runs within the SharePoint host environment. The implementation of a client web part must follow the rules of SharePoint app development.

Client web parts are supported under each of the three app hosting models. You implement a client web part in a SharePoint-hosted app by using HTML, CSS, and JavaScript. In a cloud-hosted app, you also have the option of implementing the behavior for a client web part by using server-side code in the remote web.

At first, many developers assume that a client web part is nothing more than an IFrame wrapper around an external web page. However, the client web part provides significant value beyond that. When you configure the URL within a client web part, you can use the same tokens as with the start page, such as *~appWebUrl*, *~remoteAppUrl*, and *{StandardTokens}*. Client web parts also support adding custom properties, as well. Furthermore, the page behind a client web part is often passed contextual security information that allows it to call back into the SharePoint host environment with an established app identity. You can think of the client web part as an IFrame on steroids.

When you want to add a new client web part to a SharePoint app project, you use the Add New Item command. The Add New Item dialog box in Visual Studio 2012 provides a Client Web Part item template, as shown in Figure 1-7.

When you add a new project item for a client web part, Visual Studio 2012 adds an elements. xml file to the SharePoint app project that contains a *ClientWebPart* element. The following code is a simple example of the XML definition for a client web part in a SharePoint-hosted app project that is implemented by using a page inside the app web:

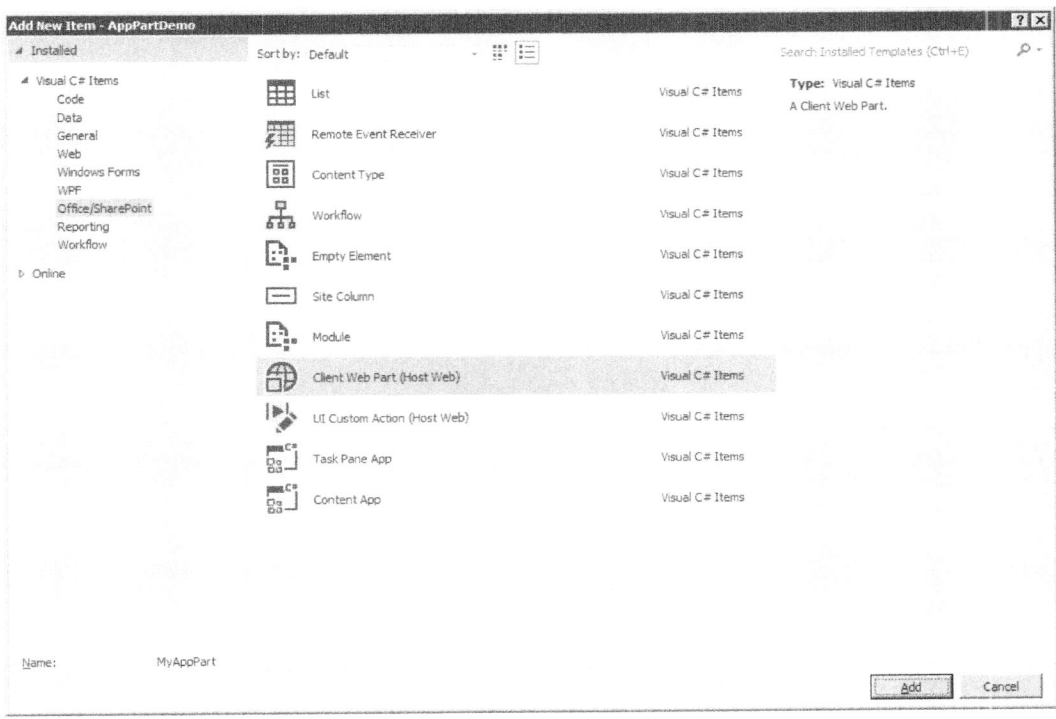

FIGURE 1-7 The Add New Item dialog provides templates for adding client web parts and UI custom actions to app projects.

```
<ClientWebPart Name="MyAppPart" Title="My App Part" Description="My description"
              DefaultWidth="300" DefaultHeight="200" >

  <Content Type="html" Src="~appWebUrl/Pages/AppPart1.aspx" />

</ClientWebPart>
```

As you can see from this example, the content displayed in a client web part is configured by assigning a URL to the *Src* attribute of the <Content> element. The web page that is referenced by this URL is usually added to either the app web or to the remote web. However, you can even reference a web page on the Internet that is neither in an app web nor in a remote web. The only important restriction is that the web page cannot be returned with the *X-Frame-Options* header in the HTTP response. This is a header used by some websites to prevent its pages from being used inside an IFrame with a type of attack known as *clickjacking*.

Here is something that can catch you off guard when creating a client web part in a SharePoint-hosted app: the default behavior of SharePoint 2013 is to add the *X-Frame-Options* header with a value of *SAMEORIGIN* in the HTTP response when it serves up pages from a SharePoint site. The result of this is that a page served up from the app web will not work when you attempt to use it as the page behind a client web part. The way to deal with this problem is to add the following directive to the top of any page in the app web referenced by a client web part to suppress the default behavior of adding the *X-Frame-Options* header:

```
<WebPartPages:AllowFraming ID="AllowFraming" runat="server" />
```

When you develop client web parts, you can add custom properties. The real value of custom properties is that they can be tailored by the user in the browser in the same fashion as a user customizes the properties of standard web parts. You define a custom property by adding a <Properties> element into the <ClientWebPart> element and then adding a <Property> element within that, as illustrated in Listing 1-2.

LISTING 1-2 Client Web Part properties

```
<Properties>
  <Property
    Name="MyProperty"
    Type="string"
    WebBrowsable="true"
    WebDisplayName="My Custom Property"
    WebDescription="Insightful property description"
    WebCategory="Custom Properties"
    DefaultValue="Some default value"
    RequiresDesignerPermission="true" />
</Properties>
```

Once you have added a custom property, you must then modify the query string at the end of the URL that is assigned to the *Src* attribute in the <Content> element. You do this by adding a query string parameter and assigning a value based on a pattern by which the property name is given an underscore before it and after it. Thus, for a property named *MyProperty*, you should create a query string parameter and assign it a value of *_MyProperty_*. This would result in XML within the <Content> element that looks like the following:

```
<Content
  Type="html"
  Src="~appWebUrl/Pages/AppPart1.aspx?MyPropertyParameter=_MyProperty_"
/>
```

Note that you can use any name you want for the query string parameter itself. It's when you assign a value to the parameter that you have to use actual property name and follow the pattern of adding the underscores both before and after.

Building UI custom actions

A UI custom action is a developer extension in the SharePoint app model with which you can add custom commands to the host site. The command for a UI custom action is surfaced in the user interface of the host site by using either a button on the ribbon or a menu command in the menu associated with items in a list or documents in a document library that is known as the Edit Control Block (ECB) menu. It is the act of installing an app with UI custom actions that automatically extends the user interface of the host site with ribbon buttons and ECB menu commands.

As in the case of the client web part, UI custom actions are supported in each of the three app hosting models. However, a UI custom action is different than the client web part because its purpose is not to display content in the host web. Instead, it provides an executable command for business users with which they can display a page supplied by the app. The page that is referenced by a UI custom action can be in either the app web or the remote web.

As a developer, you have control over what is passed in the query string for a UI custom action. This makes it possible to pass contextual information about the item or the document on which the command was executed. This in turn makes it possible for code inside the app to discover information such as the URL that can be used to access the item or document by using either the Client-Side Object Model (CSOM) or the new Representational State Transfer (REST) API, which is discussed in Chapter 2, "Client-Side Programming."

Keep in mind that an app will require additional permissions beyond the default permission set in order to access content in the host web. This topic is discussed in Chapter 3, "SharePoint App Security." This current chapter will only discuss how to create a UI custom action that passes contextual information to a page supplied by the app. Chapter 3 also covers what's required to actually use this information to call back into the SharePoint host environment.

In the dialog box shown earlier in Figure 1-6, you can see that Visual Studio 2012 provides a project item template named UI Custom Action. When you use this item template to create a new UI custom action, Visual Studio 2012 adds a new *elements.xml* file to your SharePoint app project. When you look inside the *elements.xml* file you find a <CustomAction> element that you can modify to define either an ECB menu item or a button on the ribbon.

Many SharePoint developers already have experience working with custom actions in SharePoint 2007 and SharePoint 2010. The good news is that the manner in which you edit the XML within the <CustomAction> element for a SharePoint app project works the same way as it does for a SharePoint solution project. The bad news is that many of the custom actions available when developing farm solutions are not available when developing a SharePoint app.

In particular, a SharePoint app only allows for UI custom actions that create ECB menu commands and ribbon buttons. The SharePoint app model imposes this restriction to provide a balance between functionality and security concerns. Furthermore, you are prohibited from adding any custom Java-Script code when you configure the URL for a UI custom action in a SharePoint app. If this restriction were not enforced, JavaScript code from the app could call into the host site without being granted the proper permissions.

Suppose that you want to create a UI custom action to add a custom ECB menu item to all the items in every Contacts list within the host site. You can structure the <CustomAction> element to look like that presented in Listing 1-3.

LISTING 1-3 A Custom Action definition

```
<CustomAction
  Id="CustomAction1"
  RegistrationType="List"
  RegistrationId="105"
  Location="EditControlBlock"
  Sequence="100"
  Title="Send Contact To App">

    <UrlAction Url="~appWebUrl/Pages/Action1.aspx" />

</CustomAction>
```

Once you install an app with this UI custom action, it registers an ECB menu command for every item in lists that have a list type ID of 105. This is the ID for the Contacts list type. Once the app is installed, the host web will provide a custom menu item on the ECB menu for each item in any Contacts list. An example of what the ECM menu command looks like is shown in Figure 1-8.

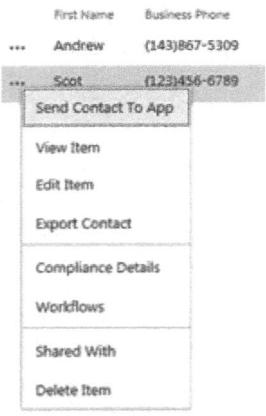

FIGURE 1-8 A custom UI action is used to add an item to the edit-control block or ribbon.

The default action of a UI custom action is to redirect the user to the page referenced by the URL configured within the <UrlAction> element. This makes sense for a scenario in which you want to move the user from the host web into the full immersion experience of the app in order to do some work. However, this default behavior will provide a distracting user interface experience for a scenario in which a user wishes to return to the host web immediately after seeing the page displayed by the app. For these scenarios, you can modify the UI custom action to display the page from the app as a dialog box in the context of the host web. The user interface experience is much better because the user can see a page from the app without ever leaving the host web.

Listing 1-4 demonstrates the technique to display the page referenced by a UI custom action as a dialog box, which involves adding three attributes to the <CustomAction> element. First, you add the *HostWebDialog* attribute and assign it a value of *true*. Next, you add the *HostWebDialogWidth* attribute and the *HostWebDialogHeight* attribute and assign them values to set the width and height of the dialog box.

LISTING 1-4 Displaying a referenced page

```
<CustomAction
  Id="CustomAction1"
  RegistrationType="List"
  RegistrationId="105"
  Location="EditControlBlock"
  Sequence="100"
  Title="Display more information about this contact"
  HostWebDialog="TRUE"
  HostWebDialogWidth="480"
  HostWebDialogHeight="240" >

    <UrlAction Url="~appWebUrl/Pages/Action1.aspx" />

  </CustomAction>
</Elements>
```

Now, let's go into more detail about configuring the *Url* attribute of the <UrlAction> element. When you configure the URL you can use the same familiar tokens that you use with the start page and with client web parts such as *~appWebUrl*, *~remoteAppUrl*, and *{StandardTokens}*, as shown in the following code:

```
<UrlAction Url="~appWebUrl/Pages/Action1.aspx" />
```

However, UI custom actions support several additional tokens beyond what is available for start pages and client web parts. These are the tokens that make it possible to pass contextual information about the item or document on which the command was executed. For example, you can pass the site-relative URL to the item or document by using the *{ItemURL}* token.

```
<UrlAction Url="~appWebUrl/Pages/Action1.aspx?ItemUrl={ItemURL}" />
```

In most scenarios, you will also need the absolute URL to the root of the host web, which can be passed by using the *{HostUrl}* token. Note that the *Url* is configured by using an XML attribute, so you cannot use the "&" character when combining two or more parameters together. Instead, you must use the XML encoded value, which is &amp, as shown in the following example:

```
<UrlAction Url="~appWebUrl/Pages/Action1.aspx?HostUrl={HostUrl}&amp;ItemURL={ItemUrl}" />
```

Note that the SharePoint host environment substitutes values into these tokens by using standard URL encoding. This means that you must write code in the app to use a URL decoding technique before you can use these values to construct a URL that can be used to access the item or document.

Table 1-2 lists the tokens that can be used in UI custom actions, beyond those that are also supported in start pages and client web parts. Note that some of the tokens work equally well regardless of whether the UI custom action is used to create an ECB menu item or a button in the ribbon. However, the *{ListID}* token and the *{ItemID}* token work with ECB menu items but not with buttons on the ribbon. Conversely, the *{SelectedListId}* token and the *{SelectedItemId}* token work with buttons on the ribbon but not with ECB menu items.

TABLE 1-2 The extra tokens available when configuring the URL for a UI custom action

Token	Purpose
{HostUrl}	Provides an absolute URL to the root of the host site
{SiteUrl}	Provides an absolute URL to the root of the current site collection
{Source}	Provides a relative URL to the page that hosts the custom action
{ListURLDir}	Provides a site-relative URL to the root folder of the current list
{ListID}	Provides a GUID-based ID of the current list (ECB only)
{ItemURL}	Provides a site-relative URL to the item or document
{ItemID}	Provides an integer-based ID of the item or document (ECB only)
{SelectedListId}	Provides a GUID-based ID of the selected list (ribbon only)
{SelectedItemId}	Provides an integer-based ID of the selected item or document (ribbon only)

Packaging and distributing apps

The final section of this chapter examines how SharePoint apps are distributed and deployed into production as well as how apps are managed over time. First, you will learn about the details of how apps are packaged into redistributable files. After that, you will see how these files are published and installed to make SharePoint apps available to users. As you will see, the SharePoint app model provides valuable support for managing apps in a production environment and upgrading to newer versions.

Packaging apps

A SharePoint app is packaged up for deployment by using a distributable file known as an *app package*. An app package is a file built by using the zip archive file format and it requires an extension of .app. For example, if you create a new SharePoint-hosted app project named MySharePointApp, the project will generate an app package named *MySharePointApp.app* as its output.

Note that the zip file format for creating an app package is based on the Open Package Convention (OPC). This is the same file format that Microsoft Office began using with the release of Office 2007 for creating Word documents (.docx) and Microsoft Excel workbooks (.xslx).

The primary requirement for an app package is that it contains the app manifest as a top-level file named *AppManifest.xml*. As discussed earlier in this chapter, the SharePoint host environment relies on metadata contained in the app manifest so that it can properly configure an app during the installation process.

An app package will usually contain an app icon file named *AppIcon.png*. The *AppIcon.png* file, like many of the other files in an app package, is paired with an XML file named *AppIcon.png.config.xml*. The purpose of this XML file is to assign the *AppIcon.png* file an identifying GUID.

Understanding the app web solution package

In addition to the *AppManifest.xml* file, the app package often contains additional files that are used as part of the app's implementation. For example, the app package for a SharePoint-hosted app contains a file for the app's start page along with other resources used by the start page such as a CSS file and a JavaScript file. These are examples of files that are added to the app web as part of the app installation process.

The distribution mechanism used by a SharePoint app to add pages and lists to the app web during installation is a standard solution package, which is a CAB file with a .wsp extension. If this sounds familiar, that's because the solution package file embedded within an app package has the exact same file format as the solution package files that developers have been using to deploy SharePoint solutions in SharePoint 2007 and SharePoint 2010. The one key difference is that the solution package used by the SharePoint app model to add files to an app web is not a stand-alone file. Instead, it is embedded as a .wsp file within the app package, as shown in Figure 1-9.

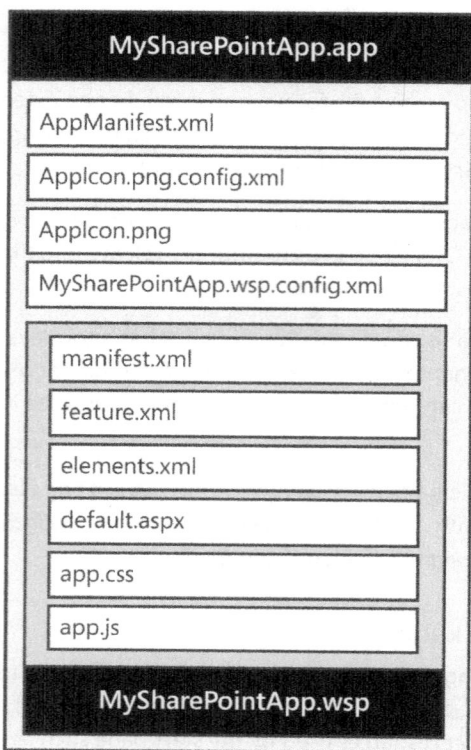

FIGURE 1-9 App packages that contain artifacts for deployment contain a separate solution package within the app package.

When a user installs a SharePoint app, the SharePoint host environment examines the app package to see if it contains an inner solution package. It is the presence of an inner solution package within the app package file that specifies to the SharePoint host environment whether it needs to create an app web during installation. If the app package does not contain an inner solution package, the SharePoint host environment installs the app without creating an app web.

The app web solution package contains a single web-scoped feature. The SharePoint host environment activates this feature automatically on the app web immediately after the app web is created. This feature is what makes it possible to add declarative elements such as pages and lists to the app web as the app is installed.

An app web solution package cannot contain a .NET assembly DLL with server-side code. Therefore, you can say that the app web solution package embedded inside an app package is constrained because it must be a fully declarative solution package. This is different from the solution packages for farm solutions and sandboxed solutions, which can contain assembly DLLs with custom .NET code written in either C# or VB.NET.

Keep in mind that the installation of a SharePoint app doesn't always result in the creation of an app web. Some apps are designed to create an app web during installation and some are not. A SharePoint-hosted app is the type of app that will always create an app web during installation. This is a requirement because a SharePoint-hosted app requires a start page that must be added to the app web.

However, things are different with a cloud-hosted app. Because a cloud-hosted app usually has a start page that is served up from a remote web, it does not require the creation of an app web during installation. Therefore, the use of an app web in the design of a provider-hosted app or an autohosted app is really just an available option as opposed to a requirement as it is with a SharePoint-hosted app.

When you design a provider-hosted app or an autohosted app, you have a choice of whether you want to create an app web during installation to store private app implementation details inside the SharePoint host. Some cloud-hosted apps will store all the content they need within their own external database and will not need to create an app web during installation. Other cloud-hosted apps can be designed to create an app web during installation for scenarios in which it makes sense to store content within the SharePoint host environment for each installed instance of the app.

Packaging host web features

This chapter has already discussed client web parts and UI custom actions. As you recall, these two types of features are used to extend the user interface of the host web, as opposed to many of the other types of elements in an app that are added to the app web. For this reason, the XML files containing the definitions of client web parts and UI custom actions are not deployed within a solution package embedded within the app package. Instead, the XML files that define client web parts and UI custom actions are added to the app package as top-level files.

Consider an example SharePoint app named MyAppParts that contains two client web parts. The contents of the app package for this app will contain a top-level *elements.xml* file for each of the client web parts and a top-level *feature.xml* file for the feature that hosts them. When Visual Studio 2012 creates these XML files and builds them into the output app package file, it adds a unique GUID to each file name to avoid naming conflicts, as illustrated in Figure 1-10.

The feature that hosts client web parts and UI custom actions is a web-scoped feature known as a *host web feature*. The SharePoint host environment is able to detect a host web feature inside an app package during app installation and activate it in the host web. When an app with a web host feature is installed at tenancy scope, that feature will be activated in more than one site.

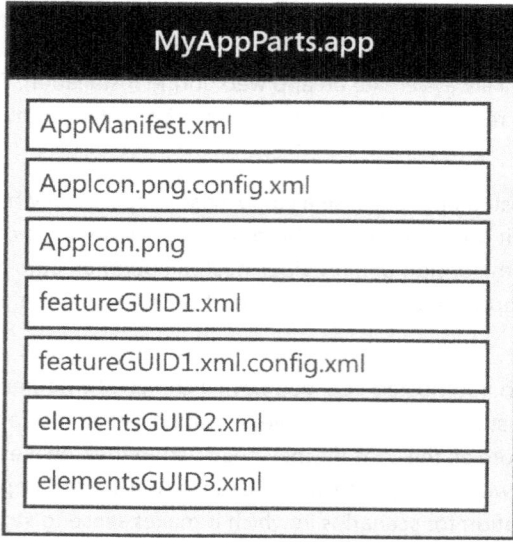

FIGURE 1-10 The XML files that define client web parts and UI custom actions are packaged as top-level files within the app package.

Packaging for autohosted apps

When it comes to packaging a SharePoint app for distribution, autohosted apps are more complicated and deserve a little extra attention. The extra complexity is required because the app package for an autohosted app must contain the resources required to create an ASP.NET application on demand to deploy the remote web. An autohosted app can also be designed to create a SQL Azure database, as well, during the app installation process.

When you create a new autohosted app, Visual Studio 2012 creates two projects. There is one project for the app itself and a second web project for an ASP.NET application to implement the remote web. For example, if you create a new autohosted app using the name MyAutoHostedApp, Visual Studio 2012 creates an app project named MyAutoHostedApp and an ASP.NET project named MyAutoHostedAppWeb, and adds them to a single Visual Studio solution.

What is important to understand is that the app package built for the MyAutoHostedApp project must contain all the necessary files to deploy the ASP.NET project named MyAutoHostedAppWeb. This is a requirement because the installation of this app package must provide the Office 365 environment with the means to provision the remote web as a Windows Azure application. This is what makes it possible for an autohosted app to create its own remote web during the installation process.

Visual Studio 2012 relies on a packaging format that Microsoft created especially for the Windows Azure environment by which all the files and metadata required to deploy an ASP.NET application are built in to a single zip file for distribution. This zip file is known as a *web deploy package*. When used within the SharePoint app model, the web deploy package is embedded within the app package of an autohosted app for distribution.

When Visual Studio 2012 builds the web deploy package for an autohosted app, it creates the file by combining the app package name together with a web.zip extension. For example, an app packaged named *MyAutohostedApp.app* will have an embedded web deploy package named *MyAutohostedApp.web.zip*.

Now, consider the scenario in which an autohosted app has an associated SQL Azure database. The Office 365 environment must create this database on demand during app installation. Therefore, the app package must contain the resources required to create a SQL Azure database containing standard database objects, such as tables, indexes, stored procedures, and triggers.

The SharePoint app packaging model takes advantage of a second packaging format that Microsoft created for Windows Azure known as a *Data Tier Application package*. In this packaging format, the metadata required to automate the creation of a SQL Azure database is defined in XML files that are built in to a zip file with an extension of .dacpac. The name of the Data Tier Application package is typically based on the name of the database. For example, a SQL Azure database named MySqlDatabase will have an associated Data Tier Application package named *MySqlDatabase.dacpac*. If you look inside a Data Tier Application package, you can locate a file named *model.xml*, which defines the database objects that need to be created.

Figure 1-11 shows the layout of an app package for an autohosted app that will trigger the Office 365 environment to create a remote and a SQL Azure database as part of the app installation process. Remember that the web deploy package is required in an autohosted app package, whereas the data tier application package is optional.

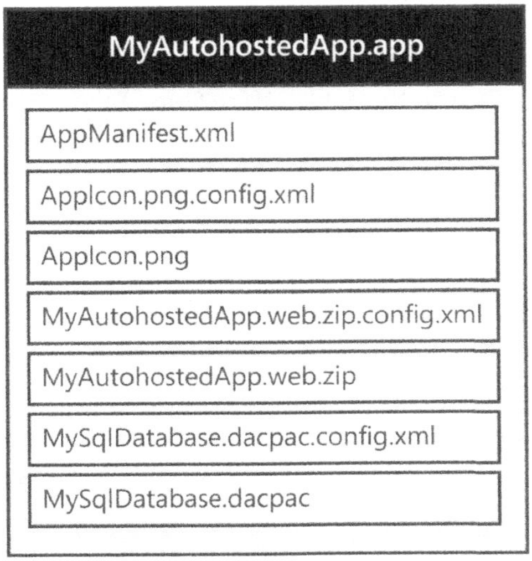

MyAutohostedApp.app

AppManifest.xml

AppIcon.png.config.xml

AppIcon.png

MyAutohostedApp.web.zip.config.xml

MyAutohostedApp.web.zip

MySqlDatabase.dacpac.config.xml

MySqlDatabase.dacpac

FIGURE 1-11 An autohosted app package contains a web deployment package to create the remote web and a data application package to create a SQL Azure database.

When you create an autohosted app, Visual Studio 2012 automatically creates the web project and takes care of setting up all that's required to build the web deploy package into the app package. However, you have to take a few extra steps to create a SQL database project and configure it to properly build the Data Tier Application package in to the app package.

The first step is to create a new SQL database project in Visual Studio 2012 and add it to the same solution that contains the autohosted project. Next, on the Properties page of the SQL Database project, go to the Project Settings tab and change the target platform setting to SQL Azure. This is the step that changes the project output to a Data Tier Application package. After this, you must build the SQL database project at least once to build the Data Tier Application package.

The final step is to configure the app project to reference the Data Tier Application package. You can accomplish this by using the property sheet for the autohosted app project. You will find that there is a project property named *SQL Package*. Once you configure the *SQL Package* property to point to the Data Tier Application package (.dacpac) file, you have made the necessary changes so that Visual Studio 2012 will begin building the Data Tier Application package into app package file.

Publishing apps

The app package is a distributable file that's used to publish SharePoint apps. Once the app package has been published, it is available for users to install. In the case of SharePoint-hosted apps and autohosted apps, the app package contains all the resources required to deploy the app during the installation process. However, provider-hosted apps require the developer to deploy the remote web independently of the publication process and the installation process.

You publish a SharePoint app by uploading its app package file to one of two different places. First, you can publish an app by uploading its app package to the public Office Store. This is the right choice to make your app available to the general public, including users with SharePoint tenancies in Office 365.

The second way to publish a SharePoint app is by uploading the app package to a special type of site known as an app catalog site. This is the option to use when you want to make the app available only to users within a specific Office 365 tenancy or within a specific on-premises farm.

Publishing SharePoint apps to the Office Store

To publish an app to the public Office Store, the developer must first create a *dashboard seller account*. You can create this type of account by navigating to *https://sellerdashboard.microsoft.com* in the browser and logging on with a valid Windows Account. Once you have logged on, you can create a new dashboard seller account that is either an individual account or a company account.

A very appealing aspect of publishing apps to the Office Store with a dashboard seller account is that it provides assistance with the management of licensing as well as collecting money from customers through credit card transactions. When you create a dashboard seller account, you are able to create a second payout account from which you supply Microsoft with the necessary details so when it collects money from customers purchasing your apps, it can transfer the funds you have earned to either a bank account or a PayPal account.

Once you have gone through the process of creating a dashboard seller account, it takes a day or two for this new account to be approved. Once your account has been approved, you can then begin to publish your apps in the Office Store. The Office Store supports publishing three types of apps: you can publish SharePoint apps, Apps for Office, and Windows Azure Catalog Apps.

You publish a SharePoint app by uploading its app package file and filling in the details associated with the app. For example, the publishing process for the Office Store requires you to provide a title, version number, description, category, logo, and at least one screenshot that shows potential customers what your app looks like.

When you publish a SharePoint app, you can also indicate via the seller dashboard whether your app is free or must be purchased. If you publish an app for purchase, you can specify the licensing fee for each user or for a given number of users. There is even an option to configure a free trial period for an app that has an associated licensing fee.

Once you have uploaded an app and provided the required information, the app must then go through an approval process. The approval process involves checking the app package to ensure that it only contains valid resources. There are also checks to validate that the app meets the minimum requirements of the user experience guidelines. For example, there is a check to ensure that the start page for the app contains the required link back to the host web.

Once the app has been approved, it is then ready for use and added to the public Office Store where it can be discovered and installed by SharePoint users.

Publishing apps to an app catalog

What should you do if you want to publish an app but you don't want to publish it to the Office Store? For example, imagine a scenario in which you don't want to make an app available to the general public. Instead, you want to publish the app to make it available to a smaller audience such as a handful of companies that are willing to pay you for your development effort. The answer is to publish the app to an *app catalog site*.

An app catalog site contains a special type of document library that is used to upload and store app package files. Along with storing the app package file, this document library also tracks various types of metadata for each app. Some of this metadata is required, whereas other metadata is optional.

In the Office 365 environment, the app catalog site is automatically added when a tenancy is created for a new customer. However, this is not the case in an on-premises farm. Instead, you must explicitly create the app catalog site by using the Central Administration site or by using Windows PowerShell. Furthermore, the app catalog is created at web application scope, so you must create a separate app catalog site for each web application.

You must have farm administrator permissions within an on-premises farm to create an app catalog site. You begin by navigating to the home page of Central Administration. On the home page, there is a top-level link for Apps. When you click the Apps link, you will be redirected to a page with a group of links under the heading of App Management. Within this group of links, locate and click the link titled *Manage App Catalog*.

The first time you click the Manage App Catalog link, you are redirected to the Create App Catalog page, which you can use to create a new app catalog site, as shown in Figure 1-12. Note that the app catalog site must be created as a top-level site within a new site collection. On the Create App Catalog page, you can select the target web app that will host the new app catalog site.

Create App Catalog

OK   Cancel

Web Application
Select a web application.

To create a new web application go to New Web Application page.

Web Application: http://wingtipserver/ ▪

Title and Description
Type a title and description for your new site. The title will be displayed on each page in the site.

Title:

Wingtip App Catlog

Description:

Web Site Address
Specify the URL name and URL path to create a new site, or choose to create a site at a specific path.

To add a new URL Path go to the Define Managed Paths page.

URL:

http://wingtipserver /sites/ ▾ AppCatalog

Primary Site Collection Administrator
Specify the administrator for this site collection. Only one user login can be provided; security groups are not supported.

User name:

WINGTIP\administrator

End Users
Specify the users or groups that should be able to see apps from the app catalog.

Users/Groups:

NT AUTHORITY\authenticated users

FIGURE 1-12 The app catalog can be created through Central Administration within a specific web app of your choice.

Note that you can also use the Create App Catalog page (shown a little later in Figure 1-14) to configure user access permissions to the app catalog site. Remember that providing users with access to the app catalog site is what makes it possible for them to discover and install apps of their own. You must provide read access to users if you want them to have the ability to discover apps and install them at site scope. However, you might decide against configuring user access to the app catalog site if you plan on installing apps at tenancy scope.

Once you have created the app catalog site within an on-premises farm, you should navigate to it and inspect what's inside. You will find that there is a document library with a title of *Apps for SharePoint* which is used to publish SharePoint apps. There is a second document library with a title of *Apps for Office* that is used to publish apps created for Office applications such as Word and Excel.

You publish a SharePoint app by uploading its app package to the Apps for SharePoint document library. The SharePoint host environment is able to automatically fill in some of the required app metadata such as the Title, Version, and Product ID by reading the app manifest as the app package is uploaded. However, there is additional metadata that must be filled in by hand or by some other means. A view of apps that have been published in the Apps for SharePoint document library is presented in Figure 1-13.

FIGURE 1-13 The Apps for SharePoint document library contains app package files and associated metadata for published apps.

You will also notice that the app catalog site supports the management of app requests from users. The idea being that a user within a site can request an app from the Office Store. The app catalog administrator can see this request and decide whether to purchase the app or not. If the app request seems appropriate, the app catalog administrator can purchase the app and make it available for site-scope installation. Alternatively, the app catalog administrator can make the app available to the requester by using a tenancy-scoped installation.

Installing apps

Once an app has been published, it can be discovered and installed by a user who has administrator permissions in the current site. If you navigate to the Site Content page within a site and click the tile with the caption *add an app*, you will be redirected to the main page for installing apps named *addanapp.aspx*. This page displays apps that have been published to the app catalog site. Remember that an Office 365 tenancy has a single app catalog site, but on-premises farms have an app catalog site per web application. Therefore, you will not see apps that have been published to an app catalog site in a different web application.

A user requires administrator permissions within a site to install an app. If you are logged on with a user account that does not have administrator permissions within the current site, you will not be able to see apps that have been published in the app catalog site. This is true even when your user account has been granted permissions on the app catalog site itself.

Once you locate an app that you want to install, you can simply click its tile to install it. The app installation process typically prompts you to verify whether you trust the app. A page appears that displays a list of the permissions that the app is requesting along with a button to grant or deny the apps permission request. You must grant all permissions that the app has requested to continue with the installation process. There is no ability to grant one requested permission to an app while denying another; granting permissions to an app during installation is always an all-or-nothing proposition.

After the app has been installed, you will see a tile for it on the Site Content page. This tile represents the app launcher that a user can click to be redirected to the app's start page. The app title also displays an ellipse to access a fly-out menu for app management, as illustrated in Figure 1-14.

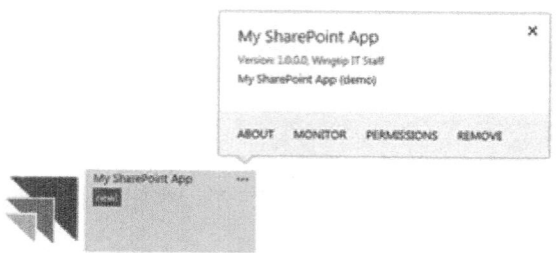

FIGURE 1-14 Once an app has been installed, it can be launched using an associated tile, which is displayed on the site content page.

Recall from earlier in the chapter what happens during app installation. Some apps require an app web. When this is the case, the app web is created as a child site under the current site where the app has been installed. If the app contains host feature elements such as client web parts and UI custom actions, these user interface extensions will be made available in the host site, as well.

Installing apps at tenancy scope

You have seen that the app catalog site provides a place where you can upload apps in order to publish them. Once an app has been published in the app catalog site, a user within the same Office 365 tenancy or within the same on-premises web application can discover the app and install it at site scope. However, the functionality of an app catalog site goes one step further: it plays a central role in installing apps at tenancy level.

You install an app at tenancy scope by installing it in an app catalog site. Just as with a site-scoped installation, you must first publish the app by uploading it to the Apps for SharePoint document library in the app catalog site. After publishing the app, you should be able to locate it on the Add An App page of the app catalog site and install it just as you would install an app in any other type of site. However, things are a bit different after the app has been installed in an app catalog site. More specifically, the app provides different options in the fly-out menu that is available on the Site Content page, as shown in Figure 1-15.

As you can see in Figure 1-15, an app that has been installed in an app catalog site has a *Deployment* menu command that is not available in any other type of site. When you click the Deployment menu command, you are redirected to a page on which you can configure the app so that you can make it available to users in other sites.

FIGURE 1-15 Once an app has been installed, the associated deployment menu can be used to make the app available to other sites.

You have several options when you configure an app in an app catalog site to make it available in other sites. One option is to make the app available to all sites within the scope of the app catalog site. Or, you can be more selective and just make the app available in sites that were created by using a specific site template or sites created under a specific managed path. There is even an option to add the URLs of site collections one-by-one if you need fine-grained control.

After you configure the criteria for a tenancy-scoped app installation to indicate the sites in which it can be used, you will find that the app does not appear in those sites instantly. That's because the SharePoint host environment relies on a timer job to push the required app metadata from the app catalog site to all the other sites. By default, this timer job is configured to run once every five minutes. During your testing you can speed things up by navigating to the Central Administration site and locating the timer job definition named App Installation Service. The page for this timer job definition provides a Run Now button that you can click to run it on demand.

Upgrading apps

The upgrade process designed by the SharePoint app model provides a much better experience compared to the upgrade process used with SharePoint solutions. When apps are published, the Office Store and app catalog sites always track their version number. When an app is installed, the SharePoint host environment sees this version number and records it for the installed app instance.

Take a simple example. Imagine you have uploaded version 1.0.0.0 of an app. After that, the app is installed in several sites via site-scoped installation. The SharePoint host environment remembers that each of these sites has installed version 1.0.0.0 of the app.

Now, imagine that you want to further develop your app. Maybe you need to fix a bug, improve its performance, or extend the app's functionality. After you have finished your testing, you decide to update the version number to 2.0.0.0 and publish the new version in the same app catalog site where you installed the original version.

One important aspect of the upgrade process of the SharePoint app model is that an updated version of an app is never forced upon the user that installed the app. Instead, the user is notified that a new version of the app is available. This user can then decide to do nothing or to update the app to the new version. Figure 1-16 shows the notification that the SharePoint host environment adds to the app tile on the Site Contents page.

My SharePoint App
An update for this app is available.

FIGURE 1-16 The tile for an app displays a notification when an updated version is available from the SharePoint Store or app catalog.

The notification depicted in Figure 1-16 contains an update link that a user can click to be redirected to a page with a button that activates the upgrade process. What actually occurs during the upgrade process is different, depending on whether the app is a SharePoint-hosted app or a cloud-hosted app.

When you are working on an updated version of a SharePoint-hosted app, you have the ability to change some of the metadata in the app manifest and to add new elements into the app web. For example, you could add a new page to the app web named *startv2.aspx* and then modify the app manifest to use this start page instead of the start page that was used in the original version of the app. You could also add other, new app web elements such as JavaScript files, lists, and document libraries. Many of the techniques used to upgrade elements in the app web are based on the same techniques developers have been using with feature upgrade in SharePoint solutions.

When it comes to updating a cloud-hosted app, things are different. That's because most of the important changes to the app's implementation are made to the remote web and not to anything inside the SharePoint host environment. If you are working with a provider-hosted app, you must roll out these changes to the remote web before you publish the new version of the app to the Office Store or any app catalog site.

It's equally important that the updated version of the remote web must continue to support customers that will continue to use the original version of the app. Remember; there is nothing that forces the user to accept an update. You should expect that some customers will be happy with the original version and will be opposed to upgrading to a new version of an app.

Once you have pushed out more than one or more updates to a provider-hosted app, you must begin to track what version each customer is using. One technique to accomplish this task is to provide a different start page for each version of the app. Many provider-hosted apps will go a step further and store the current version of app in a customer profile that is tracked in a custom database behind the remote web.

Trapping app lifecycle events

One favorable aspect of the SharePoint app model for developers is the ability to design a cloud-hosted app with custom server-side code that is automatically executed when an app is installed, upgraded, or uninstalled. By taking advantage of the ability to add code behind these three app life-cycle events, you can program against the host web and the app web with logic to initialize, update, and cleanup site elements in the SharePoint environment. These app lifecycle events also provide the necessary triggers for updating the custom database used by provider-hosted apps and autohosted apps.

The architecture of app events is based on registering app event handlers in the app manifest that cause the SharePoint host environment to call out to a web service entry point in the remote web. Due to the architecture's reliance on a server-side entry point, app events are not supported in SharePoint-hosted apps. Therefore, you can only use the app events in autohosted apps and provider-hosted apps.

It's relatively simple to add support for app events to the project for an autohosted app or a provider-hosted app. The property sheet for the app project contains three properties named *Handle App Installed*, *Handle App Uninstalling*, and *Handle App Upgrade*, as shown in Figure 1-17.

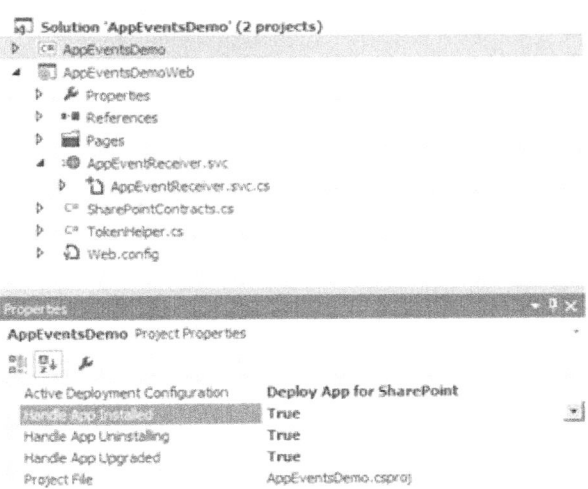

FIGURE 1-17 The property sheet for an app project provides Boolean properties for enabling lifecycle events.

The default value for each of these app event properties is *false*. The first time you change one of these properties to a value of *true*, Visual Studio 2012 adds a web service entry point into the web project with a name of *AppEventReceiver.svc*. Visual Studio 2012 also adds the required configuration information into the app manifest file, as well. If you enable all three events, the <Properties> element within <App> element of the app manifest will be updated with the following three elements:

```
<InstalledEventEndpoint>~remoteAppUrl/AppEventReceiver.svc</InstalledEventEndpoint>
<UninstallingEventEndpoint>~remoteAppUrl/AppEventReceiver.svc</UninstallingEventEndpoint>
<UpgradedEventEndpoint>~remoteAppUrl/AppEventReceiver.svc</UpgradedEventEndpoint>
```

After you have enabled one or more of the app events, you can then begin to write the code that will execute when the events occur. You write this code in the code-behind file named *AppEvent Receiver.svc.cs*. If you examine this file, you will see that Visual Studio 2012 has created a class shown in the following code that implements a special interface that the SharePoint team created for remote event handling named *IRemoteEventService*:

```
public class AppEventReceiver : IRemoteEventService {
  public SPRemoteEventResult ProcessEvent(RemoteEventProperties properties) {}
  public void ProcessOneWayEvent(RemoteEventProperties properties) { }
}
```

The *IRemoteEventService* interface is used with app events and also with other types of remote event handlers, as well. There are two methods named *ProcessEvent* and *ProcessOneWayEvent*. The SharePoint host environment makes a web service call which executes the *ProcessEvent* method when it needs to inspect the response returned from the remote web. The *ProcessOneWayEvent* method is called for cases in which the SharePoint host environment needs to trigger the execution of code in the remote web but doesn't need to inspect the response. App events always trigger to the *Process Event* method, so you can leave the *ProcessOneWayEvent* method empty in the *AppEventReceiver.svc. cs* file.

If you have registered for the *AppInstalled* event, the *ProcessEvent* method will execute whenever a user is installing the app. It is critical to supply robust error handling because an unhandled exception will be returned to the SharePoint host environment and cause an error in the app installation process.

When you implement the *ProcessEvent* method, you must return an object created from the *SPRemoteEventResult* class, as demonstrated in the following:

```
public SPRemoteEventResult ProcessEvent(RemoteEventProperties properties) {
  // return an SPRemoteEventResult object
  SPRemoteEventResult result = new SPRemoteEventResult();
  return result;
}
```

The *SPRemoteEventResult* class was designed to make it possible for code in the remote web to relay contextual information back to the SharePoint host environment. For example, imagine that you have detected that the installer's IP address is located in a country that you do not want to support. You can tell the SharePoint host environment to cancel the installation process and pass an appropriate error message, such as shown here:

```
SPRemoteEventResult result = new SPRemoteEventResult();
result.Status = SPRemoteEventServiceStatus.CancelWithError;
result.ErrorMessage = "App cannot be installed due to invalid IP address";
return result;
```

The *ProcessEvent* method passes a parameter named *properties*, which is based on a type named *RemoteEventProperties*. You can use this parameter to access important contextual information such as the URL of host web and security access token required to call back into the SharePoint host environment. Listing 1-5 shows that the properties parameter also provides an *EventType* property with which you can determine which of the three app events has caused the *ProcessEvent* method to execute.

LISTING 1-5 Handling events

```
public SPRemoteEventResult ProcessEvent(RemoteEventProperties properties) {

    // obtain context information from RemoteEventProperties property
    string HostWeb = properties.AppEventProperties.HostWebFullUrl.AbsolutePath;
    string AccessToken = properties.AccessToken;

    // handle event type
    switch (properties.EventType) {
      case RemoteEventType.AppInstalled:
        // add code here to handle app installation
        break;
      case RemoteEventType.AppUpgraded:
        // add code here to handle app upgrade
        break;
      case RemoteEventType.AppUninstalling:
        // add code here to handle app uninstallation
        break;
      default:
        break;
    }

    // return an SPRemoteEventResult object
    SPRemoteEventResult result = new SPRemoteEventResult();
    return result;

}
```

Note that debugging app event handlers can be especially tricky to set up and in many situations it doesn't work at all. That's because the SharePoint host environment must be able to call back into the remote web. For cases in which you have installed the app into an Office 365 tenancy for testing, it is a web server in the Office 365 environment that will be issuing the call to the remote web. This web server hosted in the Office 365 environment must be able to locate and access the web server that is hosting the remote web. Therefore, attempting to debug an app event handler for which the remote web is configured to use a host name such as localhost or to use a host domain name that only resolves to the proper IP address inside your testing environment will not work.

Conclusion

This chapter provided you with an introduction to SharePoint apps. You learned about the pain points of SharePoint solution development and the design goals that influenced how the architecture of the SharePoint app model was created. You also learned many details about app hosting models, user interface design, publishing, installation, and upgrade. Now, it's time to move ahead and begin learning about how to write code in an app that accesses the SharePoint host environment by using the CSOM and the new REST API.

## CHAPTER 2

Client-side programming

The Microsoft SharePoint 2013 app model does not support running server-side code within the SharePoint host environment. As a result, SharePoint developers cannot utilize the server-side API in apps. Instead, app developers must use the client-side API, which consists of the Client-Side Object Model (CSOM) and the Representational State Transfer (REST) API.

When developing apps, CSOM and the REST API can be programmed by using either C# or JavaScript. C# is used in remote webs associated with provider-hosted or autohosted apps. JavaScript can run in the browser in SharePoint-hosted, provider-hosted, or autohosted apps. The combination of languages and APIs results in the app designs outlined in Table 2-1.

TABLE 2-1 App designs

Language	API	SharePoint-hosted	Provider-hosted	Autohosted
JavaScript	CSOM	✓		
JavaScript	REST	✓	✓	✓
C#	CSOM		✓	✓
C#	REST		✓	✓

Whereas the choices outlined in Table 2-1 offer a lot of flexibility, you will find that some app designs are much more natural choices than others. For example, if you want to do most of your development in C#, you will find that CSOM in a provider-hosted or autohosted app is the most straightforward design. On the other hand, if you mostly want to create SharePoint-hosted apps for Microsoft Office 365, JavaScript against the REST API will be the easiest design.

This chapter demonstrates the use of CSOM and REST in the various app designs. Along the way, it introduces the required technical concepts necessary to understand the app designs and the best practices for developing them. The chapter starts with a short JavaScript primer followed by a review of the various patterns for creating reusable and maintainable libraries in JavaScript. It then covers the fundamentals of the CSOM and REST object models.

Because app authentication is covered in Chapter 3, "App Security," the examples in this chapter steer clear of situations that involve advanced app authentication. Instead, this chapter focuses on the fundamentals necessary to successfully develop apps against CSOM and REST. The patterns and principles presented in this chapter are subsequently applied in samples throughout the book.

Introducing JavaScript for SharePoint developers

JavaScript takes on increased importance in app development. Therefore, this section presents a brief overview of the JavaScript language and its key characteristics from the perspective of an experienced SharePoint programmer. Although you have probably written some JavaScript, you might not have spent time to understand JavaScript at the level necessary to be successful writing SharePoint apps. If you are a JavaScript expert, you can certainly skip this section. If you have only used JavaScript casually in your past SharePoint solutions, you should read this section thoroughly and pay special attention to the discussion in the section "Creating Custom Libraries."

Understanding JavaScript namespaces

As a SharePoint developer, you have probably written at least some JavaScript in a webpage; thus, you understand that JavaScript code is comprised of functions. These functions can be written directly into the webpage by using script tags or referenced in separate library files. If you are more of a casual JavaScript developer, however, you might not be aware that simply writing a named function places that function in the *global namespace*. The global namespace is the container into which all variables and functions are placed by default. In the browser, this container is the *window* object. Cluttering the global namespace with functions can easily lead to naming conflicts and "spaghetti" code.

In addition to the global namespace, you can define your own custom namespaces. Namespaces in JavaScript are essentially just containing objects defined within the global namespace. By using custom namespaces, you can isolate your code from other JavaScript in the page. This is essential for preventing naming conflicts. Custom namespaces are one of the few things that should be defined within the global namespace. Most variables and functions are generally defined within a custom namespace. The following code shows how to define a custom namespace:

```
var Wingtip = window.Wingtip || {};
```

The sample code sets a global variable named *Wingtip* to reference either an existing global variable or creates a new one if it does not exist already. This is the standard approach to creating namespaces because this line of code can exist in several different libraries without causing a naming conflict. The first library loaded with this code present establishes the namespace definition for those loaded later.

Understanding JavaScript variables

Variables in JavaScript can be declared either in a namespace or within a function. Unlike C#, JavaScript variables are not declared by using a data type keyword. Instead, JavaScript uses the *var* keyword to define a variable. Although not strictly required, variables should always be declared by using the *var* keyword. This is important because when it is not used, the variable is automatically defined within the global namespace. When the *var* keyword is used outside of a function, the associated variable is always defined within the global namespace. When it is used within a function, the associated variable is scoped to the function only. The following code shows an example of a global variable, global function, and local variable:

```
<script type="text/JavaScript">
    var myGlobalVar = "This is a global variable";
    function myGlobalFunction() {
        alert("This function is defined in the global namespace");
        for (var i=0; i<5; i++) {
            alert("This variable is local to the function: " + i);
        }
    }
</script>
```

Variables can be defined within a custom namespace by simply referencing the namespace when using the variable. The code that follows shows how to create a variable within a custom namespace. The section "Creating Custom Libraries" expands upon this idea significantly to encapsulate code and keep it out of the global namespace.

```
var Wingtip = window.Wingtip || {};
var window.Wingtip.myNamespaceVar = "This is a variable defined within a namespace";
```

Although JavaScript does not have specific data type keywords, declared variables do have a type based on the value they hold. Variable types can be examined by using the *typeof* operator. The *typeof* operator returns one of the following values when applied to a variable or function parameter:

- undefined

- string

- number

- Boolean

- function

- object

Because JavaScript is very loose with rules concerning variable and object definitions, you should be sure to always use *strict* JavaScript in your apps. Strict JavaScript is an improved version of Java-Script. You can enable it by adding the line *"use strict"* at the top of any library or function. Strict JavaScript will prevent you from making many common mistakes in your code. The following lists some of the key restrictions enabled by strict JavaScript:

- Cannot use a variable without declaring it

- Cannot write to a read-only property

- Cannot add properties to non-extensible objects

- Cannot illegally delete functions and variables

- Cannot define a property more than once in an object literal

- Cannot use a parameter name more than once in a function

- Cannot use reserved words, *eval*, or arguments, as names for functions and variables

- The value of *this* in a function is no longer the *window* object

- Cannot declare functions inside of statements

- Cannot change the members of the *arguments* array

Understanding JavaScript functions

When writing functions, you need to understand that the function signature consists of the function name, parameters, and scope. In C# programming against the SharePoint server-side API, the calling code should match the function signature by passing in parameters that are typed appropriately. Furthermore, an error is thrown when the calling code does not match the function signature. In JavaScript, however, no error is thrown when the list of parameters passed to a function does not match the function signature. Instead, all parameters are available within a function through the *arguments* array. Consider the following JavaScript function:

```
function Add(){
    var sum = 0;
    for (var i=0; i<arguments.length; i++) {
        sum += arguments[i];
    }
    return sum;
}
```

The *Add* function definition does not include any parameters. Instead, the function looks through the *arguments* array and simply adds together the values contained within it. Because of this, the following calls to the *Add* function will all succeed:

```
var sum1 = Add();
var sum2 = Add(7);
var sum3 = Add(7,11);
var sum4 = Add(7,11,21,36);
```

Functions in JavaScript are actually objects. As such, they can be assigned to a variable. The variable referencing the function can then be invoked as if it were the name of the function. A function can also be defined without a name, making it an *anonymous* function. The following code shows an example of an anonymous function assigned to a variable named *talk* and then invoked:

```
var talk = function() {
    alert("hello there!");
};
talk();
```

Understanding JavaScript closures

Because anonymous functions can be assigned to a variable, they can also be returned from other functions. Furthermore, the local variables defined within the containing function are available through the returned anonymous function. This concept is called a *closure*. Consider the following code that returns an anonymous function from a containing named function:

```
function echo (shoutText) {
    var echoText = shoutText + " " + shoutText;
    var echoReturn = function() { alert(echoText); };
    return echoReturn;
}
```

Because the return value from the named function is an anonymous function, the code that follows can be used to invoke the returned function. When the returned function is invoked, the browser displays the text "Hello! Hello!".

```
echo("Hello!")();
```

What is interesting in this example is the fact that the anonymous function is using the local variable *echoText* within its body, and the local variable is available even after the function returns. This is possible because the returned value is essentially a pointer to the anonymous function defined within the named function, which means that the local variables do not go out of scope after the named function completes. This is the essence of a closure in JavaScript.

At first glance, closures might appear to be more of a curiosity than a useful construct. However, closures are essential to the process of creating encapsulated JavaScript that is maintainable. Consider the following code:

```
function person (name) {
    var talk = function() { alert("My name is " + name); };
    return {
        speak:talk
    };
}
```

In the preceding example, an anonymous function is assigned to the local variable *talk*. The return value of the function is an object that has a key *speak*, which references the value *talk*. By using this type of closure, the function can be invoked by using method syntax, which returns the message "My name is Brian Cox".

```
person("Brian Cox").speak();
```

Notice how the code that invokes the function appears almost as if it is object-oriented. Even though JavaScript is clearly not object-oriented, by using closures, you can create functions that look and feel more familiar to C# developers and significantly improve maintainability. This concept results in several development patterns that are investigated in the section "Creating Custom Libraries."

Understanding JavaScript prototypes

A JavaScript object is really just an unordered collection of key-value pairs. Objects can be created with the key-value pairs defined at the moment they are created. The keys are then used to access the values. The following code shows a simple *customer* object with a *name* property defined:

```
customer = {Name: "Brian Cox"};
alert("My name is " + customer["Name"]);
```

Every JavaScript object is based on a *prototype*, which is an object that supports the inheritance of its properties. With prototypes, you can define the structure of an object and then use that structure to create new object instances. Listing 2-1 shows an example of defining a prototype and creating an object from it.

LISTING 2-1 Creating an object from prototypes

```
var human = Object.create(null);

Object.defineProperty(human, "name",
                    {value: "undefined",
                    writable: true,
                    enumerable: true,
                    configurable: true}
                    );

var customer = Object.create(human);

Object.defineProperty(customer, "title",
                    {value: "undefined",
                    writable: true,
                    enumerable: true,
                    configurable: true}
                    );

customer["name"] = "Brian Cox";
customer["title"] = "Developer";
alert("My name is " + customer["name"]);
alert("My title is " + customer["title"]);
```

In Listing 2-1, a null *human* prototype is created and then a single *name* property is defined. The *human* prototype is then used to create an instance called *customer*. The *customer* prototype is then modified to contain a *title* property. If you call a property on an object but the property does not exist, JavaScript will look for the property by following the *prototype chain* up the inheritance tree. In this case, the *name* property of the *customer* is defined in the *human* prototype.

Using prototypes is very efficient when you are creating large numbers of objects because the functions do not need to be created for each instance. This behavior results in development patterns that are presented in the next section.

Creating custom libraries

Even though the function-based nature of JavaScript makes it deceptively easy to get started, most developers who are new to the language simply write global functions directly in the web page. This practice, however, is seriously flawed because naming conflicts will inevitably arise between functions in libraries. Furthermore, writing reams of functions in the global namespace is simply unmaintainable. This section examines several approaches for creating custom libraries that are efficient and maintainable.

Understanding the singleton pattern

The singleton pattern creates a single instance of an object that encapsulates code within it. The singleton pattern is a straightforward implementation of an object designed to encapsulate code and keep it out of the global namespace. As an example, consider the following code that sets up a custom namespace and then defines a singleton:

```
"use strict";

var Wingtip = window.Wingtip || {};
Wingtip.Customer = {

    name: "Brian Cox",
    speak: function() { alert("My name is " + this.name); }

};
```

Within the *Customer* object, each member is added by declaring a publicly accessible key, followed by the definition of a function or object as the value. Note the use of the *this* keyword within the *speak* function to reference the *name* member object. Calling code might interact with the publically accessible members as shown in the following code.

```
Wingtip.Customer.speak();
```

The singleton pattern does a nice job of encapsulating code into the *Customer* object outside of the global namespace. Additionally, the calling code is straightforward, readable, and maintainable. The entire *Customer* definition could subsequently be packaged into a separate file (for example, *wingtip.customer.js*) and reused across several apps. The obvious disadvantage of this pattern is that you can only have one customer. In a typical SharePoint app, you are going to need to create many customer instances.

Understanding the module pattern

The module pattern and its variants use a function instead of an object as the basis for encapsulation. The advantage of the module pattern is that it can support private members, public members, and multiple instances; the exact support is based on the pattern variant that you use.

The standard module pattern uses a self-invoking function as the container. The standard module pattern can be regarded as an improved version of the singleton pattern because it still only supports one instance. Listing 2-2 shows an example of the module pattern.

LISTING 2-2 The module pattern

```
"use strict";

var Wingtip = window.Wingtip || {};
Wingtip.Customer = function () {

    //private members
    var name = "Brian Cox",
        talk = function() {alert("My name is " + name);};};

    //public interface
    return {
        fullname: name,
        speak: talk
    }

}();
```

In Listing 2-2, notice that the function definition is followed by a set of parentheses. It is these parentheses that make the function self-invoking. The return value is an object whose key-value pairs reference the private members, which effectively creates a public interface for the library. The following code shows how the module is called:

```
alert(Wingtip.Customer.fullname);
Wingtip.Customer.speak();
```

Note that the return value doesn't have to actually provide a key-value pair for every one of the private members. When the return value reveals only a subset of the members, the pattern is said to be a variant of the module pattern known as the *revealing module pattern*. The revealing module pattern allows for the definition of private members that are inaccessible through the public interface. Listing 2-3 shows an example that utilizes get and set functions to access the *name* member.

LISTING 2-3 The revealing module pattern

```
"use strict";

var Wingtip = window.Wingtip || {};
Wingtip.Customer = function () {

    //private members
    var name,
        setname = function(n) { name = n; },
        getname = function() { return name; },
        talk = function() {alert("My name is " + name);};};
```

```
        //public interface
        return {
            set_name: setname,
            get_name: getname,
            speak: talk
        }

    }();
```

If the parentheses are removed from the function, it is no longer self-invoking. To make use of the module, you must create an instance referenced by a new variable. Using this variant of the module pattern, you can create multiple customer instances for use, which should feel very familiar to C# developers. The following code shows how to create an instance if the module were not self-invoking:

```
var customer1 = new Wingtip.Customer();
customer1.set_name("Brian Cox");
customer1.speak();
```

Understanding the prototype pattern

Unlike previous patterns, the prototype pattern does not rely on closures to achieve its functionality. Instead, it relies on the inheritance of the prototype chain. The prototype provides a means of defining members in a single place for use by many instances. Every object in JavaScript has a prototype property with which you can expand to include new members. This sets up a very interesting pattern that you can utilize to define a prototype that can be used to create instances later. If you're a C# developer, this feels a lot like defining a class from which instances are created. The following code shows an example of the prototype pattern:

```
"use strict";

var Wingtip = window.Wingtip || {};
Wingtip.Customer = function (n) {
    this.name = n;
};

Wingtip.Customer.prototype.speak = function() {
    alert("My name is " + this.name);
}
```

The prototype pattern begins with the definition of a function. This function often accepts initialization parameters, which are stored in variables defined within the prototype by using the *this* keyword. The initial function definition acts as the constructor for new instances, which means that the variables defined within are also defined for each instance as part of the prototype.

The prototype associated with a function can easily be extended by referencing the prototype property and adding a new member. In the example, a *speak* function is added to the prototype. As an alternative, you can also define the prototype as an object containing many functions, as shown in the following code:

```
"use strict";

var Wingtip = window.Wingtip || {};
Wingtip.Customer = function (n) {
    this.name = n
};
Wingtip.Customer.prototype = {
    get_name: function() { return this.name; },
    set_name: function(n) { this.name = n; },
    speak: function() { alert("My name is " + this.name); }
};
```

The prototype pattern can also be combined with the module pattern by simply defining a self-invoking function in the prototype. Additionally, defining members separately is not required; you could simply define all members in the constructor as shown in the code that follows. The bottom line is that hybrid patterns are possible by combining several concepts together.

```
"use strict";

var Wingtip = window.Wingtip || {};
Wingtip.Customer = function (n) {
    this.name = n;
    this.speak = function() { alert("My name is " + this.name); };
};
```

Once the prototype is defined, you can create instances by using the *new* keyword. Each instance inherits the definition of the function prototype. The code that follows shows how to create an instance and invoke a function. The resulting code has a decidedly object-oriented feel that should make C# programmers comfortable.

```
var customer1 = new Wingtip.Customer("Brian Cox");
customer1.speak();
```

Introducing jQuery for SharePoint developers

In the same way that developers can build and reuse their own JavaScript libraries, third parties have created JavaScript libraries that can simply be referenced and used in app development. Although there are many third-party libraries available on the Internet, one library, jQuery, is so popular that it has almost become synonymous with JavaScript itself.

The reason for the popularity of jQuery is that it does two very important things extremely well: it makes it easy to select elements from the document object model (DOM) and then perform operations on the selected elements. jQuery is so important that Microsoft has baked it into the app project template in Microsoft Visual Studio 2012. Therefore, SharePoint app developers must understand how to use the jQuery library. The following sections present a brief introduction to jQuery from the perspective of a SharePoint app developer. Readers who want complete coverage of the library should visit the jQuery website at *www.jquery.com*.

Referencing jQuery

To include any JavaScript library in an app, it must be referenced by using a script tag. The script tag refers to the location of the library so that it can be downloaded. In the Visual Studio app project template, the jQuery library is included as a file and referenced in the *Default.aspx* page, as shown in the following code:

```
<script type="text/javascript" src="../Scripts/jquery-1.6.2.min.js"></script>
```

Along with directly hosting the jQuery library in your app, you can also choose to use a content delivery network (CDN). A CDN hosts the jQuery library in the cloud so that it is always available. Referencing a CDN can improve performance of public-facing apps because the library is downloaded in parallel and cached. The same version of the library can then be used across several different apps. The following code shows how to reference the Microsoft CDN for jQuery:

```
<script src="http://ajax.aspnetcdn.com/ajax/jquery/jquery-1.8.0.min.js" type="text/javascript">
</script>
```

Understanding the global function

The jQuery library is encapsulated in a single function named *jQuery*, which is known as the *global function*. Using the global function, you can easily select elements from the DOM, which is fundamental to any JavaScript solution. To select DOM elements, the global function is invoked and selector syntax is passed. The following code shows the traditional method of selecting elements in JavaScript by using the *getElementById* method, contrasted with the jQuery approach:

```
var elem1 = document.getElementById("displayDiv");
var elem2 = jQuery("#displayDiv");
```

In the preceding code, the jQuery selector syntax uses the hash sign to indicate that the selector corresponds to the ID of the desired element. You can simplify this code even further because the jQuery library uses the $ symbol as an alias for the global function. Therefore, the following code is equivalent:

```
var elem1 = document.getElementById("displayDiv");
var elem2 = $("#displayDiv");
```

Understanding selector syntax

At first, it might seem that selecting DOM elements by using jQuery is not that exciting. The power of jQuery, however, lies in the fact that the selector syntax is identical to that used in cascading style sheets (CSS). This means that you can use a rich, familiar selector syntax to reference any part of the DOM, which becomes a powerful and efficient way to manipulate the DOM elements. Table 2-2 shows common selection operations and how to accomplish them in jQuery.

TABLE 2-2 jQuery selector syntax

Operation	Example	Description
Select elements by type	`$("p")`	Selects all paragraph elements in the page
Select elements by ID	`$("#container")`	Selects the element whose ID is "container"
Select elements by class	`$(".emphasis")`	Selects all elements with a class attribute of "emphasis"
Select elements by type and ID	`$("div#displayDiv")`	Selects the <div> element whose ID is "displayDiv"
Select elements by ancestor and descendant	`$("div#displayDiv p")`	Select all paragraph elements within the <div> whose ID is "displayDiv", regardless of where they are inside the div element
Select elements based on their parent	`$("div#displayDiv > p")`	Selects all paragraph elements that are children of the <div> whose ID is "displayDiv"
Select the first child of a parent	`$("ul#displayList > li:first")`	Selects the first list item element in the unordered list whose ID is "displayList"
Select the last child of a parent	`$("ul#displayList > li:last")`	Selects the last list item element in the unordered list whose ID is "displayList"
Select elements by attribute	`$("input[name='firstName']")`	Selects the input element whose name attribute is "firstName"

Once you understand the common selection operations, you can move ahead to combine them to create more sophisticated selectors. The jQuery library also supports a number of extensions that provide yet more capabilities. A complete description of supported selectors is available on the jQuery website at *http://api.jquery.com/category/selectors/*.

Understanding jQuery methods

Once you have selected DOM elements, you will want to manipulate them. This is where jQuery methods come into play. The jQuery library has a tremendous number of methods that perform all kinds of useful DOM manipulations. These manipulations are always performed on the collection of elements returned from the jQuery global function. Table 2-3 shows some commonly used jQuery methods.

TABLE 2-3 Common jQuery methods

Method	Example	Description
Read the HTML within an element	`var x = $("#displayDiv").html();`	Returns the inner HTML of the element whose ID is "displayDiv"
Modify the HTML within an element	`$("#displayDiv").html("<p>Hello</p>")`	Sets the inner HTML of the element whose ID is "displayDiv"
Read the text of an element	`$("ul#displayList > li:first").text();`	Returns the text of the first list item in the unordered list whose ID is "displayList"
Modify the text of an element	`$("ul#displayList > li:first").text("Item 1");`	Sets the text of the first list item in the unordered list whose ID is "displayList"
Read the value of a style property	`var x = $("#displayDiv").css("marginTop");`	Returns the value of the "margin-top" CSS property for the element whose ID is "displayDiv"
Set the value of a style property	`$("#displayDiv").css("marginTop","5px");`	Sets the value of the "margin-top" CSS property for the element whose ID is "displayDiv" to "5px"
Add a CSS class to an element	`$("#displayDiv").addClass("emphasis")`	Adds the CSS class named "emphasis" to the element whose ID is "displayDiv"
Remove a CSS class from an element	`$("#displayDiv").removeClass("emphasis")`	Removes the CSS class named "emphasis" to the element whose ID is "displayDiv"
Hide an element	`$("#displayDiv").hide()`	Hides the element whose ID is "displayDiv"
Show an element	`$("#displayDiv").show()`	Shows the element whose ID is "displayDiv"
Toggle the display of an element	`$("#displayDiv").toggle()`	Hides the element whose ID is "displayDiv" if it is visible; otherwise, shows it

jQuery supports many methods for manipulating DOM elements beyond what is shown in Table 2-3. The complete reference of supported methods is available at *http://api.jquery.com/category/manipulation*. Furthermore, jQuery methods can be chained together so that you can perform several operations in a single line of code. The following code changes the inner HTML of an element, adds a class, and then displays the result, all in a single line:

```
$("displayDiv").html("<p>Hello</p>").addClass("emphasis").show();
```

Understanding jQuery event handling

Along with selecting and manipulating elements, you can use jQuery to attach event handlers to DOM elements. By handling events in jQuery, you can keep your JavaScript code out of the webpage and contained within custom libraries. This approach makes your code much more maintainable and isolated than using a more traditional approach to bind events to DOM elements.

The basic approach for binding events is to select the target DOM element by using the global function and then bind the event. The code to run in response to the event can be defined directly in the binding as an anonymous function. The following code shows a simple example of binding the click event of all paragraph elements:

```
$("p").click( function (e) {
    alert($(e.target).text());
});
```

Notice in the preceding code that the function handling the click event is defined in line with the binding. Additionally, notice how the element that caused the event can be determined by selecting *e.target* within the function. Complete documentation for the events supported by the jQuery library is available at *http://api.jquery.com/category/events*.

Of all the events available in jQuery, the most important is the *ready* event of the *document* object. This event fires when the DOM is ready for selection and manipulation. The SharePoint-hosted app project template in Visual Studio 2012 automatically adds this event handler into the *Apps.js* library of the app to act as the starting point. This is a pattern that you should follow in your apps, as well.

Working with the CSOM

SharePoint 2010 introduced the CSOM as a way to program against a Windows Communication Foundation (WCF) endpoint in SharePoint by using a style that mimicked server-side API development. Prior to the introduction of CSOM, SharePoint developers had only a limited set of web services available for use from client-side code. With the introduction of CSOM, developers had a way to access a significant portion of core SharePoint functionality from C# (called the "managed" client object model), JavaScript, and Silverlight. Although the Silverlight CSOM is still available in SharePoint 2013, its primary role is for creating mobile apps, so this chapter focuses on the managed and JavaScript implementations of CSOM.

Understanding client object model fundamentals

The managed and JavaScript client object models are maintained in separate libraries, which are located under the SharePoint system directory. The managed client object model is contained in the assemblies *Microsoft.SharePoint.Client.dll* and *Microsoft.SharePoint.ClientRuntime.dll*, which can be found in the ISAPI folder. The JavaScript client object model is contained in the library *sp.js*, which is located in the LAYOUTS folder. Although each of the models provides a different programming interface, each interacts with SharePoint through a WCF service named *Client.svc*, which is located in the ISAPI directory. Figure 2-1 shows a basic architectural diagram for the client object models.

In SharePoint 2013, CSOM has been greatly expanded to include functionality from workloads outside of SharePoint Foundation. Using CSOM, app developers now have client-side access to Enterprise Search, Business Connectivity Services, Managed Metadata, Social, and much more. This additional functionality is made available through separate assemblies and libraries that can be referenced in your apps.

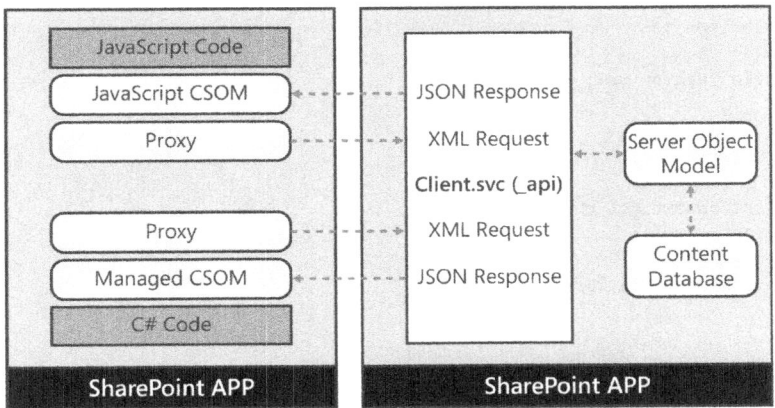

FIGURE 2-1 The client object model provides a programmatic interface to make web service calls against SharePoint by passing in an XML request and receiving a JSON response.

Each of the object models presents an object interface in front of a service proxy. Developers write client-side code using the object model, but the operations are batched and sent as a single XML request to the *Client.svc* service. When the XML request is received, the *Client.svc* service makes calls to the server-side object model on behalf of the client. The results of the server-side calls are then sent back to the calling client in the form of a JavaScript Object Notation (JSON) object.

Understanding contexts

Much like the standard code you write against the server-side object model, CSOM requires a starting point in the form of a context object. The context object provides an entry point into the associated API that can be used to gain access to other objects. Once you have access to the objects, you can interact with the scalar properties of the object freely (for example, *Name*, *Title*, *Url*, and so on). Listing 2-4 shows how to create a context in each of the models and return an object representing a site collection. After the site collection object is returned, the *Url* property is examined.

LISTING 2-4 Creating contexts

```
//Managed Client Object Model
string appWebUrl = Page.Request["SPAppWebUrl"];
using (ClientContext ctx = new ClientContext(appWebUrl))
{
    Site siteCollection = ctx.Site;
    ctx.Load(siteCollection);
    ctx.ExecuteQuery();
    string url = siteCollection.Url;
}

//JavaScript Client Object Model
var siteCollection;
var ctx = new SP.ClientContext.get_current();
siteCollection = ctx.get_site();
ctx.load(site);
ctx.executeQueryAsync(success, failure);

function success() {
    string url = siteCollection.get_url();
}
function failure() {
    alert("Failure!");
}
```

The *ClientContext* class in the managed object model inherits from the *ClientContextRuntime* class. Using the *ClientContext* class, you can get a valid runtime context by passing in the URL of a site. In Listing 2-4, the URL of the app web is retrieved from the *SPAppWebUrl* query string parameter. This URL is always available to the remote web and can be used to create a client context for scenarios in which the SharePoint app is using the "internal" security principal. Scenarios that utilize OAuth tokens for app authentication are covered in Chapter 3.

The *SP.ClientContext* object in the JavaScript client object model inherits from the *SP.ClientContext Runtime* object and provides equivalent functionality to the *ClientContext* class found in the managed client object model. Like the managed model, you can get a runtime context in the JavaScript model by using the *SP.ClientContext* class and passing a URL. In Listing 2-4, the context is created by using the *get_current* method, which returns a client context for the app web.

Loading and executing operations

The *ClientContextRuntime* class used by the managed client defines two methods for loading objects: *Load* and *LoadQuery*. You use these load methods to designate objects that should be retrieved from the server. The *Load* method specifies an object or collection to retrieve, whereas you use the *Load Query* method to return collections of objects by using a Language-Integrated Query (LINQ) request.

Executing the *Load* or *LoadQuery* method does not cause the client to communicate with the server. Instead, it adds the load operation to a batch that will be executed on the server. In fact, you can execute multiple load methods (as well as other operations) before calling the server. Each operation is batched waiting for your code to initiate communication with server. To execute the batched operations, your code must call the *ExecuteQuery* method in managed code or the *Execute QueryAsync* method in JavaScript. The *ExecuteQuery* method creates an XML request and passes it to the *Client.svc* service synchronously. The *ExecuteQueryAsync* method sends the request asynchronously. Designated success and failure callback methods receive notification when the asynchronous batch operation is complete.

The sample code in Listing 2-4 uses the *Load* method to request an object representing the current site collection. After an object is returned, you can generally access any of the scalar properties associated with the object. In cases for which you do not want to return all of the scalar properties for a given object, you can designate the properties to return. In the managed object, properties are designated by providing a series of lambda expressions. In the JavaScript object model, properties are designated by name. This technique helps to minimize the amount of data sent between the client and server. The following code shows how to request only the *Title* and *ServerRelativeUrl* properties for a site collection object:

```
//Managed CSOM references properties via lambda expressions
ctx.Load(site, s=>s.Title, s=>s.ServerRelativeUrl);

//JavaScript CSOM references properties by name
ctx.Load(site, "Title", "ServerRelativeUrl");
```

Working with the managed client object model

Because the managed client object model is supported by IntelliSense, is checked at compile time, and functions synchronously, many developers choose to develop apps that utilize remote webs and the managed CSOM to communicate with SharePoint. Using the managed client object model is a simple matter of setting a reference to the assemblies *Microsoft.SharePoint.Client.dll* and *Microsoft. SharePoint.ClientRuntime.dll*, adding a *using* statement for the *Microsoft.SharePoint.Client* namespace, and writing code. This section details how to perform basic operations with the managed client object model.

Returning collections

When working with the client object models, you will quite often be interested in returning collections of items such as all the lists in a site or all of the items in a list. Collections of items can be returned by using either the *Load* or *LoadQuery* methods. When specifying the items of a collection to return, you can use the *Load* method along with a LINQ query formatted by using *method* syntax. Additionally, you can use the *LoadQuery* method with a LINQ query formatted by using *query* syntax. Listing 2-5 shows how to return all of the list titles in a site for which the *Title* is not *NULL*.

LISTING 2-5 Returning collections by using LINQ

```
string appWebUrl = Page.Request["SPAppWebUrl"];
using (ClientContext ctx = new ClientContext(appWebUrl))
{
    //Method Syntax
    ctx.Load(ctx.Web,
            w => w.Lists.Include(l => l.Title).Where(l => l.Title != null));
    ctx.ExecuteQuery();

    foreach (List list in ctx.Web.Lists)
    {
        Response.Write(list.Title);
    }

    //Query Syntax
    var q = from l in ctx.Web.Lists
            where l.Title != null
            select l;

    var r = ctx.LoadQuery(q);
    ctx.ExecuteQuery();

    Response.Write("<ul>");
    foreach (var i in r)
    {
        Response.Write("<li>");
        Response.Write(i.Title);
        Response.Write("</li>");
    }
    Response.Write("</ul>");
}
```

Handling errors

Because of the disconnected nature of the client object model, error handling is especially important. You might see errors thrown when you attempt to access an object or value that has not yet been retrieved from the server. You might also see errors if you create a query that is not meaningful in the current context, such as trying to retrieve list items before loading the associated list. Finally, you must deal with errors that happen in the middle of batch operations on the server. All of these situations mean that you must pay special attention to error handling in your CSOM solutions.

If you attempt to access a scalar property that has not been retrieved, you will receive a *Property OrFieldNotInitializedException* error. If you make a request to the server that is deemed invalid, you will receive a *ClientRequestException* error. If your LINQ query is invalid, you will receive an

InvalidQueryExpressionException error. General errors thrown on the server during execution of a request will result in a *ServerException* error. Listing 2-6 shows code that generates the various run-time errors you might see when working with the managed client object model.

LISTING 2-6 Handling request errors

```
string appWebUrl = Page.Request["SPAppWebUrl"];
using (ClientContext ctx = new ClientContext(appWebUrl))
{
    try
    {
        //Fails because the object was not initialized
        //Requires Load() and ExecuteQuery()
        Response.Write(ctx.Web.Title);
    }
    catch (PropertyOrFieldNotInitializedException x)
    {
        Response.Write("<p>Property not initialized. " + x.Message + "</p>");
    }

    try
    {
        //Fails because Skip() and Take() are meaningless
        //in the context of a list collection
        ctx.Load(ctx.Web, w => w.Lists.Skip(5).Take(10));
        ctx.ExecuteQuery();
    }
    catch (InvalidQueryExpressionException x)
    {
        Response.Write("<p>Invalid LINQ query. " + x.Message + "</p>");
    }

    try
    {
        //Fails because InvalidObject is a meaningless object
        InvalidObject o = new InvalidObject(ctx, null);
        ctx.Load(o);
        ctx.ExecuteQuery();
    }
    catch (ClientRequestException x)
    {
        Response.Write("<p>Bad request. " + x.Message + "</p>");
    }
```

```
try
{
    //Fails because the list does not exist
    //The failure occurs on the server during processing
    ctx.Load(ctx.Web,w=>w.Lists);
    List myList = ctx.Web.Lists.GetByTitle("Non-Existent List");
    myList.Description = "A new description";
    myList.Update();
    ctx.ExecuteQuery();

}
catch (ServerException x)
{
    Response.Write("<p>Exception on server. " + x.Message + "</p>");
}
}
```

After looking over the errors that can occur during operations, the *ServerException* stands out as noteworthy. This is because the *ServerException* is thrown when an operation fails on the server. Furthermore, the failing operation could be in the middle of a large batch of operations, which can lead to unpredictable behavior. The fundamental challenge with the batch model embodied in the client object model is that you need a way to respond to errors that happen on the server so that the remainder of the batch operations can finish processing. The *ServerException* error is thrown on the client after the batch has failed, which gives you no opportunity to correct the error.

Fortunately, CSOM provides a mechanism for sending error-handling instructions to the server along with the batch operations. You can use the *ExceptionHandlingScope* object to define a *try-catch-finally* block that embodies server-side operations. If errors occur during processing on the server, it is handled on the server by the code embodied in the *ExceptionHandlingScope* object. Listing 2-7 shows how exception-handling scopes are implemented in the managed client object model.

LISTING 2-7 Handling errors in a scope

```
string appWebUrl = Page.Request["SPAppWebUrl"];
using (ClientContext ctx = new ClientContext(appWebUrl))
{
    //Set up error handling
    ExceptionHandlingScope xScope = new ExceptionHandlingScope(ctx);

    using (xScope.StartScope())
    {
        using (xScope.StartTry())
        {
            //Try to update the description of a list named "My List"
            List myList = ctx.Web.Lists.GetByTitle("My List");
            myList.Description = "A new description";
            myList.Update();
        }
```

```
using (xScope.StartCatch())
{
    //Fails if the list "My List" does not exist
    //So, we'll create a new list
    ListCreationInformation listCI = new ListCreationInformation();
    listCI.Title = "My List";
    listCI.TemplateType = (int)ListTemplateType.GenericList;
    listCI.QuickLaunchOption = Microsoft.SharePoint.Client.
                                    QuickLaunchOptions.On;
    List list = ctx.Web.Lists.Add(listCI);
}
using (xScope.StartFinally())
{
    //Try to update the list now if it failed originally
    List myList = ctx.Web.Lists.GetByTitle("My List");
    if(myList.Description.Length==0)
    {
        myList.Description = "A new description";
        myList.Update();
    }
}
}

//Execute the entire try-catch as a batch!
ctx.ExecuteQuery();
}
```

The most important aspect of the code shown in Listing 2-7 is that the *ExecuteQuery* method is called only once and it appears after the code in the exception handling scope. This means that all of the operations defined in the exception handling scope are sent to the server in a single batch. Initially, the server tries to update the description of the target list. If this operation fails, the exception handling scope assumes it is because the list does not exist. Therefore, the exception-handling scope creates a new list with the correct name. Finally, the description is updated for the newly created list.

The exception-handling scope provides a powerful way for you to deal with errors that occur during batch processing, but it does require some additional planning. For example, the code in Listing 2-7 assumes that any failure is the result of a nonexistent list. However, there are other reasons why the operation could fail, such as the end user not having the rights to update the list. Fortunately, the *ExceptionHandlingScope* provides properties that help you to understand exactly what went wrong on the server. The *ServerErrorCode*, *ServerErrorValue*, and *ServerStackTrace* properties can all be used to analyze the server error and make a decision about how to proceed.

Creating, reading, updating, and deleting

In the conditional scope shown in Listing 2-7, a new list is created if the user has the appropriate permissions. Creating new lists and items using the managed client object model is done with the creation information objects. Using the *ListCreationInformation* and *ListItemCreationInformation* objects, you can define all of the necessary values for a list or item and then send that data with the batch back to the server. Listing 2-8 shows how to use these objects to create a new list and list item.

LISTING 2-8 Creating a list and list item

```
string appWebUrl = Page.Request["SPAppWebUrl"];
using (ClientContext ctx = new ClientContext(appWebUrl))
{
    //Create a new list
    ListCreationInformation listCI = new ListCreationInformation();
    listCI.Title = "My List";
    listCI.Description += "A list for use with the Client OM";
    listCI.TemplateType = (int)ListTemplateType.GenericList;
    listCI.QuickLaunchOption = Microsoft.SharePoint.Client.QuickLaunchOptions.On;
    List list = ctx.Web.Lists.Add(listCI);
    ctx.ExecuteQuery();

    //Create a new list item
    ListItemCreationInformation listItemCI = new ListItemCreationInformation();
    ListItem item = list.AddItem(listItemCI);
    item["Title"] = "New Item";
    item.Update();
    ctx.ExecuteQuery();
}
```

If you would like to return items from a list by using CSOM, you must write Collaborative Application Markup Language (CAML) queries. CAML queries are created for the managed client object model via the *CamlQuery* object. This object has a *ViewXml* property that accepts a CAML query designating the items to return. Listing 2-9 demonstrates running a CAML query against a list.

LISTING 2-9 Using CAML to return list items

```
string appWebUrl = Page.Request["SPAppWebUrl"];
using (ClientContext ctx = new ClientContext(appWebUrl))
{
    //Read the Site, List, and Items
    ctx.Load(ctx.Web);

    List myList = ctx.Web.Lists.GetByTitle("My List");
    ctx.Load(myList);

    StringBuilder caml = new StringBuilder();
    caml.Append("<View><Query>");
    caml.Append("<Where><Eq><FieldRef Name='Title'/>");
    caml.Append("<Value Type='Text'>New Item</Value></Eq></Where>");
    caml.Append("</Query><RowLimit>100</RowLimit></View>");
```

```
CamlQuery query = new CamlQuery();
query.ViewXml = caml.ToString();
ListItemCollection myItems = myList.GetItems(query);
ctx.Load(myItems);

ctx.ExecuteQuery();
Response.Write("<p>Site: " + ctx.Web.Title + "</p>");
Response.Write("<p>List: " + myList.Title + "</p>");
Response.Write("<p>Item Count: " + myItems.Count.ToString() + "</p>");
}
```

Updating through the managed client object model is straightforward. In most cases, you will simply set the value of a property and then call the appropriate *Update* method. Listing 2-10 presents samples of updating a site, list, and list item.

LISTING 2-10 Update operations

```
//Update the Site, List, and Items
ctx.Web.Description = "Client OM samples";
ctx.Web.Update();

myList.Description = "Client OM data";
myList.Update();

foreach (ListItem myItem in myItems)
{
    myItem["Title"] = "Updated";
    myItem.Update();
}

ctx.ExecuteQuery();
Response.Write("<p>Site: " + ctx.Web.Description + "</p>");
Response.Write("<p>List: " + myList.Description + "</p>");
Response.Write("<p>Item Count: " + myItems.Count.ToString()+ "</p>");
```

Deleting objects with the managed client object model involves calling the *DeleteObject* method. This method is the same across most objects that can be deleted. The following code shows how to delete the list created earlier:

```
myList.DeleteObject();
ctx.ExecuteQuery();
```

Along with lists, you'll also want to work with libraries. Document libraries are handled in the managed client object model similarly to lists. Of course, the major difference is handling documents. Fortunately, uploading documents to libraries by using the managed client object model is very similar to using the server object model; you must upload the document using the URL of the folder in which you want to store the document. Listing 2-11 shows a full set of create, read, update, and delete operations around a file and a document library.

LISTING 2-11 Working with document libraries

```
string appWebUrl = Page.Request["SPAppWebUrl"];
using (ClientContext ctx = new ClientContext(appWebUrl))
{
    //Get site
    Web site = ctx.Web;
    ctx.Load(site);
    ctx.ExecuteQuery();

    //Create a new library
    ListCreationInformation listCI = new ListCreationInformation();
    listCI.Title = "My Docs";
    listCI.Description = "A library for use with Client OM";
    listCI.TemplateType = (int)ListTemplateType.DocumentLibrary;
    listCI.QuickLaunchOption = Microsoft.SharePoint.Client.QuickLaunchOptions.On;
    List list =site.Lists.Add(listCI);
    ctx.ExecuteQuery();

    //Create a document
    MemoryStream m = new MemoryStream();
    StreamWriter w = new StreamWriter(m);
    w.Write("Some content for the document.");
    w.Flush();

    //Add it to the library
    FileCreationInformation fileCI = new FileCreationInformation();
    fileCI.Content = m.ToArray();
    fileCI.Overwrite = true;
    fileCI.Url = appWebAppUrl + "/My%20Docs/MyFile.txt";
    Folder rootFolder = site.GetFolderByServerRelativeUrl("My%20Docs");
    ctx.Load(rootFolder);
    Microsoft.SharePoint.Client.File newFile = rootFolder.Files.Add(fileCI);
    ctx.ExecuteQuery();

    //Edit Properties
    ListItem newItem = newFile.ListItemAllFields;
    ctx.Load(newItem);
    newItem["Title"] = "My new file";
    newItem.Update();
    ctx.ExecuteQuery();

    //Delete file
    newItem.DeleteObject();
    ctx.ExecuteQuery();
}
```

Working with the JavaScript client object model

The JavaScript client object model is really only a viable choice in SharePoint-hosted apps for which C# code is not allowed and the pages have an associated SharePoint context. The SharePoint 2013 app project template for SharePoint-hosted apps provides some initial template code to implement a welcome message. This code is a good place to see the fundamentals of CSOM in action. Listing 2-12 comes from the app project template for a SharePoint-hosted app.

LISTING 2-12 Visual Studio 2012 app project template code

```
var context;
var web;
var user;

$(document).ready(function () {
    context = SP.ClientContext.get_current();
    web = context.get_web();
    getUserName();

});

function getUserName() {
    user = web.get_currentUser();
    context.load(user);
    context.executeQueryAsync(onGetUserNameSuccess, onGetUserNameFail);
}

function onGetUserNameSuccess() {
    $('#message').text('Hello ' + user.get_title());
}

function onGetUserNameFail(sender, args) {
    alert('Failed to get user name. Error:' + args.get_message());
}
```

The code in Listing 2-12 creates three variables in the global namespace named *context*, *web*, and *user* to reference objects needed globally. The *context* variable is used to setup the SharePoint context on the client side so that calls can be made back to the *Client.svc* endpoint; the *web* variable is used to reference the app web itself; and the *user* variable references the current app user.

Note This template code violates the best practice of encapsulating code in a separate namespace and using strict JavaScript. Therefore, it is best to simply delete all of the template code when creating your own apps.

To populate the variables, a call is made to the *load* method to specify that the scalar properties should be loaded, and then a call to the *executeQueryAsync* method is made to make an asynchronous call to the *Client.svc* endpoint. In the app project code, the round trip populates not only information about the app web, but also information about the current user. Combining operations in this way makes CSOM programming more efficient. Two callback functions, which the template code names *onGetUserNameSuccess* and *onGetUserNameFail*, are passed. The first callback function named is called if the round trip completes without errors. The second callback function is called if errors occur.

Returning collections

The JavaScript client object model supports both a *load* and *loadQuery* method. The *loadQuery* method can be used to store a collection into a variable other than the one referencing the desired collection. In either method, you can use query strings to request that collections be included in the returned results. Listing 2-13 illustrates how to use the JavaScript client object model to return all of the list titles in the app web along with the field names and descriptions for each list.

LISTING 2-13 Returning collections by using JavaScript

```
"use strict";

var Wingtip = window.Wingtip || {}

Wingtip.Collections = function () {

    //private members
    var site,
        listCollection,

        getListCollection = function () {
            var ctx = new SP.ClientContext.get_current();
            site = ctx.get_web();
            ctx.load(site);
            listCollection = site.get_lists();
            ctx.load(listCollection,
            'Include(Title,Id,Fields.Include(Title,Description))');
            ctx.executeQueryAsync(success, failure);
        },

        success = function () {

            var html = [];

            //List Information
            html.push("<ul>");
            var listEnumerator = listCollection.getEnumerator();
            while (listEnumerator.moveNext()) {
```

```
            //List Title
            html.push("<li>");
            html.push(listEnumerator.get_current().get_title());
            html.push("<ul>");

            //Field Names
            var fieldEnumerator =
                listEnumerator.get_current().get_fields().getEnumerator();
            while (fieldEnumerator.moveNext()) {
                html.push("<li>");
                html.push(fieldEnumerator.get_current().get_title());
                html.push("</li>");
            }

            html.push("</ul></li>");
        }
        html.push("</ul>");

        //Show results
        $("#displayDiv").html(html.join(''));
    },

    failure = function (sender, args) {
        alert(args.get_message());
    }

    //public interface
    return {
        execute: getListCollection
    }
}();

$(document).ready(function () {
    Wingtip.Collections.execute();
});
```

Handling errors

Just like the managed client object model, the JavaScript client object model must deal with the potential for server-side errors during the round trip. Because the JavaScript client object model can only make asynchronous calls, the basic error-handling pattern involves the definition of success and failure callback methods. However, you can also use error scopes in your JavaScript. Listing 2-14 shows how to set up error scopes in JavaScript. The sample performs the same functionality as presented in Listing 2-7, wherein managed code was used.

LISTING 2-14 JavaScript CSOM error scopes

```javascript
"use strict";

var Wingtip = window.Wingtip || {}

Wingtip.ErrorScope = function () {

    //private members
    var site,

    scope = function () {

        //Get Context
        var ctx = new SP.ClientContext.get_current();

        //Start Exception-Handling Scope
        var e = new SP.ExceptionHandlingScope(ctx);
        var s = e.startScope();

        //try
        var t = e.startTry();

        var list1 = ctx.get_web().get_lists().getByTitle("My List");
        ctx.load(list1);
        list1.set_description("A new description");
        list1.update();

        t.dispose();

        //catch
        var c = e.startCatch();

        var listCI = new SP.ListCreationInformation();

        listCI.set_title("My List");
        listCI.set_templateType(SP.ListTemplateType.announcements);
        listCI.set_quickLaunchOption(SP.QuickLaunchOptions.on);

        var list = ctx.get_web().get_lists().add(listCI);

        c.dispose();

        //finally
        var f = e.startFinally();
```

```
            var list2 = ctx.get_web().get_lists().getByTitle("My List");
            ctx.load(list2);
            list2.set_description("A new description");
            list2.update();

            f.dispose();

            //End Exception-Handling Scope
            s.dispose();

            //Execute
            ctx.executeQueryAsync(success, failure);

            },

        success = function () {
            alert("Success");
        },

        failure = function (sender, args) {
            alert(args.get_message());
        }

        //public interface
        return {
            execute: scope
        }
}();


$(document).ready(function () {
    Wingtip.ErrorScope.execute();
});
```

Creating, reading, updating, and deleting in the JavaScript client object model

Creating, reading, updating, and deleting list items by using the JavaScript client object model is more complex than with the managed client object model. The additional complexity comes from not only the asynchronous calls, but also the need to properly encapsulate the JavaScript so that it's separated from the global namespace. Listing 2-15 shows the basic structure of a JavaScript library used to perform create, read, update, and delete (CRUD) operations on a contacts list contained in a SharePoint-hosted app.

LISTING 2-15 CSOM library structure

```
"use strict";

var Wingtip = window.Wingtip || {};
Wingtip.Contacts;
Wingtip.ContactList = function () {

    //private members
    createItem = function (lname, fname, wphone) {
    },
    readAll = function () {
    },
    readAllSuccess = function () {
    },
    updateItem = function (id, lname, fname, wphone) {
    },
    removeItem = function (id) {
    },
    success = function () {
        readAll();
    },
    error = function (sender, args) {
        alert(args.get_message());
    }

    //public interface
    return {
        createContact: createItem,
        updateContact: updateItem,
        deleteContact: removeItem
    }

}();

$(document).ready(function () {
    Wingtip.ContactList.createContact("Cox", "Brian", "555-555-5555");
    alert("Contact Created!");
    Wingtip.ContactList.updateContact(1, "Cox", "Brian", "111-111-1111");
    alert("Contact Updated!");
    Wingtip.ContactList.deleteContact(1);
    alert("Contact Deleted!");
});
```

Before examining the implementation details for the CRUD operations, take some time to study the structure of the library. Listing 2-15 contains the definition of a namespace object and a self-invoking function, which should be familiar from other examples in this chapter. In this case, however, a new property named *Wingtip.Contacts* is also defined. This property is used to hold a reference to the list items between asynchronous calls to the SharePoint server. Within the self-invoking function, all of the CRUD operations are defined, but only the create, update, and delete functions are revealed through the public interface of the library. These functions are called from some example code contained in the *ready* event handler.

Creating new contacts is done in the *createItem* function. This function uses the *SP.ListItemCreationInformation* object to define a new list item. The first name, last name, and phone number are set on the new item, and it is added to the list. Note that in a contacts list, the "Title" field is actually the last name of the contact. Listing 2-16 presents the code for adding a new item.

LISTING 2-16 Creating new items

```
createItem = function (lname, fname, wphone) {
    var ctx = new SP.ClientContext.get_current();
    var list = ctx.get_web().get_lists().getByTitle("Contacts");
    ctx.load(list);
    var listItemCreationInfo = new SP.ListItemCreationInformation();
    var newContact = list.addItem(listItemCreationInfo);
    newContact.set_item("Title", lname);
    newContact.set_item("FirstName", fname);
    newContact.set_item("WorkPhone", wphone);
    newContact.update();
    ctx.executeQueryAsync(success, error);
}
```

After each create, update, or delete operation, the list is read and redrawn. The *readAll* function reads every item in the list by using a CAML query and then creates an HTML table to hold the contacts. The HTML is rendered in a <div> via jQuery. Listing 2-17 demonstrates how the list is read and drawn. Note the use of the *Wingtip.Contacts* property to reference the list data between asynchronous calls to the server.

LISTING 2-17 Rendering the list items

```
readAll = function () {
    var ctx = new SP.ClientContext.get_current();
    var query = "<View><Query><OrderBy><FieldRef Name='Title'/>" +
                "<FieldRef Name='FirstName'/></OrderBy></Query>" +
                "<ViewFields><FieldRef Name='ID'/><FieldRef Name='Title'/>" +
                "<FieldRef Name='FirstName'/><FieldRef Name='WorkPhone'/>
                </ViewFields></View>";
    var camlQuery = new SP.CamlQuery();
    camlQuery.set_viewXml(query);
    var list = ctx.get_web().get_lists().getByTitle("Contacts");
    ctx.load(list);
    Wingtip.Contacts = list.getItems(camlQuery);
    ctx.load(Wingtip.Contacts, 'Include(ID,Title,FirstName,WorkPhone)');
    ctx.executeQueryAsync(readAllSuccess, error);
},

readAllSuccess = function () {
    var html = [];
    html.push("<table><thead><tr><th>ID</th><th>First Name</th>");
    html.push("<th>Last Name</th><th>Title</th></tr></thead>");
```

```
    var listItemEnumerator = Wingtip.Contacts.getEnumerator();

    while (listItemEnumerator.moveNext()) {
        var listItem = listItemEnumerator.get_current();
        html.push("<tr><td>");
        html.push(listItem.get_item("ID"));
        html.push("</td><td>");
        html.push(listItem.get_item("FirstName"));
        html.push("</td><td>");
        html.push(listItem.get_item("Title"));
        html.push("</td><td>");
        html.push(listItem.get_item("WorkPhone"));
        html.push("</td><td>");
    }

    html.push("</table>");
    $('#displayDiv').html(html.join(''));
}
```

Updating list items is accomplished by using the *updateItem* function. This function retrieves the item to be updated by its ID in the list. The new values for the fields are applied to the list item and it is updated. After the roundtrip to the server, the table is redrawn with the new values for the list item visible. Listing 2-18 shows the code for updating items.

LISTING 2-18 Updating list items

```
updateItem = function (id, lname, fname, wphone) {
    var ctx = new SP.ClientContext.get_current();
    var list = ctx.get_web().get_lists().getByTitle("Contacts");
    ctx.load(list);
    var listItem = list.getItemById(id);
    listItem.set_item("Title", lname);
    listItem.set_item("FirstName", fname);
    listItem.set_item("WorkPhone", wphone);
    listItem.update();
    ctx.executeQueryAsync(success, error);
}
```

Deleting list items is done by using the *removeItem* function. The function retrieves the item to delete by its ID. The *DeleteObject* method is then called to remove the designated item from the list. After the item is removed asynchronously, the table is redrawn with the remaining list items. Listing 2-19 presents the code for deleting items.

LISTING 2-19 Deleting list items

```
removeItem = function (id) {
    var ctx = new SP.ClientContext.get_current();
    var list = ctx.get_web().get_lists().getByTitle("Contacts");
    ctx.load(list);
    var listItem = list.getItemById(id);
    listItem.deleteObject();
    ctx.executeQueryAsync(success, error);
}
```

Working with the REST API

If you are planning to create apps that are based primarily on JavaScript, you will be interested in the Representational State Transfer (REST) API. Making REST calls from JavaScript is considerably easier than making the equivalent CSOM calls. Furthermore, several libraries such as jQuery provide additional support for REST calls. All of this makes the REST API an attractive approach for app development.

Understanding REST fundamentals

Remote Procedure Call (RPC) is a software architecture that uses a generated client-side proxy to communicate with a remote web service. Simple Object Access Protocol (SOAP) is the protocol that is used along with the RPC architecture in classic SharePoint web services. When developers think about making RPCs to SharePoint, they most often think about calling into a SOAP web service to perform tasks, such as retrieve user profile information, run a search, or interact with a list.

REST is a software architecture that uses uniform resource identifiers (URI) to specify operations against a remote service. Open Data Protocol (OData) is the protocol that is used along with REST to access many cloud-based services. Although SharePoint developers are most familiar with the RPC/SOAP approach, the REST/OData approach has become important when developing cloud-based solutions.

REST-based (known more commonly as "RESTful") solutions use standard HTTP *GET, POST, PUT,* and *DELETE* verbs to perform CRUD operations against a remote source. Support for the standard HTTP verbs provides easy cross-platform data access and is ideally suited for cloud-based apps. The OData protocol returns results in either the Atom Publishing Protocol (AtomPub) or JSON.

SharePoint 2010 introduced support for RESTful access to list data through the *listdata.svc* web service. In SharePoint 2013, the *listdata.svc* service is still available, but it should not be used for any new development. Instead, the *client.svc* service has been expanded to include significant support for

RESTful operations. Nearly all of the APIs available through CSOM have a corresponding RESTful endpoint. Additionally, the *client.svc* endpoint can be reached through the alias *_api*, which makes forming appropriate URIs more natural. Figure 2-2 presents a basic architectural diagram of the SharePoint 2013 REST infrastructure.

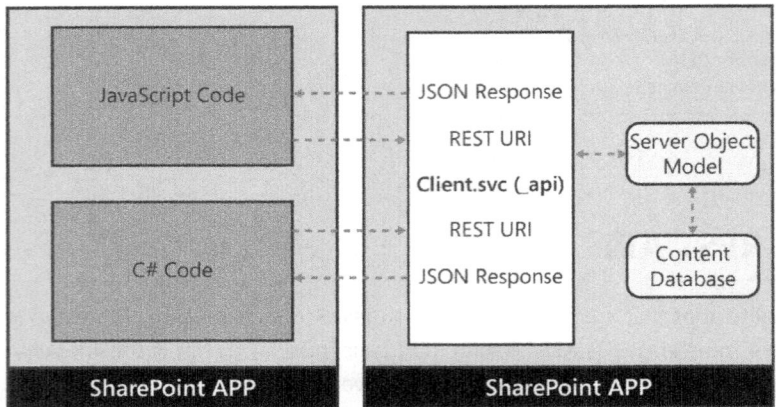

FIGURE 2-2 The REST interface supports RESTful calls made against the "underscore api" endpoint.

The essential task required to use the REST capabilities in SharePoint 2013 is to create the correct URI. One of the nice things about REST is that you can enter URIs directly in the browser and immediately see the result of the HTTP *GET* operation. By using this approach, you can experiment with the URIs quite easily to ensure that they return the desired results. For a SharePoint site collection located at wingtip.com, Listing 2-20 shows the returned XML from the URI http://wingtip.com/_api/site, which returns the site collection properties.

LISTING 2-20 Site collection properties

```
<?xml version="1.0" encoding="utf-8" ?>
<entry xml:base="http://wingtip.com/_api/" xmlns="http://www.w3.org/2005/Atom"
 xmlns:d="http://schemas.microsoft.com/ado/2007/08/dataservices"
 xmlns:m="http://schemas.microsoft.com/ado/2007/08/dataservices/metadata"
 xmlns:georss="http://www.georss.org/georss"
 xmlns:gml="http://www.opengis.net/gml">
 <id>http://wingtip.com/_api/site</id>
 <category term="SP.Site" scheme="http://schemas.microsoft.com/ado/2007/08/
    dataservices/scheme" />
 <link rel="edit" href="site" />
 <link rel="http://schemas.microsoft.com/ado/2007/08/dataservices/related/
    EventReceivers" type="application/atom+xml;type=feed"
    title="EventReceivers" href="site/EventReceivers" />
 <link rel="http://schemas.microsoft.com/ado/2007/08/dataservices/related/
    Features" type="application/atom+xml;type=feed" title="Features" href="site/
    Features" />
```

```xml
<link rel="http://schemas.microsoft.com/ado/2007/08/dataservices/related/Owner"
    type="application/atom+xml;type=entry" title="Owner" href="site/Owner" />
<link rel="http://schemas.microsoft.com/ado/2007/08/dataservices/related/
    RecycleBin" type="application/atom+xml;type=feed"
    title="RecycleBin" href="site/RecycleBin" />
<link rel="http://schemas.microsoft.com/ado/2007/08/dataservices/related/
    RootWeb" type="application/atom+xml;type=entry" title="RootWeb" href="site/
    RootWeb" />
<link rel="http://schemas.microsoft.com/ado/2007/08/dataservices/related/
    UserCustomActions" type="application/atom+xml;type=feed"
    title="UserCustomActions" href="site/UserCustomActions" />
<title />
<updated>2012-08-27T12:14:20Z</updated>
 <author>
   <name />
 </author>
 <content type="application/xml">
   <m:properties>
    <d:AllowDesigner m:type="Edm.Boolean">true</d:AllowDesigner>
    <d:AllowMasterPageEditing m:type="Edm.Boolean">true
      </d:AllowMasterPageEditing>
    <d:AllowRevertFromTemplate m:type="Edm.Boolean">true
      </d:AllowRevertFromTemplate>
    <d:AllowSelfServiceUpgrade m:type="Edm.Boolean">true
      </d:AllowSelfServiceUpgrade>
    <d:AllowSelfServiceUpgradeEvaluation
      m:type="Edm.Boolean">true</d:AllowSelfServiceUpgradeEvaluation>
    <d:CompatibilityLevel m:type="Edm.Int32">15</d:CompatibilityLevel>
    <d:Id m:type="Edm.Guid">eb53c264-14db-4989-a395-b93cbe8b178c</d:Id>
    <d:LockIssue m:null="true" />
    <d:MaxItemsPerThrottledOperation m:type="Edm.Int32">5000
      </d:MaxItemsPerThrottledOperation>
    <d:PrimaryUri>http://wingtip.com/</d:PrimaryUri>
    <d:ReadOnly m:type="Edm.Boolean">false</d:ReadOnly>
    <d:ServerRelativeUrl></d:ServerRelativeUrl>
    <d:ShowUrlStructure m:type="Edm.Boolean">true</d:ShowUrlStructure>
    <d:UIVersionConfigurationEnabled
      m:type="Edm.Boolean">false</d:UIVersionConfigurationEnabled>
    <d:UpgradeReminderDate m:type="Edm.DateTime">1899-12-30T00:00:00
      </d:UpgradeReminderDate>
    <d:Url>http://wingtip.com</d:Url>
   </m:properties>
 </content>
</entry>
```

The main entry point for RESTful URIs is through the _api endpoint, which is referenced through either the site collection or site. Using the site collection or site URI as the root establishes the context for the RESTful operation. The following code shows a typical entry point:

```
http://wingtip.com/_api
```

Following the root reference is the namespace, which refers to the workload that you want to reference, such as search or taxonomy. Table 2-4 shows some sample namespaces in URIs. If the functionality you are invoking resides in SharePoint foundation, no namespace is required. If the functionality resides in one of the many other available namespaces, it can be difficult to determine the exact URI without some form of documentation.

TABLE 2-4 Namespace sample URIs

Sample URI	Description
http://wingtip.com/_api/	SharePoint foundation namespace
http://wingtip.com/_api/search	Enterprise search namespace
http://wingtip.com/_api/sp.userProfiles.peopleManager	User profiles namespace

The namespace in the URI is followed by a reference to the object, property, indexer, or method target that you want to invoke. Objects can include site collections, sites, lists, and list items. After an object is referenced, you can go on to reference the properties, indexers, and methods of the object. Table 2-5 shows several sample URIs referencing objects, properties, indexers, and methods.

TABLE 2-5 Object sample URIs

Sample URI	Description
http://wingtip.com/_api/site	Site collection object
http://wingtip.com/_api/web	Site object
http://wingtip.com/_api/site/url	Site collection url property
http://wingtip.com/_api/web/lists	Site lists collection
http://wingtip.com/_api/web/lists('25e2737d-f23a-4fdb-ad5a-e5a94672504b')	Site lists collection indexer
http://wingtip.com/_api/web/lists/getbytitle('Contacts')	Site lists collection method
http://wingtip.com/_api/web/lists/getbytitle('Contacts')/items	List items collection

The RESTful URI ends with any OData query operators to specify selecting, sorting, or filtering. The *$select* operator is used to specify what fields to return from the query of a collection such as list items or fields. The *$order* operator specifies the sort order of the results. In general, if you do not provide a *$select* operator in your URI, all items in the collection are returned, with the exception of any field or property that might be particularly large. The *$select* operator also supports returning projected fields from related lookup lists by using the *$expand* operator. Table 2-6 shows several sample URIs selecting items to return.

TABLE 2-6 Selecting and sorting items

Sample URI	Description
http://wingtip.com/_api/web/lists/getbytitle('Modules')/items	Select all fields in Modules list.
http://wingtip.com/_api/web/lists/getbytitle('Modules')/items?$select=Title	Select Title field in Modules list.
http://wingtip.com/_api/web/lists/getbytitle('Modules')/items?$select=Title,Instructor/FullName&$expand=Instructor/FullName	Select the Title and Instructor fields from the Modules list. The Instructor field is a lookup from another list, so expand the selection to include the FullName field from the list used as a lookup.
http://wingtip.com/_api/web/lists/getbytitle('Modules')/items?$select=Title&$order=Modified	Select Title field in Modules list and sort by the modified date.

You use the *$filter* operator to filter the results of the RESTful operation. The RESTful URI can include numeric comparisons, string comparisons, and date/time functions. Table 2-7 shows sample URIs that filter returned collections.

TABLE 2-7 Filtering items

Sample URI	Description
http://wingtip.com/_api/web/lists/getbytitle('Contacts')/items?$filter=FirstName eq 'Brian'	Return the item from the Contacts list for which the FirstName is equal to "Brian"
http://wingtip.com/_api/web/lists/getbytitle('Contacts')/items?$filter=startswith(FirstName,'B')	Return all items from the Contacts list for which the first name starts with the letter B
http://wingtip.com/_api/web/lists/getbytitle('Contacts')/items?$filter=month(Modified) eq 8	Return all items from the Contacts list modified in August

The *$top* and *$skip* operators are used to implement paging for results. The *$top* operator specifies how many results to return. You can use the *$skip* operator to pass over a given number of items. Table 2-8 lists several examples using these operators.

TABLE 2-8 Paging items

Sample URI	Description
http://wingtip.com/_api/web/lists/getbytitle('Contacts')/items?$top=10	Returnthe the first 10 items in the Contacts list
http://wingtip.com/_api/web/lists/getbytitle('Contacts')/items?$top=10&$skip=10	Returns the second page of results, with 10 results on each page
http://wingtip.com/_api/web/lists/getbytitle('Contacts')/items?$sort=Title&$top=10&$skip=10	Returns the second page of results, sorted by Last Name

Working with the REST API in JavaScript

When you choose to use JavaScript with your app, you will find that by using the REST API, you can write cleaner code than CSOM. Furthermore, you will find built-in support for REST in the jQuery library, which makes it much easier to use than CSOM. This section details the fundamental operations necessary to work with the REST API through JavaScript.

Performing basic operations

The section "Working with the JavaScript Client Object Model" explains the SharePoint-hosted app project template code in CSOM. As a starting point for understanding REST, Listing 2-21 shows that CSOM code rewritten by using the REST API. Comparing the two implementations reveals that the REST version is more compact.

LISTING 2-21 Welcoming the current user

```
$(document).ready( function () {
    $.getJSON(_spPageContextInfo.webServerRelativeUrl + "/_api/web/currentuser",
      function (data) {
        $("#message").text('Hello ' + data.d.Title);
    });
});
```

As discussed in the section "Understanding jQuery Event Handling," the function *sharePointReady* is called when the jQuery library is loaded. The RESTful URI in Listing 2-22 is created by using the *_spPageContextInfo* object to retrieve a reference to the *webServerRelativeUrl* property. This property returns a URL, which can be concatenated with */_api* to form the root of the URI. The *_spPage ContextInfo* object is added to the ASPX pages in your app by the *SPWebPartManager* control, which means that you can depend on using it to form RESTful URIs in your apps.

The rewritten code makes use of the *jQuery.getJSON* method to retrieve information about the current user. As the name implies, the data returned from the call is in JSON format. JSON format is easy to transform into a JavaScript object, which simplifies your coding. Notice how easily the *Title* property for the current user is retrieved from the JSON results.

The *jQuery.getJSON* method is a shorthand AJAX function that simplifies RESTful calls where JSON is returned. For more control over the call, you can use the *jQuery.ajax* method. Listing 2-22 shows the equivalent call made by using the *jQuery.ajax* method.

LISTING 2-22 Using the *jQuery.ajax* method

```
$(document).ready( function () {
    $.ajax(
        {
            url: _spPageContextInfo.webServerRelativeUrl +
                "/_api/web/currentuser",
            type: "GET",
            headers: {
                "accept": "application/json;odata=verbose",
            },
            success: function (data) {
                $("#message").text('Hello ' + data.d.Title);
            },
```

```
                    error: function (err) {
                        alert(JSON.stringify(err));
                    }
                }
            );
        });
```

Performing CRUD in REST

Much like performing CSOM CRUD operations, CRUD operations in REST should be encapsulated by using one of the JavaScript library patterns. When you create your RESTful libraries, they can have a structure that is very similar to the ones created for CSOM. Listing 2-23 demonstrates a basic library structure for encapsulating RESTful CRUD operations on a contacts list.

LISTING 2-23 REST library structure

```
"use strict";

var Wingtip = window.Wingtip || {};
Wingtip.ContactList = function () {

    //private members
    createItem = function (lname, fname, wphone) {
    },
    readAll = function () {
    },
    readAllSuccess = function (data) {
    },
    updateItem = function (id, lname, fname, wphone) {
    },
    removeItem = function (id) {
    }

    //public interface
    return {
        createContact: createItem,
        updateContact: updateItem,
        deleteContact: removeItem
    }

}();

$(document).ready(function () {
    Wingtip.ContactList.createContact("Cox", "Brian", "555-555-5555");
    alert("Contact Created!");
    Wingtip.ContactList.updateContact(1, "Cox", "Brian", "111-111-1111");
    alert("Contact Updated!");
    Wingtip.ContactList.deleteContact(1);
    alert("Contact Deleted!");
});
```

The library structure in Listing 2-23 is similar to the structure used for the CSOM library presented in Listing 2-15. The primary difference between this REST library and the CSOM library is that no additional variable is required to reference objects between round trips to the server. Of course, the implementation details will be drastically different.

Creating new items is done by constructing a URI that refers to the collection to which the new items are to be added and using the *POST* verb to send an object containing the data for the new item. Whenever a RESTful operation changes a SharePoint resource, the request must include a form digest. The form digest is a security validation that guarantees the app page has not changed since it was delivered from the server. The easiest way to obtain the form digest is simply to read it from the form digest control on the app page. Listing 2-24 shows how to create a new item in a list by using this technique.

LISTING 2-24 Creating new items in a list

```
createItem = function (lname, fname, wphone) {
    $.ajax({
        url: _spPageContextInfo.webServerRelativeUrl +
            "/_api/web/lists/getByTitle('Contacts')/items",
        type: "POST",
        data: JSON.stringify(
            {
                '__metadata': {
                    'type': 'SP.Data.ContactsListItem'
                },
                'Title': lname,
                'FirstName': fname,
                'WorkPhone': wphone
            }),
        headers: {
            "accept": "application/json;odata=verbose",
            "X-RequestDigest": $("#__REQUESTDIGEST").val()
        },
        success: function () {
            readAll();;
        },
        error: function (err) {
            alert(JSON.stringify(err));
        }
    });
}
```

Along with the form digest, the create operation must also include the type metadata for the item that is being created. The type metadata is unique to the list and can be discovered by examining the metadata returned from a read operation. For list items, the type metadata generally follows the pattern *SP.Data*, concatenated with the name of the list, concatenated with *ListItem*. In Listing 2-25, the type metadata is *SP.Data.ContactsListItem*.

Reading items is a straightforward operation that uses a RESTful URI to request the items. This URI is called by using an HTTP *GET* verb. In the sample library, all successful calls to create, update, or delete an item result in redrawing the list in an HTML table. Listing 2-25 shows how to retrieve the list items and render a simple HTML table to display them.

LISTING 2-25 Reading items and presenting them in an HTML table

```
readAll = function () {
    $.ajax(
        {
            url: _spPageContextInfo.webServerRelativeUrl +
                "/_api/web/lists/getByTitle('Contacts')/items/" +
                "?$select=Id,FirstName,Title,WorkPhone" +
                "&$orderby=Title,FirstName",
            type: "GET",
            headers: {
                "accept": "application/json;odata=verbose",
            },
            success: function (data) {
                readAllSuccess(data);
            },
            error: function (err) {
                alert(JSON.stringify(err));
            }
        }
    );
},

readAllSuccess = function (data) {
    var html = [];
    html.push("<table><thead><tr><th>ID</th><th>First Name</th>" +
            "<th>Last Name</th><th>Title</th></tr></thead>");

    var results = data.d.results;

    for(var i=0; i<results.length; i++) {
        html.push("<tr><td>");
        html.push(results[i].ID);
        html.push("</td><td>");
        html.push(results[i].FirstName);
        html.push("</td><td>");
        html.push(results[i].Title);
        html.push("</td><td>");
        html.push(results[i].WorkPhone);
        html.push("</td></tr>");
    }
    html.push("</table>");
    $('#displayDiv').html(html.join(''));
}
```

Updating items is accomplished by creating a RESTful URI that refers to the item that will be updated. Just like item creation, item updating also requires the request to include a form digest. The URI is then invoked by using a *PUT, PATCH,* or *MERGE* verb. When a *PUT* operation is used, you must specify all writable properties in the request. When a *PATCH* or *MERGE* operation is used, you can specify only the properties you want to change. Although *MERGE* and *PATCH* accomplish the same task, the *PATCH* operation is considered more standard. Listing 2-26 shows how to update a list item by using the *PATCH* operation.

LISTING 2-26 Updating items

```
updateItem = function (id, lname, fname, wphone) {
    $.ajax(
            {
                url: _spPageContextInfo.webServerRelativeUrl +
                    "/_api/web/lists/getByTitle('Contacts')/getItemByStringId
                        ('" + id + "')",
                type: "POST",
                contentType: "application/json;odata=verbose",
                data: JSON.stringify(
                {
                    '__metadata': {
                        'type': 'SP.Data.ContactsListItem'
                    },
                    'Title': lname,
                    'FirstName': fname,
                    'WorkPhone': wphone
                }),
                headers: {
                    "accept": "application/json;odata=verbose",
                    "X-RequestDigest": $("#__REQUESTDIGEST").val(),
                    "IF-MATCH": "*",
                    "X-Http-Method": "PATCH"
                },
                success: function (data) {
                    readAll();
                },
                error: function (err) {
                    alert(JSON.stringify(err));
                }
            }
    );
}
```

When performing updates on list items, you can utilize ETags for concurrency control. ETags are version numbers assigned at the list-item level. This number determines whether the list item was altered by another process since your code last read the data. You can find the ETag for a list item by reading it from the metadata. Listing 2-25 could be updated to display ETag values by reading them with the following code:

```
results[i].__metadata.etag
```

ETag values are sent during an update operation via the *IF-MATCH* header. If the ETag sent in the update process is different from the ETag currently assigned to the list item, the update will fail. If you want to force an update regardless of ETag values, you can pass *IF-MATCH:**, which is the approach taken in Listing 2-26.

Deleting an item is accomplished by first constructing a URI that references the target item to delete. The URI is invoked by using an HTTP *DELETE* verb. The delete operation must provide a form digest and an ETag value. Listing 2-27 shows the implementation of a delete operation.

LISTING 2-27 Deleting items

```
removeItem = function (id) {
    $.ajax(
        {
            url: _spPageContextInfo.webServerRelativeUrl +
                "/_api/web/lists/getByTitle('Contacts')/getItemByStringId
                ('" + id + "')",
            type: "DELETE",
            headers: {
                "accept": "application/json;odata=verbose",
                "X-RequestDigest": $("#__REQUESTDIGEST").val(),
                "IF-MATCH": "*"
            },
            success: function (data) {
                readAll();
            },
            error: function (err) {
                alert(JSON.stringify(err));
            }
        }
    );
}
```

Working with the REST API in C#

Using the REST API from a C# application is certainly possible, but it is easily the least attractive of all the programming options. You will find that retrieving form digests, parsing out properties, and creating payloads can be tedious and messy. This section details the steps necessary to work with the REST API in C#.

Performing basic operations

In the section "Working with the REST API in JavaScript," the SharePoint-hosted app project template code was rewritten to use REST. As a starting point to understanding how to utilize REST in C#, Listing 2-28 shows the same code rewritten in a provider-hosted app. The code runs within the *Page_Load* event and welcomes the user to the app.

LISTING 2-28 Welcoming the current user

```
protected void Page_Load(object sender, EventArgs e)
{
    //Construct URI
    string appWebUrl = Page.Request["SPAppWebUrl"];
    Uri uri = new Uri(appWebUrl + "/_api/web/currentuser");

    //Perform GET operation
    HttpWebRequest restRequest = (HttpWebRequest)WebRequest.Create(uri);
    restRequest.Credentials = CredentialCache.DefaultCredentials;
    restRequest.Method = "GET";
    HttpWebResponse restResponse = (HttpWebResponse)restRequest.GetResponse();

    //Parse out Title
    XDocument atomDoc = XDocument.Load(restResponse.GetResponseStream());
    XNamespace ns = "http://schemas.microsoft.com/ado/2007/08/dataservices";
    message.Text = "Hello " + atomDoc.Descendants(ns + "Title").First().Value;
}
```

The code in Listing 2-28 begins by constructing a URI to request the current user object from the REST API. The URI is invoked by using the *HttpWebRequest* object, which uses the HTTP *GET* verb and returns the data in AtomPub format. Finally, the *Title* property is extracted from the returned XML document by using LINQ-to-XML. You can see that the mechanics of using the REST API are the same in C# as they are in JavaScript, but the implementation is not as clean.

Performing CRUD in C#

Performing CRUD operations with C# against the REST API can be a bit challenging. This is because you must go through an extra step to retrieve a form digest and because you must create the proper XML payloads by hand. Fortunately, you can encapsulate the basic CRUD functionality in a static class to make it easier. Listing 2-29 shows a basic class structure for encapsulating CRUD operations against the REST API. In keeping with previous examples, the class targets a contacts list in the app.

LISTING 2-29 A class for REST operations

```
namespace Wingtip
{
    public static class Contacts
    {
        public static string AppWebUrl;
        public static void CreateItem(string LastName,
                                      string FirstName,
                                      string WorkPhone){}
        public static List<TableRow> ReadAll(){}
```

```
        public static void UpdateItem(string ID,
                                      string LastName,
                                      string FirstName,
                                      string WorkPhone){}
        public static void RemoveItem(string ID){}
        private static string GetFormDigest(){}
    }
}
```

The structure of the static class in Listing 2-29 is similar to libraries that were shown previously in JavaScript, which contained methods for creating, reading, updating, and deleting. When using C# against the REST API, however, there are two new elements to consider. First, a static variable *AppWeb Url* is added to make the root URL of the app available to all the methods. Second, a *private* method named *GetFormDigest* is added to retrieve the form digest when necessary.

When you use C# against the REST API, it will always be from a remote web. Therefore, you don't have the luxury of the form digest control being present on the app page. Because of this, you must make a separate RESTful call back to SharePoint solely to retrieve a form digest that can be used in the CRUD operations. Listing 2-30 shows the implementation of the *GetFormDigest* method, which returns the form digest as a string.

LISTING 2-30 Retrieving the form digest

```
private static string GetFormDigest()
{
    Uri uri = new Uri(AppWebUrl + "/_api/contextinfo");
    HttpWebRequest restRequest = (HttpWebRequest)WebRequest.Create(uri);
    restRequest.Credentials = CredentialCache.DefaultCredentials;
    restRequest.Method = "POST";
    restRequest.ContentLength = 0;

    HttpWebResponse restResponse = (HttpWebResponse)restRequest.GetResponse();
    XDocument atomDoc = XDocument.Load(restResponse.GetResponseStream());
    XNamespace d = "http://schemas.microsoft.com/ado/2007/08/dataservices";
    return atomDoc.Descendants(d + "FormDigestValue").First().Value;
}
```

Creating new items in C# requires the same basic approach as JavaScript. A URI is constructed that refers to the collection to which the new items are to be added and the *POST* verb is used to send an XML chunk containing the data for the new item. In C#, you must create the XML by hand and substitute in the new values. Listing 2-31 shows the code to create a new item in the contacts list.

LISTING 2-31 Creating new items in a contacts list

```
public static void CreateItem(string LastName, string FirstName, string
                              WorkPhone)
{
    Uri uri = new Uri(AppWebUrl +
    "/_api/web/lists/getByTitle('Contacts')/items");

    string itemXML = String.Format(@"
          <entry xmlns='http://www.w3.org/2005/Atom'
           xmlns:d='http://schemas.microsoft.com/ado/2007/08/dataservices'
           xmlns:m='http://schemas.microsoft.com/ado/2007/08/dataservices/
                      metadata'>
            <category term='SP.Data.ContactsListItem'
             scheme='http://schemas.microsoft.com/ado/2007/08/dataservices/
                      scheme' />
              <content type='application/xml'>
                <m:properties>
                  <d:FirstName>{0}</d:FirstName>
                  <d:Title>{1}</d:Title>
                  <d:WorkPhone>{2}</d:WorkPhone>
                </m:properties>
              </content>
            </entry>", FirstName, LastName, WorkPhone);

    HttpWebRequest restRequest = (HttpWebRequest)WebRequest.Create(uri);
    restRequest.Credentials = CredentialCache.DefaultCredentials;
    restRequest.Method = "POST";
    restRequest.Headers["X-RequestDigest"] = GetFormDigest();
    restRequest.Accept = "application/atom+xml";
    restRequest.ContentType = "application/atom+xml";
    restRequest.ContentLength = itemXML.Length;
    StreamWriter sw = new StreamWriter(restRequest.GetRequestStream());
    sw.Write(itemXML);
    sw.Flush();

    HttpWebResponse restResponse = (HttpWebResponse)restRequest.GetResponse();
}
```

Reading items is fairly straightforward. You can simply create the URI referencing the items to return and make the call. Listing 2-32 illustrates the implementation of the *ReadAll* method for the sample. In this case, the method returns a collection of type *TableRow*, which is subsequently added to an ASP.NET Table control to display the items.

LISTING 2-32 Reading list items

```
public static List<TableRow> ReadAll()
{
    Uri uri = new Uri(AppWebUrl +
                "/_api/web/lists/getByTitle('Contacts')/items/" +
                "?$select=Id,FirstName,Title,WorkPhone" +
                "&$orderby=Title,FirstName");

    HttpWebRequest restRequest = (HttpWebRequest)WebRequest.Create(uri);
    restRequest.Credentials = CredentialCache.DefaultCredentials;
    restRequest.Method = "GET";

    HttpWebResponse restResponse = (HttpWebResponse)restRequest.GetResponse();
    XDocument atomDoc = XDocument.Load(restResponse.GetResponseStream());
    XNamespace a = "http://www.w3.org/2005/Atom";
    XNamespace d = "http://schemas.microsoft.com/ado/2007/08/dataservices";

    List<TableRow> rows = new List<TableRow>();
    foreach (var entry in atomDoc.Descendants(a + "entry"))
    {
        TableRow r = new TableRow();
        TableCell c1 = new TableCell();
        c1.Text = entry.Descendants(d + "Id").First().Value;
        TableCell c2 = new TableCell();
        c2.Text = entry.Descendants(d + "FirstName").First().Value;
        TableCell c3 = new TableCell();
        c3.Text = entry.Descendants(d + "Title").First().Value;
        TableCell c4 = new TableCell();
        c4.Text = entry.Descendants(d + "WorkPhone").First().Value;
        r.Cells.Add(c1);
        r.Cells.Add(c2);
        r.Cells.Add(c3);
        r.Cells.Add(c4);
        rows.Add(r);
    }
    return rows;
}
```

Updating items is also done by using the same basic approach presented with JavaScript. A URI is constructed that refers to the item to be updated. The XML chunk containing the new property values must be created and a form digest added to the headers. Additionally, the *PATCH* method is used to allow only the desired properties to be updated. Finally, the corresponding ETag value must be supplied or an asterisk used to force an update. Listing 2-33 shows the complete implementation of the method to update items in the contacts list.

LISTING 2-33 Updating items in a contacts list

```
public static void UpdateItem(string ID, string LastName, string FirstName,
                              string WorkPhone)
{
    Uri uri = new Uri(AppWebUrl +
    "/_api/web/lists/getByTitle('Contacts')/items(" + ID + ")");

    string itemXML = String.Format(@"
           <entry xmlns='http://www.w3.org/2005/Atom'
            xmlns:d='http://schemas.microsoft.com/ado/2007/08/dataservices'
            xmlns:m='http://schemas.microsoft.com/ado/2007/08/dataservices/
                     metadata'>
             <category term='SP.Data.ContactsListItem'
              scheme='http://schemas.microsoft.com/ado/2007/08/dataservices/
                      scheme' />
               <content type='application/xml'>
                 <m:properties>
                   <d:FirstName>{0}</d:FirstName>
                   <d:Title>{1}</d:Title>
                   <d:WorkPhone>{2}</d:WorkPhone>
                 </m:properties>
               </content>
           </entry>", FirstName, LastName, WorkPhone);

    HttpWebRequest restRequest = (HttpWebRequest)WebRequest.Create(uri);
    restRequest.Credentials = CredentialCache.DefaultCredentials;
    restRequest.Method = "POST";
    restRequest.Headers["X-RequestDigest"] = GetFormDigest();
    restRequest.Headers["IF-MATCH"] = "*";
    restRequest.Headers["X-Http-Method"] = "PATCH";
    restRequest.Accept = "application/atom+xml";
    restRequest.ContentType = "application/atom+xml";
    restRequest.ContentLength = itemXML.Length;
    StreamWriter sw = new StreamWriter(restRequest.GetRequestStream());
    sw.Write(itemXML);
    sw.Flush();

    HttpWebResponse restResponse = (HttpWebResponse)restRequest.GetResponse();
}
```

Deleting items is a simple operation compared to the other methods. To delete an item, a URI is constructed that refers to the item to be deleted. A form digest is sent in the headers and the *DELETE* verb is used to indicate that the target item should be deleted. There is no XML chunk to create for this operation. Listing 2-34 shows the implementation details for deleting items from the contacts list.

LISTING 2-34 Deleting items from a contacts list

```
public static void RemoveItem(string ID)
{
    Uri uri = new Uri(AppWebUrl +
    "/_api/web/lists/getByTitle('Contacts')/items(" + ID + ")");

    HttpWebRequest restRequest = (HttpWebRequest)WebRequest.Create(uri);
    restRequest.Credentials = CredentialCache.DefaultCredentials;
    restRequest.Method = "DELETE";
    restRequest.Headers["X-RequestDigest"] = GetFormDigest();
    restRequest.Headers["IF-MATCH"] = "*";
    restRequest.Accept = "application/atom+xml";
    restRequest.ContentType = "application/atom+xml";

    HttpWebResponse restResponse = (HttpWebResponse)restRequest.GetResponse();
}
```

Conclusion

Client-side programming against SharePoint 2013 apps is a new paradigm for all SharePoint developers. Even though previous versions of SharePoint supported some of the capabilities found in Share-Point 2013, most developers concentrated on writing server-side code. With the introduction of the app model, SharePoint developers must now become experts in client-side programming.

There are four options for client-side programming: JavaScript against CSOM, JavaScript against REST, C# against CSOM, and C# against REST. When creating SharePoint-hosted apps, you will find that JavaScript against the REST API is generally the best choice. When creating provider-hosted or autohosted apps, you will likely find that C# against CSOM is the best fit. In any case, as a SharePoint developer, you will need to focus on client-side programming much more than you have in the past.

CHAPTER 3

SharePoint app security

Let's begin with a basic question: what is a security principal? In a common scenario in a Windows network environment, a security principal can be a user with an account in Active Directory. But, the concept of a security principal goes far beyond that. A security principal can also be a user with an account in some other type of identity management system such as Microsoft ASP.NET forms-based authentication (FBA), Microsoft Account, or Facebook.

There are also common scenarios in which a security principal will not have a one-to-one mapping to a human being. For example, an Active Directory security group is a type of security principal, as is an FBA role. A computer becomes a first class security principal when it is added to an Active Directory domain. In this chapter, you will also see that a SharePoint app can also play the role of a first class security principal, as well.

Microsoft SharePoint 2010 includes support for authenticating users and providing them with controlled access to SharePoint resources. However, the security infrastructure becomes more complex in SharePoint 2013 due to the new requirements to add support for authenticating apps and managing app permissions. The goal of this chapter is to explain how app authentication and app authorization in SharePoint 2013 work from the ground up.

Reviewing the concepts of authentication and authorization

A computer security system performs two basic functions: authentication and authorization. Although you likely already understand these two concepts, this section will provide a quick review because fully understanding them is critical to all the other material in this chapter.

A security system uses authentication to determine the identity of a caller. The first part of the authentication process attempts to map the caller to an existing security principal. For example, authentication could map the caller to a user account in an Active Director domain. When this process is successful, the system establishes the caller's identity by creating a security token which contains attributes of the security principal in question.

For example, the Windows operating system creates a special type of security token known as a Windows security token when it authenticates a user. A Windows security token is an in-memory data structure that contains the user's logon name and a list of security groups in which the user is a member.

If the authentication process asks the question "who are you?", the authorization process asks "what can you do?" The authentication process must occur before the authentication process. The reason for this is that you must determine the caller's identity before you can determine what the caller can do.

Before the authorization process can begin, the authentication process must create a security token that maps the caller to a security principal. During the authorization process, the system examines information contained by the security token to determine whether the caller should be allowed access to the requested resource(s).

Understanding SharePoint 2013 authentication

Every version of SharePoint has provided support for authenticating users and configuring user permissions. However, SharePoint 2013 is the first version to add support for authenticating apps. This section will begin with a brief explanation of how user authentication works, and then it will dive into the details of app authentication.

Understanding user authentication in SharePoint 2013

The first thing to understand is that the SharePoint platform itself does not supply the actual code to authenticate users. Instead, the SharePoint platform relies on external user authentication systems such as Windows Server and Active Directory or the built-in support in ASP.NET for FBA. After an external system has authenticated a user and created a security token, the SharePoint platform is then able to create a profile around that security token to establish and track the user's identity within the SharePoint security system.

Let's quickly revisit how user authentication has evolved in SharePoint over the last decade. SharePoint 2003 was pretty limited because it only offered support for Windows authentication. This meant that each and every authenticated user required an Active Directory account.

SharePoint 2007 made a step ahead by adding support for ASP.NET FBA. The new support for FBA was a welcomed change to developers and system integrators, especially for common scenarios such as extranets and publically-facing Internet sites for which it was impractical to create and maintain an Active Directory account for each user or site member.

However, it was with SharePoint 2010 that Microsoft really changed how user authentication works with the introduction of claims-based security. Prior to SharePoint 2010, the SharePoint platform tracked user identity by using the security token created by the underlying authentication system. For example, SharePoint 2007 tracks user identity via two types of security tokens: Windows security tokens, which are created by Windows Server, and FBA security tokens, which are created by the ASP.NET runtime.

With claims-based security, the SharePoint platform moves to a single, unified format for the security tokens that are created during the user authentication process. More specifically, the user authentication process creates security tokens by using an XML-based standard known as Security

Assertion Markup Language (SAML). Within developer circles, this type of security token is commonly referred to as a *SAML token*.

Let's walk through the authentication process in a SharePoint environment configured for claims-based security. In this scenario, the user is authenticated by using either Windows security or FBA. The first part of the authentication process essentially remains unchanged with respect to the fact that it creates a Windows security token or an FBA token. The end of the authentication process is where things are different. This is because any Windows security token or FBA token must be converted into a SAML token.

Every SharePoint web server runs a local service known as the Security Token Service (STS). The STS is responsible for converting Windows security tokens and FBA tokens into SAML tokens as the final part of the authentication process. In SharePoint 2010, these SAML tokens are cached in memory on a per–web server basis and can be reused across multiple requests from the same user. SharePoint 2013 further optimizes the caching of SAML tokens with the Distributed Cache Service, which can be configured to maintain a farm-wide cache of SAML tokens.

SharePoint's adoption of claims-based security and SAML tokens has another significant effect: it has dramatically increased the number of identity providers that can be integrated with a SharePoint farm. In addition to supporting Windows authentication and FBA, claims-based security makes it possible for a SharePoint farm to authenticate users by using external identity providers such as Windows Azure Access Control Service (ACS), Windows Account, Google, and Facebook.

Configuring user authentication in web applications

The manner by which SharePoint authenticates users is configured at the web-application level. When you create a web application in a SharePoint farm, you have the option of creating it in either claims mode or classic mode. A web application created in claims mode authenticates users as described in the previous section. The important point is that a SAML token is created during the user authentication process to establish user identity.

SharePoint's support for creating classic-mode web applications is provided for backward compatibility. It should be avoided except for rare scenarios in which a SharePoint farm contains content migrated from earlier versions which rely on older custom components that need to be rewritten before they can support running within a claims-mode web application.

The bottom line is that you should avoid creating classic-mode web applications in SharePoint 2013 except for scenarios in which you are forced into it to support legacy components. With Share-Point 2013, Microsoft has deprecated the use of classic-mode web applications and removed the ability to create them through Central Administration. The only way to create a classic-mode web application is by using Windows PowerShell.

A significant reason to avoid the use of classis-mode web applications is that they do not support installing and running SharePoint apps. All of Microsoft's design and testing of the SharePoint app model assumes that apps are always installed on sites hosted by claims-mode web applications. For the remainder of this chapter you can assume that any discussion of a web application is a claims-mode web application.

Understanding how SharePoint 2013 authenticates apps

Chapter 1, "Introducing SharePoint Apps," discusses many of the significant pains with respect to SharePoint solutions. As you might recall, one of the biggest limitations with respect to developing and deploying SharePoint solutions revolves around security and the inability to configure permissions for a SharePoint solution independently of user permissions. The underlying problem is that SharePoint solutions are not recognized as first-class security principals.

From the very beginning of the design phase, Microsoft created the SharePoint app model so that apps could be authenticated and recognized as first-class security principals. The obvious benefit here is that app permissions can be configured independently of user permissions. To achieve this goal, however, Microsoft had to build new infrastructure into SharePoint 2013 that is capable of authenticating incoming calls from apps and tracking app identity.

If you already have a firm understanding of how SharePoint authenticates users, you should not assume anything is the same with respect to how it authenticates apps. The authentication mechanisms used for apps are completely different. SharePoint 2013 supports three different types of app authentication:

- Internal app authentication
- External app authentication using OAuth
- External app authentication using S2S High-trust

Note that app authentication is supported only for scenarios in which an app is calling to the SharePoint host environment by using client-side object model (CSOM) or the REST API. SharePoint 2013 does not support app authentication in any other endpoints beyond these. This means it is not possible to develop and deploy a set of custom web service entry points that support app authentication.

Whenever the SharePoint host environment receives an incoming call that targets either CSOM or the REST API, it must decide how to authenticate the call. First, the SharePoint host environment must determine whether the call was initiated by a user or by an app. If the call was initiated by an app, the SharePoint host environment must also determine whether to use internal authentication or external authentication.

The SharePoint host environment inspects an incoming request to see what type of security token has been passed. If an incoming call contains a special type of security token used for app authentication known as an *access token*, the SharePoint host will know the call was made by an app. In this scenario, the SharePoint host environment authenticates the caller by using external app authentication.

If the SharePoint host environment sees a SAML token in an incoming request, it knows that there is already an authenticated user associated with the call. However, at this point the SharePoint host environment cannot yet assume that call was initiated by a user as opposed to an app. The SharePoint host environment must additionally inspect the target URL to determine whether the call was initiated by a user or by an app.

If an incoming request with a SAML token maps to a target URL within a domain associated with an app web, the SharePoint host environment will assume that the call was made by an app. In this scenario, the SharePoint host environment uses internal authentication to authenticate the app and establish its identity. If an incoming request with a SAML token does not map to a target URL within a domain associated with an app web, the SharePoint host environment will know that the call was not made by an app and it will initialize the call context by using just the user's identity.

The diagram in Figure 3-1 shows four different scenarios for CSOM and REST API calls that target a SharePoint 2013 site. The first call (at the top) is a client-side CSOM or REST API call that has been executed from a page in the host web. The SharePoint host environment authenticates this type of call by using standard user authentication, which results in the creation of a SAML token.

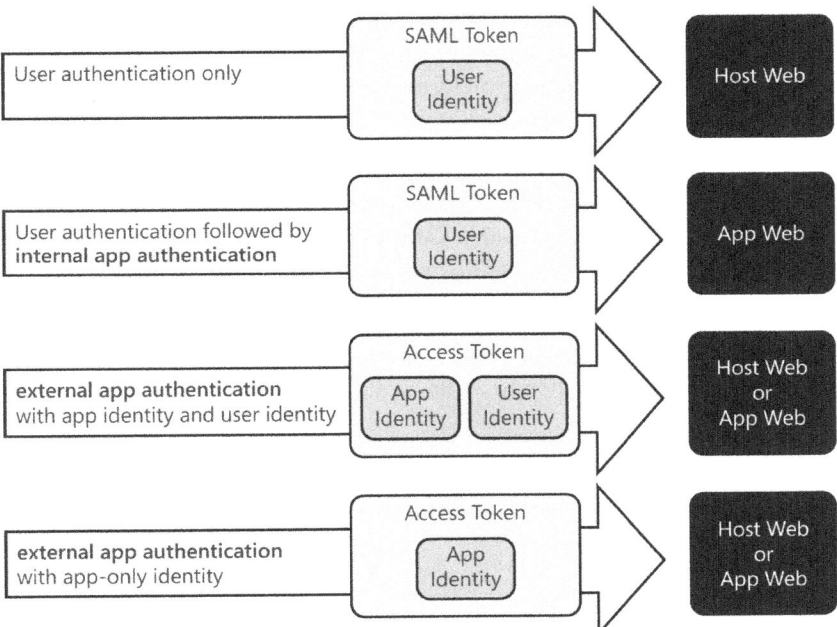

FIGURE 3-1 The SharePoint environment inspects the security tokens that are passed with incoming calls to determine which type of authentication to use.

The second call in Figure 3-1 (second down from the top) is similar to the first call in that the SharePoint host environment uses the standard user authentication process to create a SAML token with the user's identity. However, the second call is treated differently because it targets the domain of an app web. The fact that this call targets an app web is what leads the SharePoint host environment to authenticate the calling app by using internal app authentication.

The third and fourth calls in Figure 3-1 both carry an access token instead of a SAML token. When the SharePoint host environment sees an access token in an incoming CSOM or REST API call, it can assume that it should authenticate the app by using external authentication. The difference between the third call and the fourth call involves whether the access token carries a user identity along with the app identity. The third call is an example of the more common scenario in which the access token includes the identity of the current user in addition to the identity of the app. The fourth call shows an example of an access token that contains app identity but no user identity. The use of this type of access token containing app-only identity is not as common but is useful in specific scenarios, which will be described later in this chapter.

Using Internal Authentication

The most common scenario in which the SharePoint host environment uses internal authentication involves client-side calls that are initiated from pages in an app web. If you recall from Chapter 1, the SharePoint host environment creates an isolated domain whenever it creates an app web during app installation. The cross-site scripting (XSS) restrictions in the browser ensure that CSOM and REST API calls made from pages in the app web target endpoints within the same domain. This makes it possible for the SharePoint host environment to map an incoming call that targets an app web domain to a specific installed instance of an app.

When the SharePoint host environment has determined an incoming call targets a URL that maps to a specific app, it uses internal authentication to initialize the call context with the app's identity. Because this scenario involves an incoming call with a SAML token, the SharePoint host environment can further initialize the call context with the user's identity in addition to the app's identity.

SharePoint-hosted apps always use internal authentication. That's because all the pages for a SharePoint-hosted app must be added to an app web. This means that the SharePoint host environment can always use internal authentication to authenticate any CSOM or REST API call from a SharePoint-hosted app.

The app manifest for a SharePoint-hosted app should be configured to support internal authentication. This is accomplished in the app manifest by adding an <AppPrincipal> element with an inner <Internal> element.

```
<AppPrincipal>
  <Internal />
</AppPrincipal>
```

SharePoint-hosted apps are not the only type of app that can use internal authentication. A second scenario in which internal authentication is used involves client-side calls initiated from a cloud-hosted app using the *cross-domain library*. The cross-domain library is a JavaScript library included with SharePoint 2013 with which a cloud-hosted app can issue client-side calls to the SharePoint host environment from pages in the remote web.

The cross-domain library has been added to SharePoint 2013 to address the scenario in which a cloud-hosted app calls back into the SharePoint host environment by using client-side calls instead of server-side calls. For example, your user interface design might favor client-side calls over server-side calls to give pages in the remote web more of a web 2.0 look and feel.

In a different scenario, you might be required to use the cross-domain library when deploying a cloud-hosted app in an environment in which a firewall is blocking server-side code running in the remote web from calling back to the SharePoint host environment. The problem caused by the firewall can be solved by using client-side calls initiated from pages served up by the remote web. This allows the app to call back to the SharePoint host environment from the browser running on the user's computer or device.

Note that CSOM and REST API calls executed by using the cross-domain library must be routed through the app web of the calling app. Although cloud-hosted apps do not usually require an app web, this is a scenario in which they do. Therefore, you must configure a cloud-hosted app to create an app web if you plan to use the cross-domain library.

The high-level architecture of the cross-domain library involves a proxy page in the LAYOUTS directory named *AppWebProxy.aspx*. When you execute a request by using the cross-domain library, the library provides JavaScript code that sends the request to the proxy page *AppWebProxy.aspx* by using a URL scoped inside an app web. The proxy page responds by returning a response that includes the requested data in an IFrame along with some low-level JavaScript code that makes it possible for JavaScript code in the cross-domain library to extract this data by using the HTML5 post-Message API.

The cross-domain library provides two valuable yet distinct aspects. First, it abstracts away all the grungy code required to get around the browser restrictions for cross-domain scripting. Second, it provides the SharePoint host environment with the ability to authenticate calls from an app by using internal authentication.

Note that cross-domain library calls are authenticated by using standard user authentication. That means that cross-domain library calls are passed to the app web with a SAML token. As in the case with client-side calls initiated from pages inside the app web, the SharePoint host environment can inspect the sender's URL with a cross-domain library call and map the caller's URL to a specific installed instance of an app.

The programming techniques required to use the cross-domain library is covered in Chapter 4, "Developing SharePoint Apps." The goal of this chapter has been to give you a complete picture of how SharePoint 2013 uses internal authentication. Just remember that any cloud-hosted app that uses the cross-domain library must be designed to create an app web during installation.

Suppose that you wanted to create a cloud-hosted app that supports internal authentication but not external authentication. To accomplish this, you should configure the app manifest with an <AppPrincipal> element with an inner <Internal> element, just like a SharePoint-hosted app, but you should additionally add the *AllowedRemoteHostUrl* attribute, as well.

```
<AppPrincipal>
  <Internal AllowedRemoteHostUrl="~remoteAppUrl" />
</AppPrincipal>
```

Note that the ability for a cloud-hosted app to make client-side calls by using the cross-domain library is not limited to apps whose app manifest contains an <Internal> element with the *Allowed RemoteHostUrl* attribute. As is demonstrated in Chapter 4, a cloud-hosted app that has been config-ured to use external authentication can also make client-side calls from pages in the remote web and those calls will be authenticated by using internal authentication.

Using external authentication

There are many scenarios in which a cloud-hosted app makes CSOM and REST API calls to a Share-Point host that cannot be authenticated by using internal authentication. In these scenarios, the app must be configured to use external authentication. The key difference with external authentication is that the app must include an access token when calling to the SharePoint host environment.

There are two ways by which you can configure an app to use external authentication. The first is based on *OAuth authentication*, which is the only type of external authentication supported in the Microsoft Office 365 environment. The second way is based on server-to-server authentication, which is only supported in on-premises farms.

OAuth authentication requires integration with Windows Azure ACS. That means the remote web of the app requires access to Windows Azure ACS running in the cloud to acquire access tokens. How-ever, it is relatively simple to set up because the required integration between the Office 365 environ-ment and Windows Azure ACS is automatically configured for you. Your primary requirement when configuring OAuth authentication is to register an app security principal that will have an identifying GUID known as a *client ID*. The details of how to configure OAuth authentication as well as how to implement an app to acquire access tokens from Windows Azure ACS will be discussed later in the chapter.

Server-to-server (S2S) authentication doesn't require an app to access Windows Azure ACS or any other authentication service in the cloud. The only computers involved in the S2S authentication pro-cess are the web server running the remote web and a SharePoint web server in an on-premises farm. This makes this form of external authentication ideal for scenarios in which you want to avoid depen-dencies on servers across the Internet where everything needs to run inside a single, private network.

S2S authentication is configured by establishing a trust between the web servers in an on-premises SharePoint farm and the web server running the remote web of a provider-hosted app. This trust is created by using an x.509 certificate with a public/private key pair. At a high level, S2S authentication is based on the app creating an access token and signing it with the private key. Web servers in the SharePoint farm then authenticate these access tokens by using the public key.

At this point, you should have a high-level understanding of how external authentication works. External authentication can be configured by using either OAuth authentication or S2S authentica-tion. In either case, the remote web passes an access token by which the SharePoint host environment can authenticate the app and establish the app's identity.

Although an access token is required to contain information about the app's identity, it can option-ally contain information about the identity of the current user, as well. Therefore, some access tokens carry information about the identity of both the app and the current user, whereas other access tokens only carry information about the identity of the app.

Understanding app authentication flow in SharePoint 2013

Now that you have learned about the fundamental differences between internal authentication and external authentication, it's time to walk through the authentication flow used by the SharePoint host environment.

Remember that app authentication is only supported in endpoints based on CSOM and the REST API. Therefore, the SharePoint host environment uses only standard user authentication for any request that is not based on CSOM or the REST API. This includes scenarios for page requests from both the host web and the app web.

When the SharePoint host environment processes a CSOM call or a REST API call, it must do more work to determine which type of authentication to use. The diagram in Figure 3-2 shows a flow chart that details the complexity and the factors that the SharePoint host environment uses to choose the correct type of authentication.

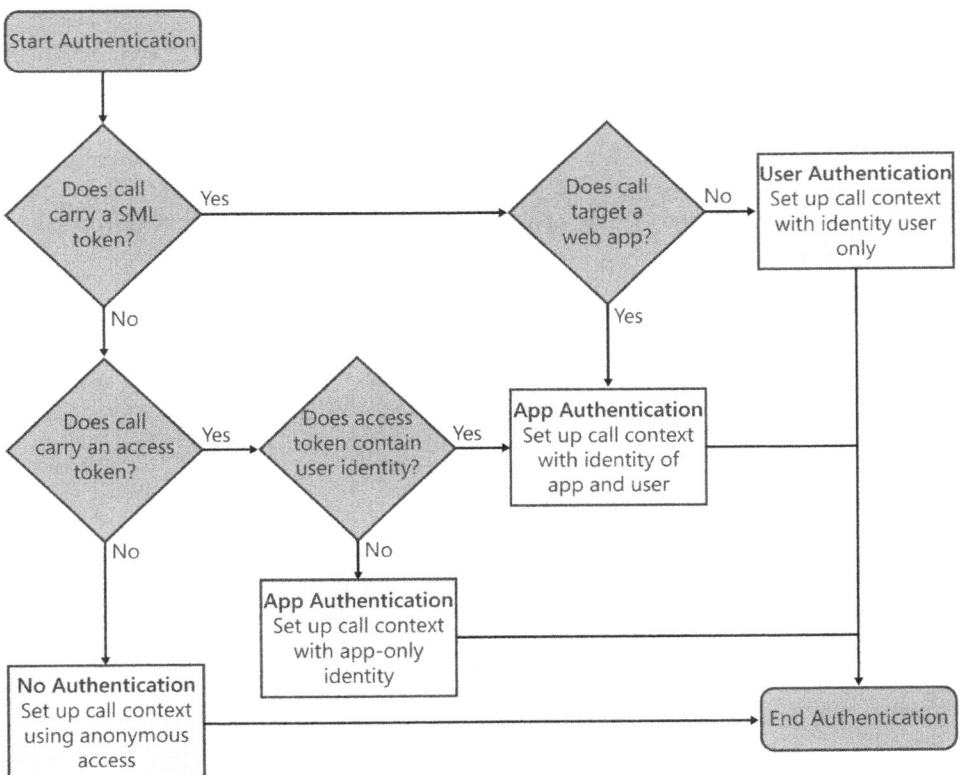

FIGURE 3-2 The SharePoint host environment looks at the tokens contained in the incoming call as well as the endpoint to determine whether to setup a user and app context.

The first question the SharePoint host environment asks after starting the authentication process for a CSOM call or REST API call is whether the call carries a SAML token with a user identity. If the incoming call does carry a SAML token, the next question is whether the request targets an app web or not. If the call does not target an app web, the SharePoint host environment uses standard user authentication and sets up the call context with just the user identity. Note that this is exactly what SharePoint does for any request that does not target a CSOM or REST API endpoint.

When an incoming call with a SAML token targets the domain of an app web, the SharePoint host environment determines that it must authenticate the app that is associated with that app web. It then uses internal authentication to authenticate the app and it sets up the call context with app identity as well as with the user identity it finds in the SAML token.

When an incoming call carries an access token instead of a SAML token, the SharePoint host environment determines that the call is from an app and it must use external authentication to authenticate it. The SharePoint host environment starts the external authentication process by determining whether the access token is an OAuth token or an S2S token and then validating the authenticity of the access token.

After the access token has been validated, the SharePoint host environment can then extract information about the identity of the app. The SharePoint host environment also inspects the access token to see if it carries information about the identity of the current user. If it does, the SharePoint host environment sets up the call context with both app identity and user identity. If the access token does not contain information about the identity of a user, it sets up the call context only with app identity.

The last scenario involves a request that carries neither a SAML token nor an access token. In this case, the SharePoint host environment can establish neither app identity nor user identity. This leads to the SharePoint host environment setting up the call context by using anonymous access. A call executing under anonymous access will experience an access denied error in all scenarios except the case for which the site has been configured to allow CSOM and REST API calls from the anonymous user.

Managing app permissions

This chapter has already explained the various ways by which SharePoint 2013 is able to authenticate apps. The process of app authentication is what makes it possible to establish app identity and to map incoming calls from an app to a unique ID for the app which is tracked in the App Management Service database known as the app identifier. This, in turn, makes it possible for the SharePoint host environment to create and track app permissions by associating each one with an app identifier.

When you begin to think about app identity and app permissions, you should keep in mind that an app must be installed before it can be used and that the installation of an app creates a new app instance. For example, if you install the same SharePoint app into two different Office 365 tenancies, you will create two separate app identities as opposed to creating a single app identity that is recognized across tenancy boundaries.

SharePoint 2013 uses app identifiers that are made by combining a GUID that identifies the app instance together with the unique identifier for the hosting tenancy. Each time the SharePoint host environment creates an app permission, it must tag this permission with an app identifier to map it back to an installed instance of an app.

Note that much of the Microsoft documentation on app security often uses the generic term "realm" in place of the SharePoint-specific term "tenancy." When you hear someone talking about the hosting realm for an app, he is really just talking about the tenancy in which the app was installed. The realm identifier is just the identifier for the current tenancy.

When you install a SharePoint-hosted app, the app identifier is created and configured automatically as part of the app installation process. After a SharePoint-hosted app has been installed, the SharePoint host environment is able to use internal authentication map CSOM and REST API calls from pages in the app web to an existing app identifier. The process of internal authentication was discussed in depth earlier in this chapter.

Managing app identifiers becomes more complicated with apps that use external authentication. In certain scenarios, you must explicitly create the app identifier by registering an app principal before the app is installed. It is the act of registering the app principal that actually creates the app identifier. The details of when and how to register app principals will be covered later in this chapter; however, you now have the required background to begin learning about how SharePoint 2013 manages app permissions.

Understanding app permission policies

Now, it's time to discuss what happens after a call from an app has been authenticated and mapped to an app identifier. That's the point in time when the SharePoint host environment inspects permissions on the target object to determine whether the calling app should be able to succeed in what it is attempting to do. If the SharePoint host environment does not find that the correct set of permissions has been granted to the app, an access denied error will be returned to the caller.

As you might expect, an app must be granted the appropriate app permission to read or modify an object in a SharePoint site such as a list or a list item. Moreover, the default authorization policy for apps requires that the current user has the appropriate permissions, as well. Let's look at a simple example to illustrate how the default app authorization policy works.

Imagine that an app has been granted write access to the host web. This means that it has the required permissions to create a new list item in the host site. However, for the app to create a new list item by using CSOM or the REST API, the current user requires the permissions to create a new list item, as well. When the app is launched by a site administrator, it can succeed in creating a list in the host web. If the app is launched by a user without write permissions such as a visitor, an attempt by the app to create a new list item will fail with an access-denied error.

A key point here is that the default app authorization policy used for calls from apps checks user permissions as well as app permissions. Therefore, you need to understand how the SharePoint host environment manages user permissions as well as app permissions before you can fully understand how the app authorization process works. For this reason, this chapter will review how user permissions are managed for those readers who require this background. After that, the chapter will then focus on creating and managing app permissions. As you will see, the way in which the SharePoint host environment manages app permissions is significantly different from the way it manages user permissions.

Reviewing how SharePoint manages user permissions

SharePoint 2013 doesn't introduce any significant changes with respect to how it manages user permissions. If you understand how user permissions are managed in SharePoint 2010, you already know the important aspects of how they are managed in SharePoint 2013. The next few paragraphs will provide a quick primer for readers who need to solidify their understanding of how user permissions are managed.

The SharePoint host environment tracks user permissions at site-collection scope. Within the scope of a site collection there are three types of securable objects: sites, lists, and list items. The SharePoint host environment provides a user-interface experience for privileged users such as a site administrator to configure permissions on securable objects such as the top-level site, child sites, lists, and list items. The SharePoint host environment tracks these user permissions by adding them to access control lists (ACLs) that are maintained in the content database associated with the current site collection.

Within the scope of a site collection, user permissions are maintained within a hierarchy of securable objects. The securable object at the top of the hierarchy in any site collection is the top-level site. When a user attempts to access a securable object such as a list or list item, the SharePoint host environment checks to see if that securable object has its own unique ACL. If it does, the SharePoint host environment uses that ACL to determine whether to allow the current user access to the securable object. However, it is quite common that a securable object under the top-level site will not have its own unique ACL.

If a user attempts to access a securable object that does not have its own unique ACL, the SharePoint host environment moves up the hierarchy of securable objects to see if that securable object's parent has a unique ACL. If the parent object does not have a unique ACL, the SharePoint environment moves further up the hierarchy until it finds a securable object that has its own unique ACL, which it can use to determine whether the user is authorized. The only securable object in a site collection that is guaranteed to have its own unique ACL is the top-level site. It's not uncommon for a site collection to have just one ACL on the top-level site that is used to control access to all the child sites, lists, and list items within it.

Even though user permissions are most often managed within the scope of a site collection, it is also possible to grant permissions to a user by configuring a web app with a user policy. Creating a user policy in this manner provides a more efficient means to grant a user or an Active Directory group with access to all the site collections within a web app at once. For example, you can create a user policy to give a specific user read access to every site collection within a specific web app. It is important to note that a web app policy will override any user permissions that are configured at site-collection level.

In summary, user permissions are most commonly configured within the scope of a site collection. However, user policy can be created to quickly and effectively provide a user permission to access every site collection within a specific web app. Now, it's time to move on and discuss how app permissions are configured and tracked by SharePoint 2013.

Requesting and granting app permissions

The SharePoint host environment configures a set of default permissions for an app to provide it with full control over its app web. This means that an app that creates an app web during installation always has a place to create new lists and document libraries without having to request additional permissions.

In many scenarios, the default permissions granted to an app will not suffice. Think about the common scenario in which an app is required to create a new list in the host site. In such a scenario an app will require additional permissions beyond the default app permissions.

An app acquires additional permissions by using *permission requests*. A permission request is an XML-based element that the app developer adds to the app manifest file. When a user or administrator attempts to install a SharePoint app that contains one or more permissions requests, the SharePoint host environment displays a prompt asking the installing user to grant or deny the permissions that the app has requested.

Figure 3-3 shows a screenshot of the page that the SharePoint host environment uses to prompt the person who is installing an app with permission requests. The user must either click the Trust It button to grant the app's permission requests or click the Cancel button the deny them.

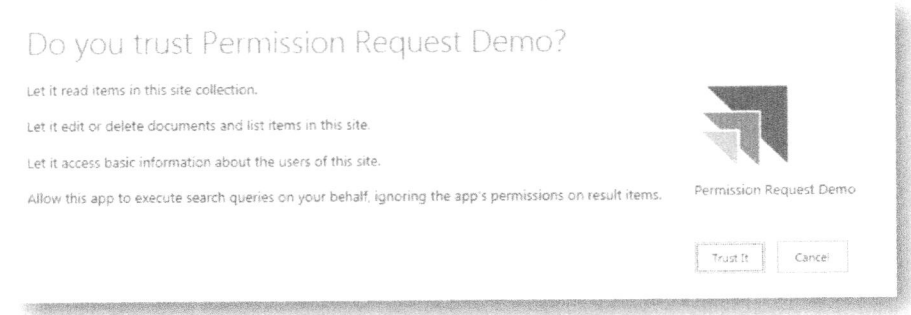

FIGURE 3-3 The user is prompted to grant or deny permission requests when an app is installed.

If the user clicks the Cancel button to deny the app's permission requests, the SharePoint host environment aborts the installation. In other words, you must grant all the permissions requested by an app to install it. It is not possible to selectively grant some permissions an app has requested while denying other permission requests. Granting permission requests during app installation is an all or nothing proposition.

It is also important to note that a user must possess any permissions that are granted to an app. For example, an app might request write capabilities on the site collection or the tenancy in which the host web is located. The user must also possess write permissions on the hosting site collection or the hosting tenancy in order to grant that permission to an app during installation. Therefore, you can encounter scenarios in which a site administrator cannot install an app because the app is requesting permissions that the installing user does not possess.

If the installing user clicks the Trust It button to grant the app's permission requests, the SharePoint host environment tracks these permissions in one or more of the SharePoint databases. The permissions that are specific to a site or a site collection are stored in the content database associated with the hosting site collection. Other types of permissions that are scoped above the site-collection level are stored in the App Management Service database.

Permission requests are created by adding <AppPermissionRequest> elements into the *AppManifest.xml* file within the scope of a top-level <AppPermissionRequests> element. Each <AppPermissionRequest> element must contain the *Scope* attribute and the *Right* attribute, as shown in Listing 3-1.

LISTING 3-1 Permissions requests inside the app manifest

```
<AppPermissionRequests>

  <AppPermissionRequest
    Scope="http://sharepoint/content/sitecollection/web"
    Right="Read" />

  <AppPermissionRequest
    Scope="http://sharepoint/content/sitecollection/web/list"
    Right="Write" />

</AppPermissionRequests>
```

The *Scope* attribute is used to define the type of object for which the permissions are being requested. The value of the *Scope* attribute is a URI that contains several distinct parts. Consider the URI value of the *Scope* attribute from the previous listing.

```
http://sharepoint/content/sitecollection/web
```

The first part of the Scope URI defines the *Product*, which in this example is *sharepoint*. In some scenarios, an app might need to request permissions from another Microsoft product such as *exchange* or *lync*.

The second part of the Scope URI defines the *permission provider*, which in this example is *content*. SharePoint 2013 provides several other permission providers such as *search*, *social*, and *bcs*.

The final part of the Scope URI defines the *target object type*, which in this example is *sitecollection/web*. This is the target object type used to define the host web. Note that this Scope URI will also include any child sites below the host web.

The *Right* attribute defines the type of permission you are requesting. The SharePoint Foundation platform defines four common rights, which include *Read*, *Write*, *Manage*, and *FullControl*. The various teams that have created SharePoint 2013 have tried to use these four basic rights as consistently as possible. However, some permission providers have added rights beyond these four. For example, the search permission provider defines the *QueryAsUserIgnoreAppPrincipal* right.

```
<AppPermissionRequest
  Scope="http://sharepoint/search"
  Right="QueryAsUserIgnoreAppPrincipal"
/>
```

You can encounter scenarios in which the *Scope* attribute does not provide enough control to specify a certain type of object. For example, imagine that you have an app that needs the *Manage* right on all document libraries in the host web. The *Scope* attribute will let you define a more general target object type for all lists, including document libraries as well as all the other list types.

```
<AppPermissionRequest
  Scope="http://sharepoint/content/sitecollection/web/list"
  Right="Manage"
/>
```

However, the app that requests permissions with this Scope URI is requesting the *Manage* right on every type of list, which is more permissions than the app actually needs. You can add a <Property> element into an <AppPermissionRequest> element to filter the object type beyond what is possible by using the Scope URI alone. Here's an example of adding the *BaseTemplateId* property with a value of *101* to filter the permission request to just document libraries:

```
<AppPermissionRequest
  Scope="http://sharepoint/content/sitecollection/web/list"
  Right="Manage" >

  <!-- add filter property to permission request -->
  <Property Name="BaseTemplateId" Value="101" />

</AppPermissionRequest>
```

In certain cases, you are not required to make direct edits to the *AppManifest.xml* file to add permission requests. The *Permissions* tab of the app manifest designer supplied by Microsoft Visual Studio 2012 makes it easy to add and configure permissions requests without having to work with the XML elements directly. The screenshot in Figure 3-4 shows what the Permissions tab looks like when you are configuring permission requests.

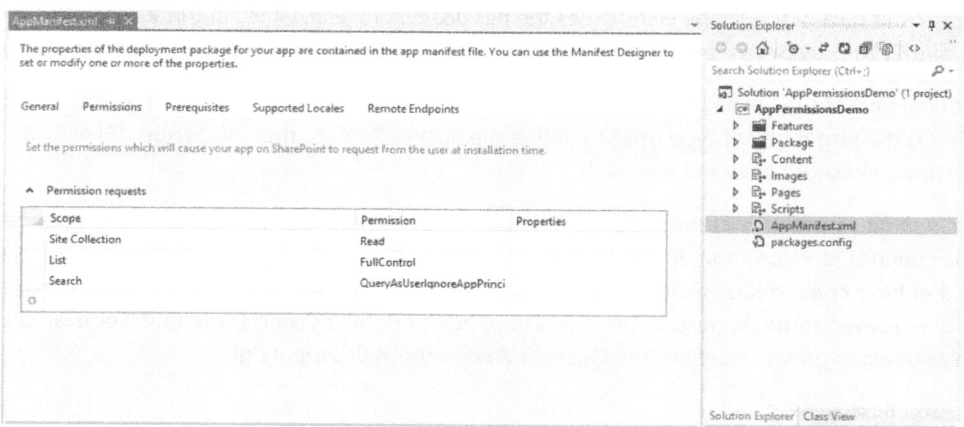

FIGURE 3-4 App permission requests are made by using the manifest designer in Visual Studio.

There are several different types of permissions that an app can request in SharePoint 2013. Table 3-1 provides a listing of the more common ones that can be used in app development in SharePoint 2013.

TABLE 3-1 Permission types in SharePoint 2013

Object type	Scope URI	Rights
Tenancy	*http://sharepoint/content/tenant*	Read, Write, Manage, FullControl
Site collection	*http://sharepoint/content/sitecollection*	Read, Write, Manage, FullControl
Host web	*http://sharepoint/content/sitecollection/web*	Read, Write, Manage, FullControl
Lists	*http://sharepoint/content/sitecollection/web/list*	Read, Write, Manage, FullControl
Search	*http://sharepoint/search*	QueryAsUserIgnoreAppPrincipal
BCS	*http://sharepoint/bcs/connection*	Read
Managed metadata	*http://sharepoint/taxonomy*	Read, Write
Social core	*http://sharepoint/social/core*	Read, Write, Manage, FullControl
Social tenancy	*http://sharepoint/social/tenant*	Read, Write, Manage, FullControl
Microsofeed	*http://sharepoint/social/microfeed*	Read, Write, Manage, FullControl

Requesting app-only permissions

For certain scenarios, the authorization system for SharePoint apps makes it possible for an app to call into the SharePoint host environment with app identity but not user identity. This relaxes the rules of app authorization because only the app needs permissions to access an object instead of both the app and the current user. In such a scenario, calls from an app are authorized by using *app-only permissions*.

App-only permissions are used for two specific scenarios. The first scenario is to elevate the permissions of the app above the permissions of the current user. For example, consider the case in which the app has been granted permissions to create a new list but the current user doesn't possess the same permissions. By using the default app authorization policy, the app cannot create a new list. However, an app using app-only permissions would be able to create a new list even when the current user doesn't have those permissions.

The second scenario for using app-only permissions involves an app that accesses the SharePoint host environment in a time when there is no current user. Imagine a scenario in which an app has been automated to run a job every night at midnight to update a set of documents in the host web. In this scenario there is no current user. However, the app still needs to be authorized to access the host web.

You must make a modification to the *AppManifest.xml* file if you require an app to make calls that are authorized by using app-only permissions. The way this is accomplished is by adding the *Allow AppOnlyPolicy* attribute to the <AppPermissionRequests> element in the app manifest.

```
<AppPermissionRequests AllowAppOnlyPolicy="true" >

  <AppPermissionRequest
    Scope="http://sharepoint/content/sitecollection/web"
    Right="Manage" />

</AppPermissionRequests>
```

Adding the *AllowAppOnlyPolicy* attribute to the <AppPermissionRequests> element alone is not enough to execute calls from an app run with app-only policy. You must additionally create an access token with app identity but not user identity. The details of how to create an app-only access token will be covered in the next section of this chapter.

It is worth noting that running with app-only permissions is only possible when using external authentication. Executing calls from an app with app-only permissions is not possible when using internal authentication. Therefore, running with app-only permissions is not possible from SharePoint-hosted apps. Calls from a SharePoint-hosted app always require that app permissions and user permissions succeed.

Establishing app identity by using OAuth

OAuth is a standard Internet protocol for authentication and authorization which provides a cross-platform mechanism for managing app identity and app permissions. Although the original version OAuth 1.0 is still being used by some software companies, a second version, OAuth 2.0, was created to simplify development while still providing app authentication and specific authorization flows for web apps, desktop applications, and mobile devices.

Today, the OAuth 2.0 protocol is used by software companies such as Microsoft, Google, Facebook, and Salesforce.com. When Microsoft began to design the external authentication infrastructure for provided-hosted apps and autohosted apps in Office 365, it made a decision to build its implementation on top of the OAuth 2.0 protocol. More specifically, it decided that access tokens used for external authentication in the Office 365 environment would be created in accordance with the OAuth 2.0 specification.

Microsoft's implementation of OAuth 2.0 is built on top of the Windows Azure ACS. ACS is a cloud-hosted service on the Internet that is sponsored by Microsoft. The SharePoint host environment in Office 365 has been configured with a trust to ACS. This allows ACS to act as an S2S that creates access tokens that can be authenticated by Office 365. In most cases, the access tokens created by ACS will contain both app identity and user identity. However, ACS is also capable of creating access tokens with only app identity for scenarios in which an app requires app-only permissions.

Note that the OAuth 2.0 specification provides a way to add permissions into an access token. However, this aspect of the OAuth specification not used in the SharePoint 2013 implementation. SharePoint 2013 makes use of OAuth for app authentication but not for any type of authorization or permissions management. Instead, it tracks and manages app permissions independently of the app authentication scheme in use so that app permissions works the same way as you switch between internal app authentication and external app authentication using either OAuth or S2S authentication.

Understanding where OAuth fits in

At a high level, it is fair to say that OAuth is primarily used for external app authentication in the Office 365 environment, whereas S2S authentication is used for external app authentication in on-premises farms. A common question is whether a company can use OAuth in on-premises farms. The answer to this question is—of course—it depends.

Although it is technically possible to configure OAuth support for external app authentication in an on-premises farm, you have to remember that the OAuth implementation in SharePoint 2013 is tightly coupled to Windows Azure ACS. The technical requirements for configuring OAuth support in an on-premises farm include obtaining an Office 365 tenancy from Microsoft and synchronizing user accounts between the on-premises farm and this Office 365 tenancy. Additional configuration is required to create trusts so that the local on-premises SharePoint farm and the remote web can both communicate with Windows Azure ACS.

The key takeaway is that OAuth is only supported in scenarios in which it is acceptable to have dependencies on Microsoft-hosted authentication servers in the cloud. OAuth cannot be used in a scenario in which you are required to avoid dependencies outside the LAN in which you are hosting an on-premises SharePoint farm and the remote web for a provider-hosted app.

Understanding OAuth terms and concepts

The OAuth 2.0 protocol defines a flow for app authentication, which involves the following four participants.

1. Content owners

2. Client app

3. Content server

4. Authentication server

Content owners represent the users who can grant access to the content in a site. In a SharePoint 2013 environment, a content owner has permissions to access objects such as sites, lists, and items, and can consequently grant these same permissions to an app.

The client app represents that part of a website that runs across the network. In a SharePoint 2013 environment, the client app is the portion of the app that runs in the remote web.

The content server is the web server that hosts the site with content. In a SharePoint 2013 environment, the content server is a web server hosted within the Office 365 environment that provides access to SharePoint sites within an Office 365 tenancy for a specific customer.

The authentication server is a server that creates access tokens used for app authentication. The authentication server must be trusted by both the content server and the client app. In a SharePoint 2013 environment, the authentication server is always Windows Azure ACS.

Understanding app principals

The SharePoint 2013 implementation of the OAuth protocol requires any app using external authentication to have an associated security principal known as an app principal. You can think of an app principal as a type of security account similar to a user account. The app principal for a cloud-hosted app in the Office 365 environment must be registered within the context of an Office 365 tenancy. A key point is that the app principal is similar to a user account because it is used to establish an identity during the app authentication process.

When you register an app principal within the context of an Office 365 tenancy, the SharePoint host environment tracks it in the App Management Service database. As part of the same registration process, the Office 365 environment also forwards information about the new app principal to Windows Azure ACS. This makes it possible for Windows Azure ACS to keep its configuration data for app principals in sync with each Office 365 tenancy.

The profile for an app principal contains five important properties:

- Client ID

- Client secret

- Title

- App host domain

- Redirect URL

The client ID is a GUID that is used to identify the app principal associated with a cloud-hosted app. Note that the client ID is sometimes referred to as the *app ID*. Don't be confused into thinking that the client ID and the app ID are different. They are just two terms that are used to refer to the same thing.

The client secret (also known as the *app secret*) is a security key created by using a Base64-encoded string which is used to perform symmetric encryption. The client secret is shared between the client app, the hosting Office 365 tenancy, and Windows Azure ACS. The client secret is an integral part of the app authentication process because it facilitates communication among these three parties in a way that makes it possible for messages to be encrypted and authenticated.

The title is a human-readable string for the app principal which is displayed to users within the Office 365 tenancy.

The app host domain is the base URL for the domain in which the remote web is hosted. The registration of app host domain is important because it makes it possible for both the hosting Office 365 tenancy and Windows Azure ACS to ensure that calls from the remote web of an app have originated from the well-known URL.

The redirect URL is a property that is used for scenarios in which external applications and external websites need to request permissions on the fly. This property is optional. You can register an app principal without a redirect URL. The scenario in which a redirect URL is used will be covered later in this chapter.

Deploying the remote web by using Secure Sockets Layer

Note that the remote web associated with an app in a production should always be deployed by using Secure Sockets Layer (SSL). The reason for this is that SSL significantly lowers the risk of an attack by which the attacker calls to the Office 365 host environment pretending to originate from the app host domain when in fact it is being made from some other domain.

Registering app principals

When it comes to registering the app principal for an autohosted app, things are pretty easy. That's because the app principal is registered transparently behind the scenes as part of the app installation process.

When it comes to registering the app principal for a provider-hosted app, there are extra steps involved. The app principal must be explicitly registered by a user that possesses administrative permissions within the hosting Office 365 tenancy.

There are several ways by which you can register an app principal for a provider-hosted app in an Office 365 tenancy. The easiest way to do so is to use a standard application page named *AppReg New.aspx* that was added to SharePoint 2013, as shown in Figure 3-5. As you can see, the *AppRegNew. aspx* page uses the terms *App Id* and *App Secret* instead of client ID and client secret. However, you have already learned that these are just different terms that refer to the client ID and the client secret.

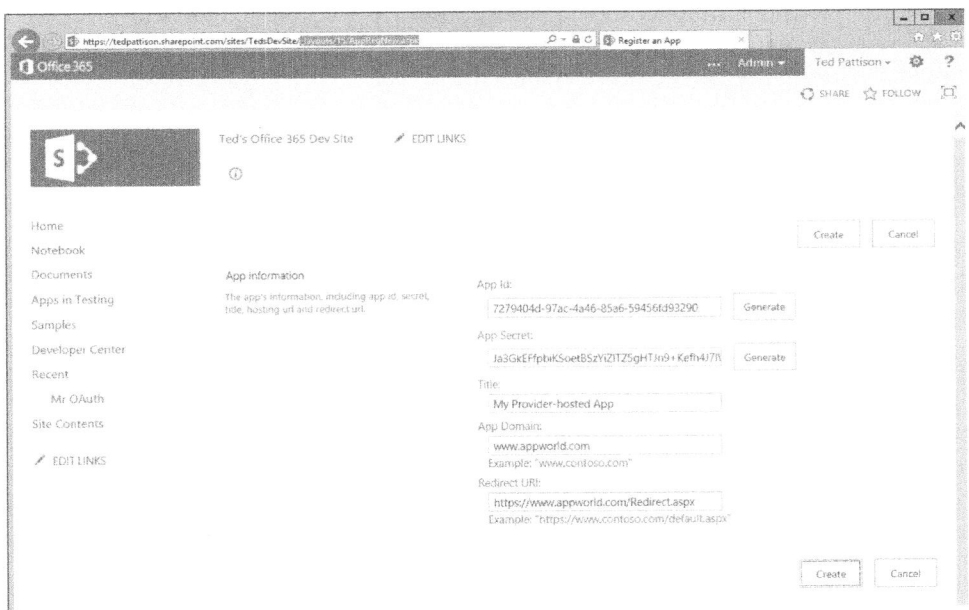

FIGURE 3-5 The *AppRegNew.aspx* page can be used to register an app principal for a provider-hosted app.

A second way to register an app principal for a provider-hosted app in the Office 365 environment involves using the *SharePoint Online Windows PowerShell Library*. This is a Windows PowerShell library that you install on a local computer that provides cmdlets with which you can create a remote connection to your Office 365 tenancy. After you have established an authenticated connection, the SharePoint Online Windows PowerShell Library provides additional cmdlets with which you can manage various aspects of your Office 365 tenancies, including creating and managing app principals.

Understanding app authentication flow in Office 365

The OAuth 2.0 protocol involves passing various types of security tokens between Windows Azure ACS, the hosting Office 365 tenancy, and the remote web. The following list shows the different types of security tokens that are passed between the participants when authenticating an app by using OAuth.

1. Context token
2. Refresh token
3. Access token
4. Authorization code

The context token is a security token that's used to pass contextual information such as the identity of the current user, the URL of the host web, and the ID of the current tenancy. The context token is created by Windows Azure ACS and initially passed to the SharePoint host environment. The SharePoint host environment is then able to pass the context token to the remote web, where it can be accessed and used by server-side code in the remote web.

The refresh token is included within the context token that is passed to the remote web. The value of the refresh token is that it can be used by code in the remote web to obtain an access token from Windows Azure ACS.

When a refresh token is created, it's good for a period of 6 months, whereas an access token is only good for 12 hours. Therefore, it often makes sense for an app to store refresh tokens in a database from which they can be retrieved and reused to create access tokens on demand.

The access token is what the server-side code in the remote web actually needs to execute authenticated calls back to the SharePoint host environment by using CSOM or the REST API. Therefore, the remote web requires code to explicitly call into Windows Azure ACS and obtain access tokens when required. After the code in the remote web has retrieved an access token, it must pass the access token in an HTTP header each time it makes a CSOM or REST API call by using programming techniques that will be discussed later in this chapter.

An authorization code is a special type of security token used for a scenario in which an external website that has never been installed as a SharePoint app wants to acquire permissions on the fly to call in to a SharePoint site. The use of authorization code will be explained later in this chapter.

Now that you have learned about the different types of security tokens, you can understand how the app authentication flow works in a typical scenario with a cloud-hosted app that has been installed in an Office 365 tenancy. Figure 3-6 shows 10 different stages within the OAuth authentication flow as security tokens are passed back and forth between the Office 365 tenancy, Windows Azure ACS, and the remote web of the cloud-hosted app.

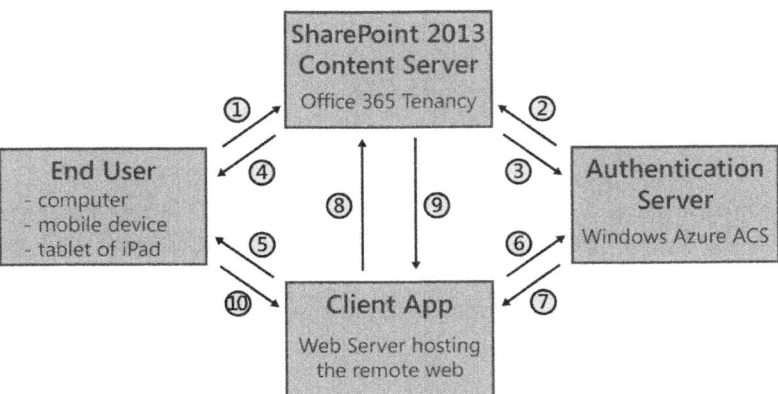

FIGURE 3-6 Apps use context tokens and access tokens to validate incoming calls and create outgoing calls.

Let's begin with stage 1, when the user first accesses a page in a SharePoint site within an Office 365 tenancy. The user is authenticated and a SAML token is created that contains information about the user identity such as the user's logon name.

In stage 2, the user navigates to the Site Contents page in which the SharePoint host environment must display a tile that the user can employ to launch the app. When the SharePoint host environment needs to create a tile with an app launcher, it must first call to Windows Azure ACS and request creation of a context token.

When the SharePoint host environment calls to Windows Azure ACS to create a context token, it passes information about the current user, the host web, and the current tenancy. Windows Azure ACS needs this information because it must add information about the current user, the host web, and the current tenancy inside the context token. In stage 3, Windows Azure ACS creates the context token and returns it to the SharePoint host environment.

In stage 4, the SharePoint host environment has the context token returned from Windows Azure ACS. The SharePoint host environment makes use of the context token by adding it into the JavaScript code for the app launcher on the Site Contents page.

Stage 5 occurs when the user clicks the tile for the app on the Site Contents page and launches the app. The JavaScript code behind the app launcher redirects the user to the app's start page in the remote web by using an HTTP *POST* request. When the HTTP *POST* request is executed, the context token is passed to the remote web by using a form variable named *SPAppToken*.

In stage 6 the client app retrieves the context token from *SPAppToken* in the incoming request to the state page. The client app is then able to read what's inside the context token to obtain information about the current user, the host web, and the current tenancy. The client app also has the ability to extract the refresh token from the context token.

Stage 6 is where the client app calls to Windows Azure ACS to request an access token. When requesting an access token, the client app must pass the refresh token. In stage 7, Windows Azure ACS creates the access token from the refresh token and passes it back to the client app. Note that Windows Azure creates an access token that has both the identity of the app as well as the identity of the current user.

Once the client app has obtained an access token from Windows Azure ACS, it is finally at a point at which it can make an authenticated call to the host web by using either CSOM or the REST API. Stage 8 shows the client app making a CSOM or REST API call on the host web. When making this type of call, the client app must include explicit programming to ensure that the access token is passed in each call using an HTTP header.

In Stage 9, the SharePoint host environment is able to authenticate the call from the app by using the access token. As long as the SharePoint host environment is able to determine that the authenticated app and the current user both have the proper permissions, it returns content back to the client app.

In the final stage, stage 10, the client app is able to return a page from the remote web that displays content from the host web that was retrieved during stages 8 and 9.

You have now seen the end-to-end flow of authentication that's used in an OAuth scenario.

Developing with OAuth

There are three important requirements to keep in mind when developing cloud-hosted apps that will be installed within an Office 365 tenancy. First, the app manifest file must be properly configured to indicate whether the app is a provider-hosted app or an autohosted app. Secondly, the *web.config* file in the ASP.NET project for the remote web must be configured to track the client ID and the client secret. Finally, you must write server-side code that creates and manages access tokens.

The app manifest file for a provider-hosted app must be configured with a <RemoteWeb Application> element that contains an inner *ClientId* attribute which tracks the GUID identifying an app principal.

```
<AppPrincipal>
  <RemoteWebApplication ClientId="00000000-0000-0000-0000-000000000001" />
</AppPrincipal>
```

If you are developing an autohosted app, on the other hand, the app manifest should be configured with an <AutoDeployedWebApplication> element. The <AutoDeployedWebApplication> element is different from the <RemoteWebApplication> element because it does not contain an attribute for a client ID.

```
<AppPrincipal>
  <AutoDeployedWebApplication/>
</AppPrincipal>
```

The next aspect of configuring a cloud-hosted app for use in the Office 365 environment is configuring the *web.config* file of the remote web with two settings that are set the same, regardless of whether you are developing a provider-hosted app or an autohosted app. In particular, you must add two *appSettings* variables into the *web.config* file to track the client ID and the client secret. These *appSettings* variables must be named *ClientId* and *ClientSecret*.

```
<configuration>
  <appSettings>
    <add key="ClientId" value="00000000-0000-0000-0000-000000000001" />
    <add key="ClientSecret" value="rdYuzdeP9LX67rJJLTDjL1E5pvqbrLe4VTs2apITF4g=" />
  </appSettings>
</configuration>
```

At this point, you might be wondering what these two *appSettings* variables are for. As it turns out, these two variables are used by a utility class named *TokenHelper* that Visual Studio 2012 automatically adds to ASP.NET projects that will be used to implement a remote web. The last step in getting up and running with OAuth is learning how to program with the *TokenHelper* class to create access tokens and to pass these access tokens when making CSOM and REST calls back to the SharePoint host environment.

Programming with the TokenHelper class

If you plan on developing cloud-hosted apps, you must learn to work with the *TokenHelper* class. The *TokenHelper* class provides a public set of static methods for working with several different types of security tokens including context tokens, refresh tokens, and, most importantly, the access tokens.

Let's start with a simple example. Examine the server-side C# code in Listing 3-2 which shows an implementation for the *Page_Load* method. This code is very similar to the "hello world" code snippet that Visual Studio 2012 automatically adds to the start page of a cloud-hosted app that uses OAuth. This code has been written to retrieve the context token passed by the SharePoint host environment and then to obtain an access token from Windows Azure ACS.

LISTING 3-2 The *TokenHelper* class used to acquire access tokens to make authenticated CSOM and REST API calls

```
protected void Page_Load(object sender, EventArgs e) {

    // get context token from incoming HTTP form variable
    var contextToken = TokenHelper.GetContextTokenFromRequest(Page.Request);

    // get host web URL from incoming query string parameter
    var hostWeb = Page.Request["SPHostUrl"];

    // call to Window Azure ACS to acquire access token
    using (var clientContext =
            TokenHelper.GetClientContextWithContextToken(hostWeb,
                                                         contextToken,
                                                         Request.Url.Authority))
    {

        // Make CSOM call to SharePoint host passing access token
        clientContext.Load(clientContext.Web, web => web.Title);
        clientContext.ExecuteQuery();

        // display site title on start page
        Response.Write(clientContext.Web.Title);
    }
}
```

Now that you have seen a simple example of using the *TokenHelper* class, it's time to explain how to program against this class in a bit more detail. When a user is redirected from a host web in an Office 365 tenancy to the start page in the remote web, the SharePoint host environment passes several important pieces of data to the app's remote web by using an HTTP POST operation.

For example, the SharePoint host environment passes several querying string parameters, including one named *SPHostUrl* which contains the base URL of the host web. When you are writing server-side code behind the start page for a cloud-hosted app, you can retrieve the host web URL by using the following code:

```
string urlHostWeb = Request.QueryString["SPHostUrl"]
```

In addition to query string parameters, the SharePoint host environment also passes several form parameters when posting to the start page in the remote web, including one named *SPAppToken*, which contain the context token. You can access the context token as a raw string by using the following code:

```
string contextTokenString = Request.Form["SPAppToken"]
```

As you have already seen in Listing 3-2, you can retrieve the context token by using a *TokenHelper* method named *GetContextTokenFromRequest*. When you make the call to *GetContextTokenFrom Request*, you pass the ASP.NET *Request* object as the one and only parameter value.

```
// when calling GetContextTokenFromRequest, you must pass the ASP.NET Request object
string contextTokenString = TokenHelper.GetContextTokenFromRequest(Request);
```

The code in Listing 3-2 demonstrates passing the context token as a raw string when calling *Get ClientContextWithContextToken*. The implementation of this method extracts the refresh token from the context token and then uses it to call to Windows Azure ACS to obtain an access token. After the access token has been returned, the *GetClientContextWithContextToken* method uses it to initialize a CSOM session with a special client context that automatically passes the access token when sending a request to execute CSOM commands on the SharePoint host environment.

If you need to read information from inside the context token, you can convert the context token string to a strongly typed object by calling the *TokenHelper* method *ReadAndValidateContextToken*.

```
string remoteWebUrl = Request.Url.Authority;
string contextTokenString = TokenHelper.GetContextTokenFromRequest(Request);

SharePointContextToken contextToken;
contextToken = TokenHelper.ReadAndValidateContextToken(contextTokenString, remoteWebUrl);
```

The call to *ReadAndValidateContextToken* returns a *SharePointContextToken* object that makes the information inside the context token accessible to your code through simple properties. The code in Listing 3-3 demonstrates the type of information that you can read from the context token.

LISTING 3-3 Accessing information within the context token

```
string remoteWebUrl = Request.Url.Authority;
string contextTokenString = TokenHelper.GetContextTokenFromRequest(Request);

SharePointContextToken contextToken;
contextToken = TokenHelper.ReadAndValidateContextToken(contextTokenString,
remoteWebUrl);

// ID of the current user on behalf of which the current call is executing
string nameId = contextToken.NameId;

// Client ID of the app principal used for external authentication
string clientId = contextToken.ActorToken.ActorToken.Id;

// ID of the hosting tenancy in Office 365
string realm = contextToken.Realm;

// Environment ID for Office 365
string targetPrincipalName = contextToken.TargetPrincipalName;

// ID of the authentication server which is Windows Azure ACS
string issuer = contextToken.Issuer;

// URL used when communicating with Windows Azure ACS
string  securityTokenServiceUri = contextToken.SecurityTokenServiceUri;
```

```
// time when context token became valid
DateTime validFrom = contextToken.ValidFrom;

// time when context token expires
DateTime validTo = contextToken.ValidTo;

// refresh token
string refreshToken = contextToken.RefreshToken;

// caching key for caching refresh tokens and access tokens
string cacheKey = contextToken.CacheKey;
```

If you look toward the end of Listing 3-3, you can see that the code demonstrates how to retrieve both the refresh token and the cache key from the context token. The refresh token is what the app must pass to Windows Azure ACS to obtain an access token. Although you do not have to work directly with refresh tokens in all scenarios, it can be helpful to store refresh tokens in a database where they are good for 6 months to retrieve access tokens. Remember that an access token is only good for 12 hours.

Recall that all refresh tokens and the majority of access tokens contain information about one specific user. Therefore, any scheme you design to cache or store refresh tokens and/or access tokens must ensure that caching is user-specific when required. It would be bad to use the refresh token associated with one user to retrieve an access token for a different user.

The context token contains a special string value named *cacheKey*. The cache key holds a string value that will always be unique for the combination of current user, the host web site, and app. The idea is that you can use the *cacheKey* as a dictionary lookup key when caching or storing access tokens in memory or refresh tokens inside a database.

Working with access tokens

At this point, you have already seen the code required to execute CSOM commands by using OAuth. Executing a REST API call by using OAuth is different because you must work directly with access tokens in your code. Listing 3-4 shows the code required to retrieve an access token. After the access token has been acquired, it must be converted into a string and added as an HTTP header before making a REST API call.

LISTING 3-4 Making a simple REST API call by using OAuth

```
// get context token as a SharePointContextToken object
string remoteWebUrl = Request.Url.Authority;
string contextTokenString = TokenHelper.GetContextTokenFromRequest(Request);
SharePointContextToken contextToken;
contextToken = TokenHelper.ReadAndValidateContextToken(contextTokenString,
                                                       remoteWebUrl);

// retrieve host web information
string hostWebUrl = Request.QueryString["SPHostUrl"];
Uri hostWebUri = new ri(hostWebUrl);
string hostWebAuthority = hostWebUri.Authority;

// get access token by passing context token and host web authority
OAuth2AccessTokenResponse accessToken = TokenHelper.GetAccessToken(contextToken,
                                                        hostWebAuthority);

// get access token as a base 64 encoded string
string accessTokenString = accessToken.AccessToken;

// prepare HttpWebRequest to execute REST API call
HttpWebRequest request1 =
  (HttpWebRequest)HttpWebRequest.Create(hostWebUrl.ToString() +
                                "/_api/Web/title");

// add access token string as Authorization header
request1.Headers.Add("Authorization", "Bearer " + accessTokenString);

// execute REST API call and inspect response
HttpWebResponse response1 = (HttpWebResponse)request1.GetResponse();
StreamReader reader1 = new StreamReader(response1.GetResponseStream());
XDocument doc1 = XDocument.Load(reader1);
string SiteTitle = doc1.Root.Value;
```

Let's step through some of the code in Listing 3-4. There is a call to the *TokenHelper* method *GetAccessToken*, which retrieves an access token from Windows Azure ACS. When you call *GetAccess Token*, you must pass a strongly typed context token and the authority of the host web.

```
// get access token by passing context token and host web authority
OAuth2AccessTokenResponse accessToken = TokenHelper.GetAccessToken(contextToken,
                                                        hostWebAuthority);

// get access token as a base 64 encoded string
string accessTokenString = accessToken.AccessToken;
```

When passing the second parameter for the host web authority, you must pass the URL of the host web but without the protocol in front. For example, the host web authority is a string such as *tenancy01.sharepoint.com*, as opposed to the host web URL, which has the protocol at the beginning with a value such as *https://tenancy01.sharepoint.com*.

You can see that calling *GetAccessToken* returns a strongly typed object of type *OAuth2Access TokenResponse*. However, you must usually work with the access token in its raw form as a Base64-encoded string. You retrieve the string for the access token by reading the *AccessToken* property of the *OAuth2AccessTokenResponse* object.

The code in Listing 3-4 demonstrates creating a *HttpWebRequest* object and adding the string-based access token as an HTTP header named *Authorization*. You should take note that the *Authorization* header value is created by combining the word "Bearer" together with the access token, with a blank space between them.

```
string restUri = hostWeb + "/_api/Web/title";
HttpWebRequest request1 = (HttpWebRequest)HttpWebRequest.Create(restUri);

// add access token to Authorization header
request1.Headers.Add("Authorization", "Bearer " + accessTokenString);
```

After you have added the *Authorization* header with the access token string, you can then issue as many REST API calls as required by using the programming techniques you learned in Chapter 2, "Client-Side Programming."

JavaScript Object Notation Web Tokens

OAuth security tokens such as context tokens, refresh tokens, and access tokens are created by using the JSON Web Token (JWT) standard. A JWT is created in a text-based, human-readable format by using JavaScript Object Notation (JSON), which allows you to read the information inside.

```
{ "token_type":"Bearer",
  "access_token":"eyJ0eXAiOiJKV1QiLCJhbGciOiJSUzI1NiIsIng1dCI6Ik5HVEZ2k5HVE2ZEst...",
  "expires_in":"43199",
  "not_before":"1355269661",
  "expires_on":"1355312861",
  "resource":"00000003-0000-0ff1-ce00-000000000000/tenancy01.sharepoint.com@23d..." }
```

Although JWTs are initially created in a human-readable form, they must be converted into a Base64-encoded format before they are passed across the network. After a security token has been converted into a Base64-encoded format, it loses any trace of human readability.

eyJ0eXAiOiJKV1QiLCJhbGciOiJIUzI1NiJ9.eyJhdWQiOiJmOWIONmIwZiO4YjM2LTQ2ODYtYWY5MiOwMmRhODY3
NGNiYzEvbG9jYWxob3N0OjQ0MzA0QDIzZDkO0WF1LWIzNzEtNGJmMS1iNzVmLTg5ZjAwMjk5NDY1ZiIsImlzcyI6
IjAwMDAwMDAxLTAwMDAtMDAwMC1jMDAwLTAwMDAwMDAwMDAwMEAyMQ5NDlhZS1iMzcxLTRiZjEtYjc1Zi04OWYw
MDI5OTQ2NWYiLCJuYmYiOjEzNTUyNjk2NTgsImV4cCI6MTM1NTMxMjg1OCwiYXBwX3R4c2VuZGVyIjoiMDAwMDAw
MDMtMDAwMC0wZmYxLWN1MDAtMDAwMDAwMDAwMDAwQDIzZDkO0WF1LWIzNzEtNGJmMS1iNzVmLTg5ZjAwMjk5NDY1Z
iIsImFwcGN0eCI6IntcIkNhY2h1S2V5XCI6XCJnK2k1UVFLYjZnMnRt

Working with app-only access tokens

In the majority of scenarios, an access token will carry the identity of the current user in addition to the identity of the app itself. However, there are scenarios for which it makes sense to create an access token that contains app identity but not user identity. This type of security token is known as an app-only access token.

As discussed earlier in the chapter, there are two primary scenarios in which you should use app-only access tokens. The first scenario involves a requirement to elevate the permissions for an app so that they are not constrained by the permissions of the current user. For example, an app-only access token makes it possible for an app to create a list in the host web even when the current user lacks the permissions to do so.

The second scenario in which it makes sense to create app-only access tokens is during a time when there is no current user. This might be the case if an app runs a batch job every night at midnight to update a set of document in the host web. In this scenario, the app is running but not in the context of any specific user. However, the app is still required to create an access token to make CSOM or REST API calls against the host web.

You can retrieve an app-only access token by calling the *TokenHelper* method named *GetAppOnly AccessToken*. This method accepts three parameters, including the target principal name, the host web authority, and the realm which identifies the hosting tenancy in Office 365.

```
// get app-only access token as a strongly-typed object
OAuth2AccessTokenResponse appOnlyAccessToken =
    TokenHelper.GetAppOnlyAccessToken(contextToken.TargetPrincipalName,
                                      hostWebAuthority,
                                      contextToken.Realm);

// get access token in a string form to pass across the network
string appOnlyAccessTokenString = appOnlyAccessToken.AccessToken;
```

After you have obtained the app-only access token from Windows Azure ACS and converted it into its string format, you can use it to set up the *Authorization* header, just as you do with standard access tokens, as shown back in Listing 3-4. If you want to execute CSOM commands by using app-only permissions, you must first obtain the string value for an app-only access token. You can pass the app-only access token string when calling the *GetClientContextWithAccessToken* method to establish a new CSOM session, which executes its commands by using app-only permissions.

```
ClientContext appOnlyClientContext =
    TokenHelper.GetClientContextWithAccessToken(hostWebUrl, appOnlyAccessTokenString);
```

The SHAREPOINT\APP account

When the SharePoint host environment authenticates an app by using an access token containing a user identity, it uses the user identity to initialize the calling context. However, things are different when the SharePoint host environment authenticates a call from an app that has passed on app-only access token. When the SharePoint host environment authenticates a CSOM or REST API call with an app-only access token, it initializes the calling context with a special SharePoint system account named SHAREPOINT\APP.

Acquiring permissions on the fly by using authorization code

So far, this chapter has discussed authentication and authorization scenarios involving SharePoint apps that have been installed into a specific SharePoint tenancy. SharePoint 2013 provides another option which can be used by standard websites that were not developed as SharePoint apps. This allows any type of website on the Internet to request permissions to access a SharePoint 2013 site on the fly.

Although this approach does not involve creating or installing a SharePoint app, it does require you to preregister an app principal within the scope of the target tenancy where the permissions will be requested. Enabling this capability for an external website to request permissions on the fly is the primary scenario in which you must register an app principal with a redirect URL.

For example, imagine that you have developed an ASP.NET website whose base URL is https://appserver.wingtip.com, and you want this website to be able to request permissions from a SharePoint site in Office 365 on the fly. First, you need to register an app principal in the scope of the host tenancy for the SharePoint site. When registering the app principal you must set the redirect URL to point to a page in the ASP.NET website such as https://appserver.wingtip.com/RedirectAccept.aspx.

After you have registered the app principal with the proper redirect URL, the next step involves writing code in the external website to create the authorization URL. This step is greatly simplified if you add the *TokenHelper* class that is also used in the remote web of a cloud-hosted app. The *Token Helper* class provides a method named *GetAuthorizationUrl*.

The code in Listing 3-5 demonstrates how to call the *GetAuthorizationUrl* method in an external website. This method accepts three parameters, including the URL of the host web, the permission being requested (for example, *Web.Read*), and a redirect URL. The redirect URL is important because it is what the SharePoint host environment uses to call back to the external website if a user with sufficient permissions grants the permission request.

LISTING 3-5 The code required to generate a permission request by using an authorization URL

```
string urlHostWeb = "https://tenancy01.sharepoint.com/ ";
string urlRedirectAccept = "https://AppServer.wingtip.com/ RedirectAccept.aspx";
string urlAuthorization = TokenHelper.GetAuthorizationUrl(urlHostWeb,
                                                          "Web.Read",
                                                          urlRedirectAccept);


// redirect
Response.Redirect(urlAuthorization, true);
```

The *GetAuthorizationUrl* method parses together a URL that targets a standard SharePoint 2013 application page named *OAuthAuthorize.aspx*. The authorization URL also includes query string parameters to pass a GUID for the client ID, the requested permissions, and the redirect URL. As shown in Listing 3-6, you can redirect the user to the authorization URL automatically by calling *Response.Redirect*.

When the user is redirected to the authorization URL within the host web, the SharePoint host environment responds by displaying a page on which the user can either grant or deny the permission request. Just as in the case of a permission request in a SharePoint app, a user must possess any permissions that are granted in a permission request. If the user grants the permission request, the SharePoint host environment responds by passing an authorization code back to the external website by using an HTTP *POST* operation that targets the page configured as the redirect URL.

Listing 3-6 shows an example of code behind the redirect page that has been written to retrieve the authorization code and use it to create an access token. The authorization code is passed from the SharePoint host environment to the redirect page by using a query string parameter named *code*.

LISTING 3-6 An external website acquiring an authorization code to access a SharePoint site

```
string authorizationCode = Request.QueryString["code"];
string targetPrincipalName = "00000003-0000-0ff1-ce00-000000000000";  // Office
                                                                         365 ID
string targetRealm = "79597708-fc2e-4c79-acfa-710bb435db25";          // tenancy
                                                                         ID
string urlHostWeb = "https://tenancy01.sharepoint.com/ ";             // host web
string urlRedirectAccept = "https://AppServer.wingtip.com/RedirectAccept.aspx";
Uri uriRedirectAccept = new Uri(urlRedirectAccept);

ClientContext context =
  TokenHelper.GetClientContextWithAuthorizationCode(urlHostWeb,
                                                    targetPrincipalName,
                                                    authorizationCode,
                                                    targetRealm,
                                                    uriRedirectAccept);

context.Load(context.Web);
context.ExecuteQuery();
context.Dispose();
```

After you have retrieved an authorization code, you can pass it in a call to the *GetClientContext WithAuthorizationCode* method or an overloaded implementation of the *GetAccessToken* method. The code in Listing 3-6 demonstrates calling the *GetClientContextWithAuthorizationCode* method to create a CSOM client context with an access token that makes it possible for the website to make CSOM calls on the host web.

Establishing app identity by using S2S trusts

In this chapter, you have learned that SharePoint 2013 supports external app authentication by using both OAuth and S2S trusts. Although OAuth is primarily intended for use in the Office 365 environment, the S2S trust infrastructure was specifically designed to work in on-premises farms with provider-hosted apps.

Using an S2S trust for external app authentication is similar to OAuth in the sense that code in the remote web passes an access token when calling to the SharePoint host environment. However, the manner in which the access token is created and the parties involved are very different.

One significant difference from using OAuth is that an S2S trust does not require any communications with Windows Azure ACS or any other authentication server in the cloud. The only servers involved in an S2S trust are the web server that hosts the remote web and the web servers of an on-premises SharePoint 2013 farm. Therefore, all of the servers required with an S2S trust can all run within the same LAN or private network.

A second significant difference involves authenticating the current user. When using OAuth, the SharePoint host environment authenticates the current user and then passes this user's identity to the remote web by using the context token.

Things work very differently when using an S2S trust. The SharePoint host environment doesn't pass the identity of the current user to the remote web. In fact, the SharePoint host environment doesn't pass a context token at all. The context token, which is a central figure in OAuth, doesn't even exist in the authentication flow of an S2S trust.

When a provider-hosted app is configured to authenticate by using an S2S trust, its remote web takes on the responsibility of authenticating the current user independently of any user authentication that has taken place in the SharePoint host environment. Once the remote web has authenticated the current user, it can then create an access token that contains both the app identity and the identity of the current user.

When using OAuth, the remote web must call to Windows Azure ACS to acquire an access token. However, a provider-hosted app using an S2S trust can create an access code on its own by using the *TokenHelper* class.

After the remote web for a provider-hosted app has created an S2S access token, it can then pass the access token to the SharePoint host environment when executing CSOM command or REST API calls. The programming aspects of passing the access token string using the Authentication header in a provider-hosted app by using an S2S trust works the same way as it does when using OAuth.

High-trust configurations vs. full-trust configurations

A provider-hosted app using an S2S trust is often referred to as a high-trust configuration. The term "high trust" is used to imply that the provided-hosted app authenticates the current user independently of the SharePoint host environment. When the provider-hosted app makes a CSOM or REST API call, the SharePoint host environment cannot verify identity of the current user. Therefore, the SharePoint host environment must trust that the provider-hosted app has properly authenticated the user and passed the true identity of the current user in the access token.

Do not confuse the term "high trust" with "full trust." Code that runs with full trust, such as server-side code in a farm solution, runs without security restrictions. Full-trust code can do whatever it wants to do. This is very different from a provider-hosted app running at high trust, which is constrained by whatever set of permissions has been granted to the app.

Architecture of an S2S trust

The architecture of an S2S trust is based on a X.509 certificate which contains a public/private key pair. The public and private keys are used to perform asymmetric encryption. The critical underlying concept is that the provider-hosted app uses the private key to sign the access token. The SharePoint host environment uses the public key to verify that the access token has been created and signed by a party that possesses the private key. This, in turn, makes it possible for the SharePoint host environment to authenticate calls from a provider-hosted app that is configured to use an S2S trust.

Figure 3-7 shows the high-level architecture of an S2S trust. Unlike a scenario involving OAuth, the remote web does not need to communicate with Windows Azure ACS to acquire access tokens. Instead, it is able to create access tokens on its own which must be signed with the private key. One important observation is that the remote web requires access to the private key at runtime whenever it needs to create an access token.

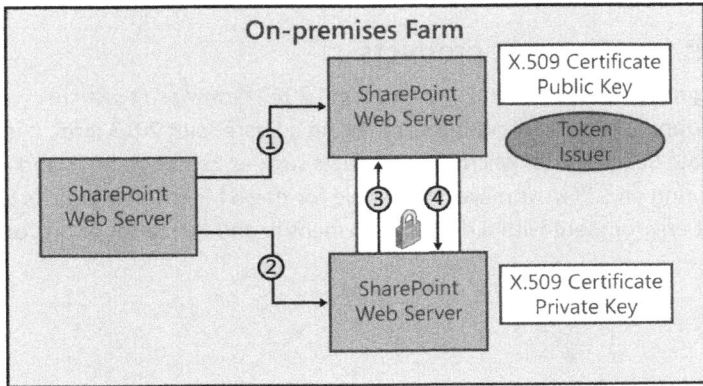

FIGURE 3-7 A server to server trust is based on a public private key pair that allows apps to create access tokens that carry a digital signature.

A second requirement for an S2S trust is that the hosting SharePoint farm must be configured with a special type of secure token service known as a *trusted security token issuer*. You will learn how to configure a trusted security token issuer by using a public key file and a Windows PowerShell script later in the chapter.

Let's follow the stages of the S2S authentication flow that are shown in Figure 3-7. In stage 1, the user navigates to a SharePoint site and is prompted to log on. When the user supplies a valid set of credentials and logs on, the SharePoint host environment creates a SAML token to track the user's identity. However, the identity of the user is never passed to a provider-hosted app using an S2S trust.

In stage 2, the user navigates to the Site Settings page and sees the tile for a provider-hosted app which has been configured to use an S2S trust. When the user clicks this tile, the SharePoint host environment uses an app launcher to redirect the user to the start page in the remote web.

When the SharePoint host environment redirects the user to the start page of a provider-hosted app with an S2S trust, it passes many of the same query string parameters as in an OAuth scenario such as the *SPHostUrl* parameter. However, the SharePoint host environment does not pass a context token. This means that the SharePoint host environment passes nothing to indicate who the user is. This puts the responsibility on the remote web to authenticate the user.

Stage 3 occurs after the user has been authenticated and there is a need to create an access token. When code in the remote web creates an access token by using the *TokenHelper* class, it adds information into the access token about the identity of the app and the identity of the current user. Next, the remote web then must acquire the value of the private key file to sign the access token. After the remote web has created and signed the access token, it can pass the access token by using the *Authorization* header each time it executes a CSOM command or a REST API call.

In stage 4, the SharePoint host environment uses external authentication to authenticate a call from a provider-hosted app that is using the S2S trust. For this to work, the hosting SharePoint farm must first be configured with a trusted security token issuer that is based on the public key. During the external authentication process, the SharePoint host environment inspects the access token and uses the trusted security token issuer to verify its authenticity.

Configuring S2S trusts for Microsoft products

The infrastructure for configuring S2S trusts within a SharePoint 2013 farm wasn't just created exclusively for custom app development. When configuring a SharePoint 2013 farm, it is sometimes necessary to create S2S trusts for Microsoft products such as Exchange 2013 and Workflow Manager. Configuring an S2S trust makes it possible for these Microsoft products to call into the SharePoint host environment with a distinct app identity and with a set of preconfigured permissions.

Configuring an S2S trust

The first step in configuring an S2S trust for a provider-hosted app is generating a public/private key pair by creating an X.509 certificate. To obtain an X.509 certificate for use on production servers, it is recommended that you go through an established certification authority (CA) that has experience creating professional-grade certificates. For development and other scenarios with lower-security concerns, you can create the required X.509 certificate with a public/private key pair by using two command-line tools named makecert.exe and certmgr.exe, both of which are available on any web server on which SharePoint 2013 has been installed.

The Windows PowerShell script shown in Listing 3-7 demonstrates how to create an X.509 certificate with a public/private key pair. You use the makecert.exe tool to create a certificate file named *appserver.wingtip.com.cer* that contains both the public key and the private key. Use the certmgr.exe tool to register the certificate with IIS so that it can be used to enable SSL on an IIS website.

LISTING 3-7 A Windows PowerShell script creating an X.509 certificate with a public/private key pair

```
$makecert = "C:\Program Files\Microsoft Office Servers\15.0\Tools\makecert.exe"
$certmgr = "C:\Program Files\Microsoft Office Servers\15.0\Tools\certmgr.exe"

# specify domain name for SSL certificate (optional)
$domain = "appserver.wingtip.com"

# create output directory to create SSL certificate file
$outputDirectory = "c:\Certs\"
New-Item $outputDirectory -ItemType Directory -Force -Confirm:$false | Out-Null

# create file name for SSL certificate files
$publicCertificatePath  = $outputDirectory + $domain + ".cer"
$privateCertificatePath = $outputDirectory + $domain + ".pfx"

Write-Host "Creating .cer certificate file..."

& $makecert -r -pe -n "CN=$domain" -b 01/01/2012 -e 01/01/2022 -eku
1.3.6.1.5.5.7.3.1
             -ss my -sr localMachine -sky exchange -sy 12
             -sp "Microsoft RSA SChannel Cryptographic Provider"
$publicCertificatePath

Write-Host "Registering certificate with IIS..."
& $certmgr /add $publicCertificatePath /s /r localMachine root

# get certificate to obtain thumbprint
$publicCertificate = Get-PfxCertificate -FilePath $publicCertificatePath
$publicCertificateThumbprint = $publicCertificate.Thumbprint
```

```
Get-ChildItem cert:\\localmachine\my |
  Where-Object {$_.Thumbprint -eq $publicCertificateThumbprint} |
  ForEach-Object {
    Write-Host "  .. exporting private key for certificate (*.PFK)"
    $privateCertificateByteArray = $_.Export("PFX", "Password1")
    [System.IO.File]::WriteAllBytes($privateCertificatePath,
                              $privateCertificateByteArray)
    Write-Host "  Certificate exported" -ForegroundColor Gray
  }
```

There is code at the end of the Windows PowerShell script in Listing 3-7 that exports the certificate's private key to a password-protected file named *appserver.wingtip.com.pfx*. This means that the remote web requires access to this PFX file and the password in order to retrieve the private key to sign access tokens.

After you have created the .cer file with the public key, you must copy it to a web server in the hosting SharePoint farm to create a trusted security-token issuer. The Windows PowerShell script in Listing 3-8 shows how to create the trusted security-token issuer by using a SharePoint Power-Shell cmdlet named *New-SPTrustedSecurityTokenIssuer*. Note that a trusted security-token issuer is registered with an identifying GUID. You should record this GUID because it must be used from the provider-hosted app.

LISTING 3-8 A SharePoint PowerShell script to register a trusted security-token issuer

```
Add-PSSnapin "Microsoft.SharePoint.PowerShell"

$issuerID = "11111111-1111-1111-1111-111111111111"
$targetSiteUrl = "http://wingtipserver"
$targetSite = Get-SPSite $targetSiteUrl
$realm = Get-SPAuthenticationRealm -ServiceContext $targetSite

$registeredIssuerName = $issuerID + '@' + $realm

$publicCertificatePath = "C:\Certs\appserver.wingtip.com.cer"
$publicCertificate = Get-PfxCertificate $publicCertificatePath

Write-Host "Create token issuer"
$secureTokenIssuer = New-SPTrustedSecurityTokenIssuer
                        -Name $issuerID
                        -RegisteredIssuerName $registeredIssuerName
                        -Certificate $publicCertificate
                        -IsTrustBroker
```

Although this example demonstrates registering a trusted security-token issuer by using a public key from a .cer file, SharePoint 2013 also supports registering one by using a metadata endpoint exposed by the provider-hosted app. This is typically the way registry is done when the app is a product such as Microsoft Exchange 2013 or Workflow Manager.

After you have registered a trusted security-token issuer, the next step is to register an app principal. This can be done by using the *AppRegNew.aspx* page in the exact same way as you would register an app principal for an app that uses OAuth. You can also register the app principal for an S2S trust by using a SharePoint PowerShell cmdlet named *Register-AppPrincipal* as shown in Listing 3-9.

LISTING 3-9 Registering the app principal for an S2S trust by using *Register-AppPrincipal*

```
# register an app principal for a provider-hosted app using an S2S trust
$appDisplayName = "My S2S High Trust App"
$clientID = "22222222-2222-2222-2222-222222222222"

$targetSiteUrl = "https://intranet.wingtip.com"
$targetSite = Get-SPSite $targetSiteUrl
$realm = Get-SPAuthenticationRealm -ServiceContext $targetSite

$fullAppPrincipalIdentifier = $clientID + '@' + $realm

Write-Host "Register new app principal"
$registeredAppPrincipal = Register-SPAppPrincipal
                            -NameIdentifier $fullAppPrincipalIdentifier
                            -Site $targetSite.RootWeb
                            -DisplayName $AppDisplayName
```

There are a few scenarios in which the *Register-SPAppPrincipal* cmdlet does not provide enough control to properly configure an app principal. More specifically, the *Register-SPAppPrincipal* cmdlet does not allow you to configure an app domain for the remote web nor a redirect URI. For scenarios in which you need to configure an app principal with an app domain and/or a redirect URI, you can write a SharePoint PowerShell script that uses the *SPAppPrincipalManager* class in the server-side object model, as shown in Listing 3-10.

LISTING 3-10 Registering an app principal by using the *SPAppPrincipalManager* class

```
Add-PSSnapin "Microsoft.SharePoint.PowerShell"

# set intialization values for new app principal
$appDisplayName = "App Principal for My High Trust App"
$clientID = "33333333-3333-3333-3333-333333333333"
$appHostDomainUrl = "http://localhost:43002/"
$appRedirectUrl = $appHostDomainUrl + "redirect.aspx"

# provide site isnide target tenancy (aka realm)
$targetSiteUrl = "http://wingtipserver"

# get App Principal Manager
$web = Get-SPWeb $targetSiteUrl
$appPrincipalManager = [Microsoft.SharePoint.SPAppPrincipalManager]::
                        GetManager($web)
```

```
# initialize creation parameters for App Principal host domain
$applicationEndPointAuthorities = new-object System.Collections.Generic.
List[string]
$applicationEndPointAuthorities.Add($appHostDomainUrl);

# initialize creation parameters for App Principal security credentials
$symmetricKey = New-Object System.Security.SecureString;
$datetimeNow = [System.DateTime]::Now

$credential = [Microsoft.SharePoint.SPAppPrincipalCredential]::CreateFromSymmetr
icKey($symmetricKey,

$datetimeNow,

$datetimeNow)

# create new object for App Principal creation parameters
$creationParameters =
New-Object Microsoft.SharePoint.SPExternalAppPrincipalCreationParameters(
                                        $clientID,
                                        $appDisplayName,

$applicationEndPointAuthorities,

                                        $credential)

# assign redirect Uri to creation parameters
$creationParameters.RedirectAddresses.Add( (New-Object System.Uri
$appRedirectUrl) )

# create app principal
$appPrincipal = $appPrincipalManager.CreateAppPrincipal($creationParameters)
```

Developing provider-hosted apps by using S2S trusts

Before you begin to develop a provider-hosted app with a S2S trust, you should first complete the following steps.

1. Create a .cer certificate file containing a public/private key pair.

2. Use the .cer file to register a trusted security token issuer.

3. Register an app principal with a client ID to help track app identity.

4. Export the private key to a password-protected .pfx file.

5. Make the .pfx file accessible on the server running the remote web.

After you have completed these steps, it is relatively simple to create a new provider-hosted app with Visual Studio 2012 and configure it to use an S2S trust. The first step is to update the app manifest with the client ID of an app principal that has already been registered.

```xml
<AppPrincipal>
  <RemoteWebApplication ClientId="22222222-2222-2222-2222-222222222222" />
</AppPrincipal>
```

The next step is to update the *web.config* file of the remote web with four *appSettings* variables that track the IDs of the trusted security-token issuer and the app principal as well as the file path and password required to extract the private key from the .pfx file at run time. Note that these four *appSettings* variables are used by Microsoft-supplied code in the *TokenHelper* class. The information in these four variables is used each time the *TokenHelper* class creates an S2S access token.

```xml
<appSettings>
  <add key="ClientId" value="22222222-2222-2222-2222-222222222222" />
  <add key="ClientSigningCertificatePath" value="C:\Certs\appserver.wingtip.com.pfx" />
  <add key="ClientSigningCertificatePassword" value="Password1" />
  <add key="IssuerId" value="11111111-1111-1111-1111-111111111111" />
</appSettings>
```

At this point, you have seen all the steps required to configure an S2S trust. All that's left to do is to write the code to create access tokens and to pass them to the SharePoint host environment in the *Authentication* header. The code in Listing 3-11 demonstrates how to create an S2S access token by calling the *GetS2SAccessTokenWithWindowsIdentity* method of the *TokenHelper* class. After you have created an S2S access token string, you can add it as an *Authorization* header by using the exact same code as you would have in an app which uses OAuth.

LISTING 3-11 Creating an S2S access token

```csharp
string hostWebUrl = Request.QueryString["SPHostUrl"];
Uri hostWebUri = new Uri(hostWebUrl);
WindowsIdentity currentUser = Request.LogonUserIdentity;

string accessTokenString =
      TokenHelper.GetS2SAccessTokenWithWindowsIdentity(hostWebUri, currentUser);

// prepare HttpWebRequest to execute REST API call
HttpWebRequest request1 =
   (HttpWebRequest)HttpWebRequest.Create(hostWebUrl.ToString() + "/_api/Web/
title");

// add access token string as Authorization header
request1.Headers.Add("Authorization", "Bearer " + accessTokenString);

// execute REST API call and inspect response
HttpWebResponse response1 = (HttpWebResponse)request1.GetResponse();
StreamReader reader1 = new StreamReader(response1.GetResponseStream());
XDocument doc1 = XDocument.Load(reader1);
string SiteTitle = doc1.Root.Value;
```

Calling *TrustAllCertificates*

While you are working in a development environment, it is common to use test certificates as opposed to production-grade certificates. The *TokenHelper* class provides a static method named *TrustAllCertificates* which can be called if you need to relax the rules used in the certificate verification process.

```
TokenHelper.TrustAllCertificates();
```

A call to *TrustAllCertificates* can be helpful to get things working in a development environment where you are using test certificates. However, any calls to *TrustAllCertificates* should be removed before your code.

Conclusion

This chapter explained the concepts, configuration details, and programming techniques associated with app authentication and app permission management. You learned that SharePoint 2013 authenticates CSOM and REST API calls from apps by using either internal authentication or external authentication. SharePoint-hosted apps use internal authentication, whereas external authentication is used by cloud-hosted apps that have server-side code running inside the remote web.

The chapter also explained how SharePoint 2013 manages app permissions and enforces a security policy that by default requires both the app and the current user to possess the required permissions to accomplish a specific task. In certain scenarios, you can execute calls with app-only permissions so that your code is not constrained by the permissions of a specific user.

The security model for SharePoint apps often requires you to add permission request to the app manifest file. Permission requests are the mechanism that your app uses to acquire the permissions it needs to read and modify content in the host web.

The second half of the chapter discussed configuration details and programming techniques that are specific to OAuth and S2S trusts. You saw that OAuth and S2S trusts both require you to write code to obtain access tokens and to pass them to the SharePoint host environment by using the *Authorization* header. However, you also learned that there is quite a difference between the way that OAuth and S2S trusts work behind the scenes.

## CHAPTER 4

Developing SharePoint apps

The previous chapters in this book have focused on the core concepts necessary for developers to be successful in building SharePoint 2013 apps. This final chapter presents patterns and samples that will assist you in developing professional apps with compelling capabilities. After completing this chapter, you should be well positioned to begin creating apps intended for commercial use.

Understanding app patterns

Chapter 2, "Client-Side Programming," outlined the permutations of JavaScript, C#, Client-Side Object Model (CSOM), and Representational State Transfer (REST) development, recommending development scenarios involving JavaScript with REST and C# with CSOM. This section details app patterns that can be used with these development scenarios. Specifically, the Model-View-ViewModel (MVVM) pattern is presented for JavaScript with REST and the Model-View-Controller (MVC) pattern is presented for C# with CSOM.

Building MVVM apps

The MVVM pattern provides a flexible way to build JavaScript/REST apps that promotes code reuse, simplifies app maintenance, and supports testing. The pattern consists of three different components. The Model component is defined as the entities on the SharePoint server such as lists, libraries, and service applications. The View component is defined as the webpages that make up the app user interface. The ViewModel component is defined as the JavaScript that binds the Model and the View together. Figure 4-1 shows a simple block diagram of the MVVM pattern.

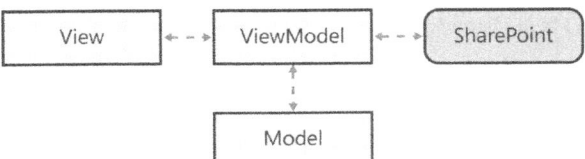

FIGURE 4-1 You use the MVVM pattern to isolate data, business logic, and display functionality.

The goal of the MVVM pattern is to separate the display of data from the business logic, which is in turn separated from the underlying data. In practical terms, this means that all JavaScript is removed from the app webpages and segregated into libraries. These libraries are responsible for interacting with the back-end data, applying business logic, and feeding data to the webpages for display.

Understanding JavaScript challenges

The biggest challenge in implementing apps with JavaScript is the intimate relationship between the webpages and the libraries. In many JavaScript implementations, the code in the libraries must have detailed knowledge of the markup in the webpages. As an example, Listing 4-1 shows a snippet of code first presented in Chapter 2 that reflects a tight binding between the webpages and JavaScript code.

LISTING 4-1 Generating HTML in JavaScript

```
readAll = function () {
    $.ajax(
        {
            url: _spPageContextInfo.webServerRelativeUrl +
                "/_api/web/lists/getByTitle('Contacts')/items/" +
                "?$select=Id,FirstName,Title,WorkPhone" +
                "&$orderby=Title,FirstName",
            type: "GET",
            headers: {
                "accept": "application/json;odata=verbose",
            },
            success: function (data) {
                readAllSuccess(data);
            },
            error: function (err) {
                alert(JSON.stringify(err));
            }
        }
    );
},

readAllSuccess = function (data) {
    var html = [];
    html.push("<table><thead><tr><th>ID</th><th>First Name</th>" +
            "<th>Last Name</th><th>Title</th></tr></thead>");

    var results = data.d.results;
```

```
        for(var i=0; i<results.length; i++) {
            html.push("<tr><td>");
            html.push(results[i].ID);
            html.push("</td><td>");
            html.push(results[i].FirstName);
            html.push("</td><td>");
            html.push(results[i].Title);
            html.push("</td><td>");
            html.push(results[i].WorkPhone);
            html.push("</td></tr>");
        }

        html.push("</table>");
        $('#displayDiv').html(html.join(''));
    }
```

Listing 4-1 uses the jQuery *ajax* method to select items from a contacts list. If the call is success-ful, an HTML table is constructed and assigned to the inner HTML of a <div> element. Note how the JavaScript must understand that the webpage requires a table for display. Because of this design, the library cannot be reused to display the data in a different way. If you wanted to show the items in a list, for example, you would need to rewrite the success handler to generate a list instead of a table. This is the challenge that the MVVM pattern seeks to address.

Introducing knockout

JavaScript does not natively support the kind of loose coupling that the MVVM pattern requires. Therefore, additional support must be introduced in the form of a third-party library. Although there are many third-party libraries available for JavaScript, few of them implement the MVVM pattern. One library that does implement it successfully is *Knockout*, which you can find at *http://knockoutjs.com*.

Knockout is a JavaScript library that you can add to your apps to implement the MVVM pattern. With Knockout, you can create ViewModel components in JavaScript that effectively bind the server-side SharePoint data sources to the webpages in your apps. The primary capabilities of Knockout that makes the MVVM pattern possible are declarative bindings and dependency tracking.

Declarative bindings make it possible for you to bind a ViewModel to HTML elements in a web-page. Instead of writing HTML elements in your JavaScript, the declarative bindings are defined within the app web page. This approach removes the knowledge of the webpage structure from the JavaScript code and creates the loose binding required by MVVM. Listing 4-2 presents an example of declarative bindings in Knockout.

LISTING 4-2 Declarative bindings

```html
<div id="resultsDiv" style="overflow: auto">
    <table>
        <thead>
            <tr>
                <th>Last Name</th>
                <th>First Name</th>
                <th>Phone</th>
            </tr>
        </thead>
        <tbody id="resultsTable" data-bind="foreach: get_contacts()">
            <tr>
                <td data-bind="text: get_lname()"></td>
                <td data-bind="text: get_fname()"></td>
                <td data-bind="text: get_phone()"></td>
            </tr>
        </tbody>
    </table>
</div>
```

In Listing 4-2, the *data-bind* attribute binds a method from the ViewModel to HTML elements in the webpage. Note how the table body uses a *foreach* construct to iterate through a set of contacts returned from the *get_contacts* method and build a table row for each contact. The last name, first name, and phone number associated with each contact is then bound to a table cell within a row.

When you develop a ViewModel, you start by creating a library to hold the data for binding. Listing 4-3 shows a JavaScript library that holds the data for an individual contact. Note how the properties of the contact are exposed through public methods, and these methods are the ones referenced in the associated HTML of Listing 4-2.

LISTING 4-3 The contact data library

```javascript
"use strict";

var Wingtip = window.Wingtip || {}
window.Wingtip.Contact = function (ln, fn, ph) {

    //private members
    var lname = 'undefined',
        fname = 'undefined',
        phone = 'undefined',
        set_lname = function (v) { lname = v; },
        get_lname = function () { return lname; },
        set_fname = function (v) { fname = v; },
        get_fname = function () { return fname; },
        set_phone = function (v) { phone = v; },
        get_phone = function () { return phone; };
```

```
        //Constructor
        lname = ln;
        fname = fn;
        phone = ph;

        //public interface
        return {
            set_lname: set_lname,
            get_lname: get_lname,
            set_fname: set_fname,
            get_fname: get_fname,
            set_phone: set_phone,
            get_phone: get_phone
        };
    }
```

The associated ViewModel performs the queries against the back-end data source and populates the data objects. The ViewModel also provides the public interface that is referenced in the *data-bind* attribute of the HTML for retrieving the collection of list items. Listing 4-4 demonstrates a complete ViewModel that queries a contacts list and creates an array of contact information.

LISTING 4-4 The contacts ViewModel

```
"use strict";

var Wingtip = window.Wingtip || {}

Wingtip.ContactViewModel = function () {

    //private members
    var contacts = ko.observableArray(),
        get_contacts = function () { return contacts; },

        load = function () {
            $.ajax(
                {
                    url: _spPageContextInfo.webServerRelativeUrl +
                        "/_api/web/lists/getByTitle('Contacts')/items/" +
                        "?$select=Id,FirstName,Title,WorkPhone" +
                        "&$orderby=Title,FirstName",
                    type: "GET",
                    headers: {
                        "accept": "application/json;odata=verbose",
                    },
```

```
                    success: onSuccess,
                    error: onError
                }
            );
        },

        onSuccess = function (data) {
            var results = data.d.results;

            contacts.removeAll();

            for (var i = 0; i < results.length; i++) {
                contacts.push(
                    new Wingtip.Contact(
                    results[i].Title,
                    results[i].FirstName,
                    results[i].WorkPhone));
            }

        },

        onError = function (err) {
            alert(JSON.stringify(err));
        };


    //public interface
    return {
        load: load,
        get_contacts: get_contacts
    };

}();
```

The difference between Listing 4-4 and Listing 4-1 is significant. Listing 4-1 relies on intimate knowledge of the user interface to create a table and push it onto the webpage for display. The View-Model in Listing 4-4 simply creates an array of contacts. You can then easily bind this array to various display forms such as a table or unordered list.

The most important aspect of the ViewModel is its use of the *ko.observableArray* type for handling the collection of contacts. The Knockout library provides the *ko.observableArray* type specifically to implement dependency tracking. With dependency tracking, automatic updating of the user interface occurs whenever data elements in the array change. When your app initializes, it should load the observable array and then bind the data. Knockout initializes the data binding when you call the *applyBindings* method. Listing 4-5 illustrates how to initialize the data bindings with the ViewModel.

LISTING 4-5 Initializing data bindings

```
$(document).ready(function () {
    Wingtip.ContactViewModel.load();
    ko.applyBindings(Wingtip.ContactViewModel, $get("resultsTable"));
});
```

Utilizing promises

When developing more complex apps against the REST API, you must often make multiple asynchronous RESTful calls. For example, an initial RESTful call might retrieve master data, whereas subsequest calls fill in child data. The challenge with multiple calls is that they need to happen sequentially, but each call is made asynchronously. So the only solution is to nest dependent calls within the "success" callback functions. Listing 4-6 shows an example of nested RESTful calls, wherein the first call retrieves the current user's account name and the nested call returns the social feed for the account name.

LISTING 4-6 Nested RESTful calls

```
"use strict";

var Wingtip = window.Wingtip || {};

Wingtip.FeedViewModel = function () {

    var init = function () {

        //Get the current user's account information
        $.ajax({
                url: _spPageContextInfo.webServerRelativeUrl +
                    "/_api/SP.UserProfiles.PeopleManager/GetMyProperties",
                method: "GET",
                headers: {
                    "accept": "application/json;odata=verbose",
                },
                success: function (data) {

                    //Now get the current user's social feed
                    var accountName = data.d.AccountName;

                    $.ajax({
                            url: _spPageContextInfo.webServerRelativeUrl +
                                "/_api/social.feed/actor(item='" +
                                    accountName +"')/Feed",
                            method: "GET",
                            headers: {
                                "accept": "application/json;odata=verbose",
                            },
                            success: function (data) {
                                var feedData = data.d;
                            },
```

```
                    error: function (err) {
                        alert(JSON.stringify(err));
                    }
                }
            );
        },
        error: function (err) {
            alert(JSON.stringify(err));
        }
    }
    );
    };


    return {
        init: init
    }
}();
```

The challenge with the code in Listing 4-6 is that is can rapidly become unmaintainable. Multiple levels of nested asynchronous calls simply creates a pile of "spaghetti" code. What is needed is a mechanism to separate out the various asynchronous calls while still maintaining the dependency between them. That is the function of a *promise*.

A promise—also known as a *deferred*—is a pattern that returns an object immediately from an asynchronous call. This object will later be populated with the result of the asynchronous call, but its immediate return simplifies the code structure making it much more maintainable. Furthermore, promises provide a built-in caching mechanism so that the same query does not have to be run again if the promise has already been successfully fulfilled.

There are several techniques for implementing promises, but one of the easiest is to make use of the jQuery *$.Deferred* method. Using the *$.Deferred* method, you can create a deferred object, which can be immediately returned from an asynchronous call. The deferred object has resolve and reject methods, which are called on success or failure respectively. Using deferreds makes it possible for you to separate the JavaScript code that performs the asynchronous call. As an example, Listing 4-7 shows how to implement the pattern to get the user's profile information.

LISTING 4-7 The promise pattern

```
"use strict";

var Wingtip = window.Wingtip || {};

Wingtip.ProfileQuery = function () {

    var deferred = $.Deferred(),

        execute = function () {

        $.ajax(
                {
                    url: _spPageContextInfo.webServerRelativeUrl +
                        "/_api/SP.UserProfiles.PeopleManager/GetMyProperties",
                    method: "GET",
                    headers: {
                        "accept": "application/json;odata=verbose",
                    },
                    success: function (data) {
                        deferred.resolve(data);
                    },
                    error: function (err) {
                        deferred.reject(err);
                    }
                }
            );

        return deferred;
    };

    return {
        execute: execute
    }
}();
```

The deferred object exposes a "promise" object that has a method named "then." The "then" method takes two arguments: the first argument is a success function, the second is a failure function. So the library in Listing 4-7 can be invoked easily by using the code in Listing 4-8.

LISTING 4-8 Invoking the asynchronous call

```
Wingtip.ProfileQuery.execute().promise().then(
    //success
    function (data) {
        var accountName = data.d.AccountName;
    },
    //failure
    function(err) {
        alert(JSON.stringify(err));
    }
);
```

The promises pattern significantly simplifies JavaScript code when your app must make multiple, nested asynchronous calls, and that makes it very powerful. However, the promise object also acts like a caching mechanism in that the success or failure function will be called immediately if the promise has already been fulfilled. This opens up additional ideas such as creating arrays of promises that contain fulfilled data so that apps do not have to run queries that have already successfully executed.

Building MVC apps

The MVC pattern has many of the same goals as the MVVM pattern. The MVC pattern looks to support code reuse, maintenance, and testing. The pattern also consists of three different components that are similar to the ones found in the MVVM pattern. The Model component is defined as the entities on the SharePoint server, such as lists, libraries, and service applications. The View component is defined as the webpages that make up the app user interface. The Controller binds the Model and the View together. The big difference between the MVVM pattern and the MVC pattern is that the MVVM pattern assumes that the data in the ViewModel will persist across create, read, update, and delete (CRUD) operations. The MVC pattern, on the other hand is stateless. Because of the differences in how state is managed, the MVC pattern lends itself to the development of SharePoint apps by using C# and CSOM. Figure 4-2 shows a simple block diagram of the MVC pattern.

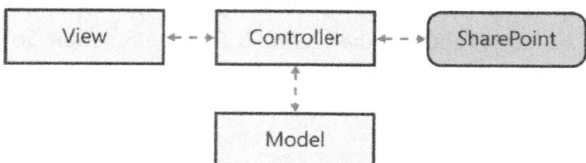

FIGURE 4-2 You use the MVC pattern to isolate logic, data, and display functionality.

Understanding web form challenges

When developers think of creating SharePoint apps with C# and CSOM, they might immediately think of using ASP.NET to create a remote web. In fact, this is the default template used in Microsoft Visual Studio for provider-hosted and autohosted apps. This approach involves the development of a set of Active Server Pages (ASPX) that contain web forms, server controls, and associated C# code. The advantage of the web forms pattern is that it is stable, mature, and well understood by web developers. However, the web forms pattern has some limitations that negatively impact code reuse, maintenance, and testing. Listing 4-9 presents a web forms app that loads data from a contacts list in the host web and displays it in a grid.

LISTING 4-9 Using web forms in an app

```
protected void Page_Load(object sender, EventArgs e)
{
    var contextToken = TokenHelper.GetContextTokenFromRequest(Page.Request);
    var hostWeb = Page.Request["SPHostWebUrl"];

    using (var clientContext = TokenHelper.GetClientContextWithContextToken(
                            hostWeb, contextToken, Request.Url.Authority))
    {
        clientContext.Load(clientContext.Web);
        List list = clientContext.Web.Lists.GetByTitle("Contacts");
        clientContext.Load(list);

        StringBuilder caml = new StringBuilder();
        caml.Append("<View><Query><OrderBy/></Query>");
        caml.Append("<ViewFields><FieldRef Name='ID'/>
                    <FieldRef Name='FirstName'/>");
        caml.Append("<FieldRef Name='Title'/><FieldRef Name='WorkPhone'/>
                    </ViewFields>");
        caml.Append("<RowLimit>100</RowLimit></View>");

        CamlQuery query = new CamlQuery();
        query.ViewXml = caml.ToString();
        Microsoft.SharePoint.Client.ListItemCollection
            listItems = list.GetItems(query);
        clientContext.Load(listItems);
        clientContext.ExecuteQuery();

        List<Contact> contacts = new List<Contact>();

        foreach (Microsoft.SharePoint.Client.ListItem listItem in listItems)
        {
            Contact contact = new Contact()
            {
                Id = listItem["ID"].ToString(),
                LastName = listItem["Title"].ToString(),
                FirstName = listItem["FirstName"].ToString(),
                WorkPhone = listItem["WorkPhone"].ToString()
            };
            contacts.Add(contact);
        }
        contactsGrid.DataSource = contacts;
        contactsGrid.DataBind();
    }
}
```

Listing 4-9 is a classic example of querying a data source and binding a grid when an ASPX page loads. Even though this code works fine, you can see that the code and the user interface are tightly bound. First, the code is placed directly in the load event of the page. Second, the grid displaying the data is directly referenced in the code. Experienced ASP.NET developers will immediately object that such problems can be fixed in the web forms pattern by separating the code into layers and utilizing data binding. Although these points are certainly valid, years of experience has taught us that web forms apps are typically constructed with tight bindings between the various layers. Furthermore, there is no universally accepted framework for web forms that supports the kind of separation envisioned in the MVC pattern.

Web forms were initially envisioned to support a rapid application development approach by which the developer is abstracted away from the request-response details of HTTP and HTML. Web forms are designed to simulate a stateful environment even though HTTP is stateless. Server controls are intended to abstract away the details of HTML so that developers can use a visual designer to create web forms. To produce the illusion of a stateful environment, ASP.NET stores the last state of a web form—called the *viewstate*—in a hidden field between postbacks. For complex systems, this can be a serious issue as the viewstate becomes larger. Abstracting away the HTML also limits the ability of the developer to support various browser types and incorporate JavaScript libraries such as Knockout and jQuery. Even though these limitations can be addressed in various ways, many developers are realizing that the web forms pattern is not well suited to developing cloud-based apps that must support millions of users and many types of browsers.

Introducing MVC4

MVC4 is the latest edition of the MVC framework available in Visual Studio 2012 that implements the MVC model and is ideally suited for developing SharePoint apps with C# and CSOM. When you develop a SharePoint 2013 app by using MVC4, you build models, controllers, and views, not web forms. Visual Studio 2012 helps you with the process by providing tools, designers, and wizards that support the MVC4 framework. If you are interested in creating SharePoint apps based on the MVC4 framework, you'll need to do some work to swap out the web forms project for an MVC4 project.

To get started, first create a provider-hosted or autohosted app. When the new remote web is created, open the associated web.config file and copy the settings for the *ClientId* and *ClientSecret* entries. You will need to transfer these settings to the new MVC4 remote web. After you have copied the settings, delete the default web project. Then, you can add a new MVC4 project to the solution. In the New ASP.NET MVC 4 Project Wizard, select the Internet Application template, as shown in Figure 4-3.

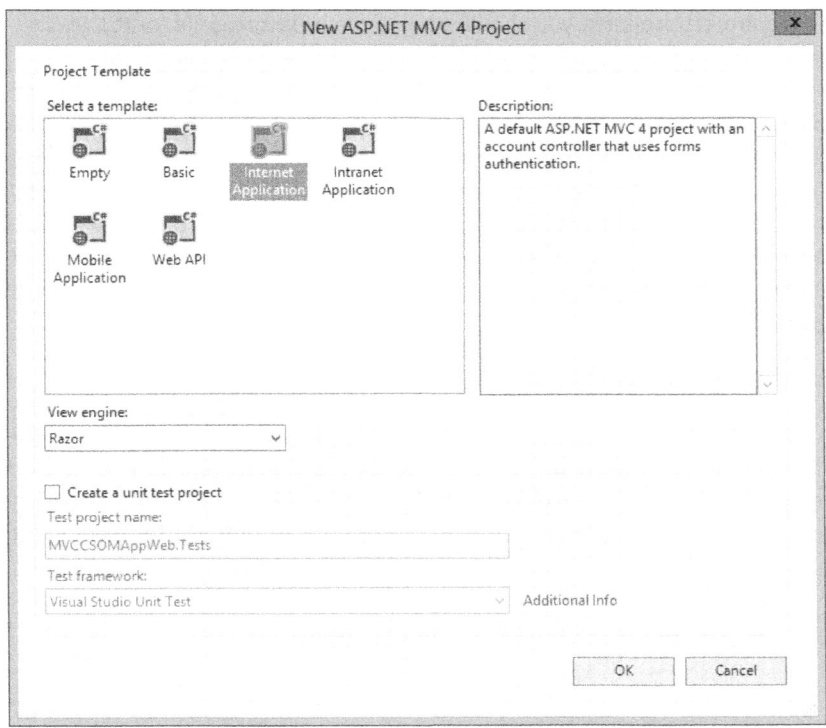

FIGURE 4-3 Use the MVC4 Project Wizard to start a new project.

After the new web project is created, you must associate it with the SharePoint app by setting the Web Project property in the SharePoint app project. This property contains a drop-down list of the web projects in the solution. Figure 4-4 shows the property.

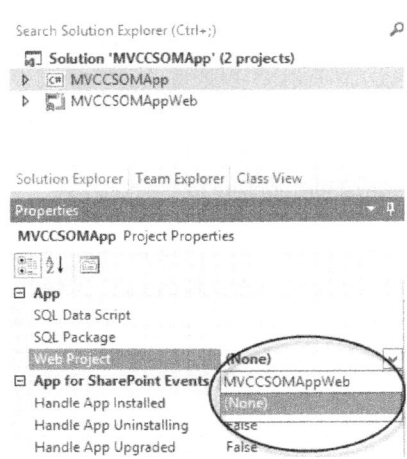

FIGURE 4-4 Use the Web Project property to associate a web project with a SharePoint app.

After setting the Web Project property, you should update the web.config file for the MVC4 project so that it contains the required *ClientId* and *ClientSecret* entries you copied earlier. Now, turn your attention to the app project. In the *AppManifest.xml* file, ensure that the *AppPrincipal* setting is correct for your deployment scenario. Next, set the <StartPage> element to refer to the start page of the MVC4 project. MVC4 uses a URL format that references the controller and then the method as opposed to webpages. The default MVC4 project template has a controller named *HomeController* that you can reference to get started. After these changes, you should be able to run the app in debug mode because the MVC4 web project template is already coded to show off some basic functionality with three built-in pages. The following code shows a sample <StartPage> URL that will work for the default template:

```
<StartPage>~remoteAppUrl/Home?{StandardTokens}</StartPage>
```

To add your own functionality to the app, you start by creating a new controller. In the MVC4 web project, right-click the Controllers folder, and the in the settings menu that appears, click Add and click Controller. When prompted, you can give the controller a name, ensuring that the name ends with the string "Controller". Figure 4-5 shows the addition of a *ContactsController* for reading list items from a contacts list.

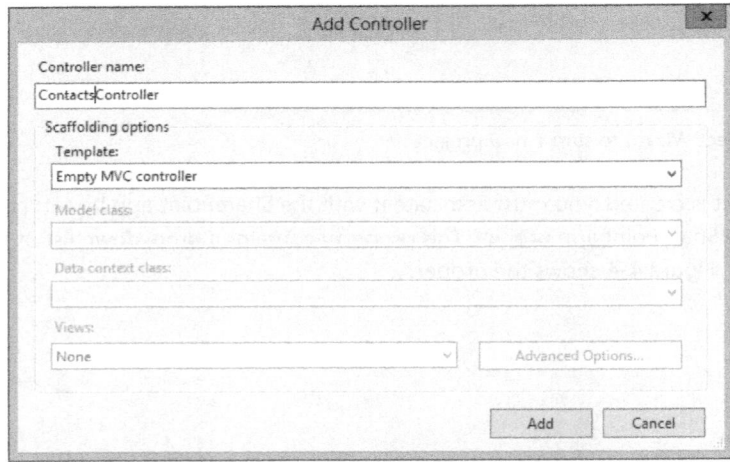

FIGURE 4-5 By creating a new controller, you can add custom page-level functionality to a remote web.

Controllers expose public methods that return Views. Each controller has a default method named *Index*, but they can have as many custom methods as you like. Custom methods can also accept arguments that correspond to the query string parameters contained in a URL. Listing 4-10 shows the implementation of a method named *ReadAll*, which uses CSOM to read the list of clients from the app web and return a View.

LISTING 4-10 Adding a method to a controller

```
public ActionResult ReadAll(string SPHostUrl, string SPLanguage, string
    SPAppWebUrl)
{
    using (ClientContext ctx = new ClientContext(SPAppWebUrl))
    {
        ctx.Load(ctx.Web);
        List list = ctx.Web.Lists.GetByTitle("Contacts");
        ctx.Load(list);

        StringBuilder caml = new StringBuilder();
        caml.Append("<View><Query><OrderBy/></Query>");
        caml.Append("<ViewFields><FieldRef Name='ID'/>
                    <FieldRef Name='FirstName'/>");
        caml.Append("<FieldRef Name='Title'/><FieldRef Name='WorkPhone'/>
                    </ViewFields>");
        caml.Append("<RowLimit>100</RowLimit></View>");

        CamlQuery query = new CamlQuery();
        query.ViewXml = caml.ToString();
        Microsoft.SharePoint.Client.ListItemCollection listItems =
            list.GetItems(query);
        ctx.Load(listItems);
        ctx.ExecuteQuery();

        List<Contact> contacts = new List<Contact>();

        foreach (ListItem listItem in listItems)
        {
            Contact contact = new Contact()
            {
                Id = listItem["ID"].ToString(),
                LastName = listItem["Title"].ToString(),
                FirstName = listItem["FirstName"].ToString(),
                WorkPhone = listItem["WorkPhone"].ToString()
            };
            contacts.Add(contact);
        }
        ViewBag.Contacts = contacts;
    }
    return View();
}
```

If you compare Listing 4-10 to Listing 4-9, you will see that the code to retrieve the list items is largely the same. What is different is that the MVC4 code does not bind directly to a grid. Instead, the code builds a list of contacts and saves them into the *Contacts* property of the *ViewBag* object. The *ViewBag* makes data from the Controller available when the View is generated. A Controller can add properties to the *ViewBag* dynamically, making it simple to pass data from the Controller to the View. In this example, the *Contact* class is the Model in the MVC pattern. The MVC4 project template contains a Models folder into which you can easily add data classes that help transfer data between the Controller and View.

A View can be added for any Controller by right-clicking within the Controller code, and then from the settings menu that appears, clicking Add and then clicking View. Within the View, you can define both static and dynamic elements. Static elements set *ViewBag* properties to a fixed value, whereas dynamic elements use properties of the *ViewBag* populated by the Controller to generate results. Listing 4-11 shows a View to generate a static title for a page and a dynamic table containing the list items retrieved from the contacts list.

LISTING 4-11 Adding a view

```
@{
    ViewBag.Title = "SharePoint 2013 MVC App";
}

<table id="contactsTable">
    <thead><th>ID</th><th>Last Name</th><th>First Name</th><th>Work Phone</th>
        </thead>
    @foreach (var contact in ViewBag.Contacts)
    {
        <tr><td>
                @contact.Id
            </td><td>
                @contact.LastName
            </td><td>
                @contact.FirstName
            </td><td>
                @contact.WorkPhone
            </td></tr>
    }
</table>
```

The code in Listing 4-11 is obviously not a complete webpage. This is because the MVC4 framework supports the idea of shared views that can be merged with the partial views to create a complete webpage. In the default template, a shared view named *_Layout* is used to generate the basic page that is merged with the custom Views you add.

After the Views and Controllers are created, you can invoke them through a URL. The URL format determines which Controller method is invoked. The associated View is then used to render the webpage. The formula for invoking a Controller method follows the format /[Controller]/[Method]?[Parameters]. In order to invoke the start page of your MVC4 remote web from a SharePoint app, you must update the <StartPage> element of the *AppManifest.xml* file to reflect this formula. As an example, the following URL would invoke the *ReadAll* method of the *ContactsController* when the SharePoint 2013 app is launched:

```
~remoteAppUrl/Contacts/ReadAll?{StandardTokens}
```

Using the chrome control

Although apps are isolated from the host web, the end-user experience should feel like an app is just a natural extension of the host web. To achieve a seamless feel, apps should take on some of the styling elements of the host web and provide a navigation system that incorporates a link back to the host web. If you are creating a SharePoint-hosted app, these issues are addressed by the app project template in Visual Studio. However, if you are creating a provider-hosted or autohosted app, the remote web will need some help in achieving these goals. This is the purpose of the chrome control.

With the chrome control, a remote web can use the header elements of a specific SharePoint site (usually the host web) without knowing the styles ahead of time. In addition to styling, the chrome control also provides a link back to the host web. Optionally, the chrome control can define a drop-down list box similar to the Site Settings menu and a Help menu. Figure 4-6 shows a remote web displaying a table of contacts with the host web chrome visible at the top of the page. The Figure also shows the link back to the host web as well as the drop-down list.

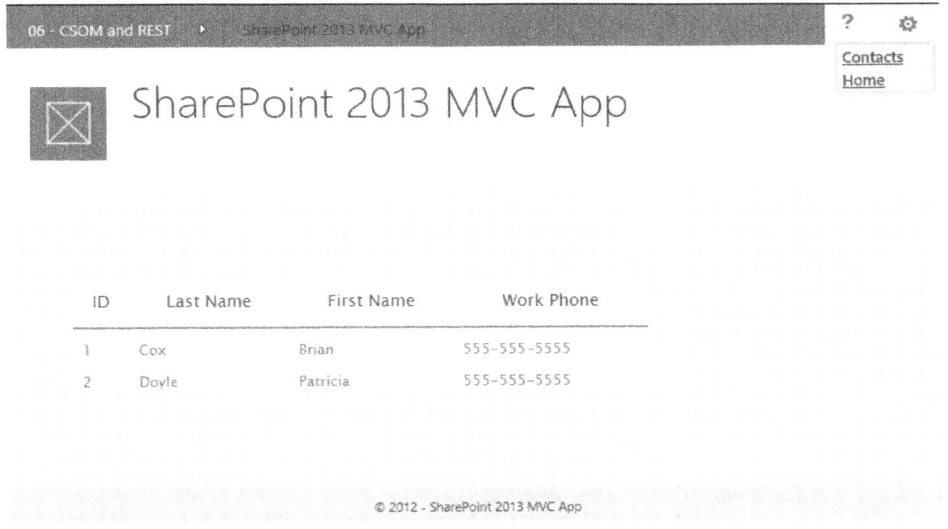

FIGURE 4-6 You can use the chrome control to incorporate the styles of a host web into an app.

The chrome control is contained within the library *sp.ui.controls.js*, which is located in the LAYOUTS directory. The simplest way to use the library is to copy it into the remote web project. The library contains the definition for the *SP.UI.Controls.Navigation* object, which can retrieve the style sheet from the host web for use in the remote web. The *SP.UI.Controls.Navigation* object makes a call to the handler *defaultcss.ashx* to retrieve the URL for the host web style sheet. The host web style sheet is then downloaded for use by the chrome control. The chrome control then generates a header section for the app into a target <div> element, which you specify.

The chrome control relies on four parameters in the query string for its functionality: *SPHostUrl*, *SPHostTitle*, *SPAppWebUrl*, and *SPLanguage*. If your app uses the *{StandardTokens}* query string in the manifest and has an associated app web, the start URL will include the *SPHostUrl*, *SPAppWebUrl*, and *SPLanguage* parameters. However, you will need to add the *{HostTitle}* token to include the *SPHost Title* parameter, as shown in Figure 4-7.

Query string: {StandardTokens}&SPHostTitle={HostTitle}

FIGURE 4-7 Setting the query string in the app.

You can use the chrome control either programmatically or declaratively. When used programmatically, you typically provide a target <div> element in the app page and create a library to set the options for the *SP.UI.Controls.Navigation* object. Listing 4-12 presents a complete library for using the chrome control.

LISTING 4-12 Using the chrome control

```
"use strict";

var Wingtip = window.Wingtip || {};

Wingtip.ChromeControl = function () {

    render = function () {
        var options = {
            "appIconUrl": "../Images/AppIcon.png",
            "appTitle": "SharePoint 2013 MVC App",
            "appHelpPageUrl": "../Help?" + document.URL.split("?")[1],
            "settingsLinks": [
                {
                    "linkUrl": "../Contacts/ReadAll?" +
                    document.URL.split("?")[1],"displayName": "Contacts"
                },
                {
                    "linkUrl": "../Welcome/Message?" +
                     document.URL.split("?")[1],"displayName": "Home"
                }
            ]
        };

        var nav = new SP.UI.Controls.Navigation(
                            "chrome_ctrl_placeholder",
                            options
                    );
        nav.setVisible(true);
    },

    getQueryStringParameter = function (p) {
        var params =
            document.URL.split("?")[1].split("&");
```

```
        var strParams = "";
        for (var i = 0; i < params.length; i = i + 1) {
            var singleParam = params[i].split("=");
            if (singleParam[0] == p)
                return singleParam[1];
        }
    }

    return {
        render: render
    }
}();

$(document).ready(function () {
    Wingtip.ChromeControl.render();
});
```

When the *ready* event of the document fires, the *render* method of the *Wingtip.ChromeControl* object is called. This method sets the options for the *SP.UI.Controls.Navigation* object. Notice the options make it possible for the icon, title, help link, and navigation links to be defined. After they are defined, the *SP.UI.Controls.Navigation* object is instantiated with the options and the identifier of the <div> element where the chrome should be rendered.

When using the chrome control declaratively, you set the options directly in the markup of the target <div> element. The chrome control will automatically render within the target <div> element if it declares the attribute *data-ms-control="SP.UI.Controls.Navigation"*. Listing 4-13 demonstrates the declarative equivalent of Listing 4-12.

LISTING 4-13 Using the chrome control declaratively

```
<div
    id="chrome_ctrl_container"
    data-ms-control="SP.UI.Controls.Navigation"
    data-ms-options=
        '{
        "appIconUrl": "../Images/AppIcon.png",
        "appTitle": "SharePoint 2013 MVC App",
        "appHelpPageUrl": "../Help?" + document.URL.split("?")[1],
        "settingsLinks": [
            {
                "linkUrl": "../Contacts/ReadAll?" + document.URL.split("?")[1],
                "displayName": "Contacts"
            },
            {
                "linkUrl": "../Welcome/Message?" + document.URL.split("?")[1],
                "displayName": "Home"
            }
        ]
        }'>
</div>
```

Calling across domains

Because of the strong emphasis on client-side programming in the SharePoint 2013 app model, developers will often need to cope with restrictions designed to prevent cross-site scripting (XSS). XSS is an attack wherein script is injected into the pages of an otherwise safe site. The injected script can be designed to steal passwords and personal information from the user and send them to a service running in a malicious domain. To prevent XSS attacks, browsers only run scripts and call services that originate from the same domain as the webpage.

The challenge for SharePoint developers is that retrieving data from different sources to create a *mash-up* is a common scenario for apps. Therefore, a mechanism is needed to securely call services in other domains from an app. SharePoint 2013 offers two approaches to solving the problem: the *cross-domain library*, and the *web proxy*. Using the cross-domain library, a remote web can access data in a SharePoint app web from client-side JavaScript. With the web proxy, an app can call services in another domain by using SharePoint to make the call on your behalf.

Using the cross-domain library

The cross-domain library is contained in the JavaScript file *SP.RequestExecutor.js*, which is located in the LAYOUTS directory. You can use the cross-domain library when a remote web needs to access data in an app web, but barriers such as a firewall prevent the normal approach of calling back through CSOM with an OAuth token. The cross-domain library works in concert with several components to make cross-site calls possible. Figure 4-8 shows the complete architecture.

At the heart of the cross-domain call architecture is the *AppWebProxy.aspx* page, which provides the functionality to execute the object model commands requested by the remote web on the target app web. Because the *AppWebProxy.aspx* page is located in the LAYOUTS directory, its location is well known to every remote web. The remote web loads the *SP.RequestExecutor* object and initializes it with the URL of the target app web. At this point, the *SP.RequestExecutor* object creates a hidden IFrame within the remote web and loads the *AppWebProxy.aspx* page from the target app web. The *SP.RequestExecutor* object uses the HTML5 postMessage API to send commands from the remote web to the *AppWebProxy.aspx* page, which in turn executes them against the target app web. Any response passes back across the IFrame to the remote web.

When the cross-domain library is first invoked, the user of the remote web will likely not be signed in to the target app web. In this case, the cross-domain library returns a 401 unauthorized response. The library subsequently redirects the user to the SharePoint logon page. After the user logs on, the cross-domain library attempts the original call again.

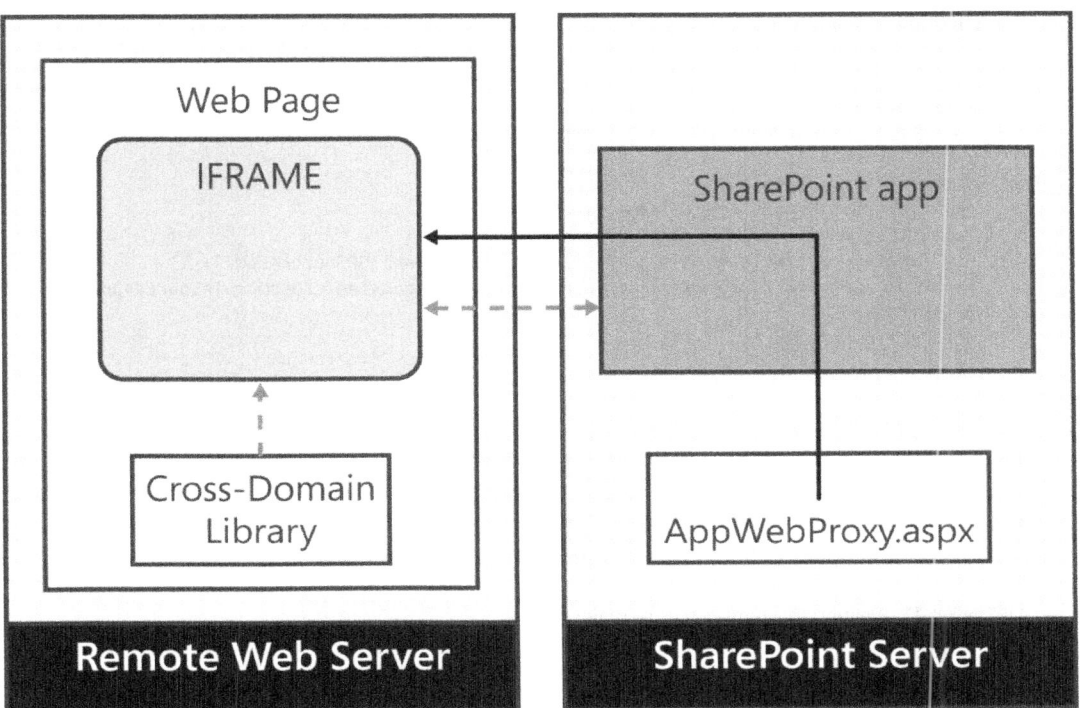

FIGURE 4-8 An overview of the cross-domain call architecture.

For a remote web to access an app web by using the cross-domain library, the target app web must explicitly permit the call. If the app is using the *Internal* principal, the *AllowedRemoteHostUrl* attribute must be set in the app manifest. If you are creating a provider-hosted or autohosted app, the domain you register for OAuth authentication will automatically be trusted for calls to the cross-domain library. The app must also be provided specific permission grants in the app manifest, just as it would for any OAuth calls. Finally, the app web associated with the remote web needs to provide the URL to the target app web as a query string parameter in the <StartPage> element of the manifest.

In many cases, the target app web and the app web associated with the remote web will be the same. This is the scenario in which the remote web wants to call back into the associated app web but is blocked by a firewall. The target app web can be different, however. All that is required is that the target app web allows the remote web to make the call and the app web associated with the remote web requests for the appropriate permission grants. Listing 4-14 shows some typical settings for app webs that might or might not be in the same manifest, depending upon your scenario.

LISTING 4-14 Manifest settings

```
<AppPrincipal>
  <Internal AllowedRemoteHostUrl="http://crossdomain.wingtip.com/" />
</AppPrincipal>
<Properties>
  <Title>Cross Domain App</Title>
  <StartPage>
    ~remoteAppUrl/Welcome/Message?{StandardTokens}&amp;SPSourceAppUrl=
    http://app-4d277429be4d8d.apps.wingtip.com/cloudhosted/CrossDomainSourceApp
  </StartPage>
</Properties>
```

The simplest way to start using the cross-domain library is to add it directly to the remote web project. After that, an instance of the *SP.RequestExecutor* object can be initialized. The URL for the target app web is retrieved from the query string passed to the remote web and used in the initialization process. After it is initialized, RESTful requests can easily be made to the target app web. Listing 4-15 shows a sample that reads list items from a contacts list in the target app web.

LISTING 4-15 Reading list items across domains

```
"use strict";

var Wingtip = window.Wingtip || {};
Wingtip.CrossDomain = function () {

    load = function () {
        var appweburl = getQueryStringParameter("SPSourceAppUrl");
        var executor = new SP.RequestExecutor(appweburl);

        executor.executeAsync(
        {
            url:
            appweburl +
            "/_api/web/lists/getByTitle('Contacts')/items/" +
                        "?$select=Id,FirstName,Title,WorkPhone,Email" +
                        "&$orderby=Title,FirstName",
            method: "GET",
            headers: { "Accept": "application/json;odata=verbose" },
            success: successHandler,
            error: errorHandler
        })
    },
```

```
    successHandler = function (data) {
        //Take action on returned data
    },

    errorHandler = function (data, errorCode, errorMessage) {
        //Handle the error
    },

    getQueryStringParameter = function (paramToRetrieve) {
        //Get querystring value and return it
    }

    return {
        load: load
    }

}()

$(document).ready(function () {
    Wingtip.CrossDomain.load();
});
```

Using the web proxy

The web proxy is a server-side proxy that can make calls to services in other domains and return them to an app. The web proxy differs from the cross-domain library in that it supports calling any endpoint, not just those contained in an app web. The web proxy is ideal for accessing multiple data sources and creating mashed-up displays in your apps.

You access the web proxy via the *SP.WebRequestInfo* object, which is available in the *sp.js* library. To use the web proxy, the *SP.WebRequestInfo* object is instantiated and initialized with a RESTful URI. The proxy is then invoked, which makes an asynchronous RESTful call. The returned XML can then be processed to extract the desired values. Listing 4-16 shows part of a custom library that makes a call to the publically available MusicBrainz API to search for songs based on the name of an artist.

LISTING 4-16 Using the web proxy

```
"use strict";

var Wingtip = window.Wingtip || {};
Wingtip.ResponseDocument;

Wingtip.SongViewModel = function () {
```

```
    var load = function (artist) {

        var ctx = SP.ClientContext.get_current();
        var request = new SP.WebRequestInfo();

        request.set_url(
            "http://www.musicbrainz.org/ws/2/recording?query=artist:" +
                artist
            );
        request.set_method("GET");
        window.Wingtip.ResponseDocument = SP.WebProxy.invoke(ctx, request);

        ctx.executeQueryAsync(onSuccess, onError);

    },

    onSuccess = function () {
        var xmlDoc = $.parseXML(window.Wingtip.ResponseDocument.get_body());
        //Process XML to extract values
    },

    onError = function (err) {
        alert(JSON.stringify(err));
    };

    return {
        load: load,
    };

}();
```

For cross-domain calls to succeed by using the web proxy, the app must explicitly declare that a domain is trusted. This is accomplished by setting the <RemoteEndpoint> element in the app manifest. The following code shows how the element is set for the MusicBrainz sample:

```
<RemoteEndpoints>
    <RemoteEndpoint Url="http://www.musicbrainz.org"/>
</RemoteEndpoints>
```

Going beyond the basics

This book has concentrated on introducing the foundational concepts associated with app development in SharePoint 2013. However, the app development model offers a rich set of capabilities that go beyond performing CRUD operations on a list. This section provides some examples of advanced app capabilities and APIs that will be important in many scenarios. The examples presented here are by no means the extent of what is possible in app development. For more detailed coverage of advanced topics, I recommend reading *Inside Microsoft SharePoint 2013*.

Using remote event receivers

SharePoint apps support event handlers—known as remote event receivers—with which code can be invoked when key events happen in the life of an app. Remote event receivers are similar in concept to the standard event handlers that SharePoint developers already build in SharePoint 2010 except that the receiver is a remote endpoint instead of an assembly. Remote event receivers support events at the web, app, list, and list-item level, which can be both synchronous and asynchronous.

Remote event receivers can be added to an app through either the Add New Item dialog box or the Properties dialog box. If the remote event receiver is to handle anything other than app lifecycle events, it should be added to the app by using the Add New Item dialog. If the remote event receiver is to handle one of the app lifecycle events, it is added by setting one of the event properties for the app, as shown in Figure 4-9.

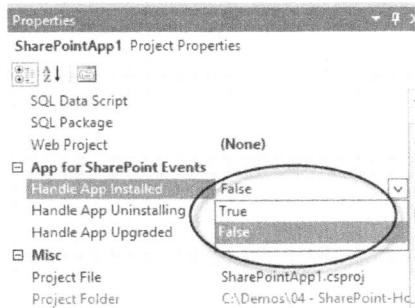

FIGURE 4-9 Adding an app event handler.

If the remote event receiver is added through the Add New Item dialog box, you will be further prompted to select the event scope and event types to handle. After the scope and type are defined, Visual Studio will automatically add a new web project to your app to handle the events. This web project is automatically set as the associated remote web for the app so that it will start during the debugging process.

The selected events are bound to the remote event receiver through an elements file that is nearly identical to the one routinely used in SharePoint 2010 for standard event handlers. The only difference is that the file adds a <Url> element that refers to the endpoint of the remote event receiver. This is the endpoint that is invoked when an event occurs. Listing 4-17 presents a typical elements file handling the *ItemAdding*, *ItemAdded*, and *ItemDeleting* events.

LISTING 4-17 Declaring event handlers

```xml
<?xml version="1.0" encoding="utf-8"?>
<Elements xmlns="http://schemas.microsoft.com/sharepoint/">
  <Receivers ListTemplateId="10000">
    <Receiver>
      <Name>AnnouncementsReceiverItemAdding</Name>
      <Type>ItemAdding</Type>
      <SequenceNumber>10000</SequenceNumber>
      <Url>~remoteAppUrl/AnnouncementsReceiver.svc</Url>
    </Receiver>
    <Receiver>
      <Name>AnnouncementsReceiverItemDeleting</Name>
      <Type>ItemDeleting</Type>
      <SequenceNumber>10000</SequenceNumber>
      <Url>~remoteAppUrl/AnnouncementsReceiver.svc</Url>
    </Receiver>
    <Receiver>
      <Name>AnnouncementsReceiverItemAdded</Name>
      <Type>ItemAdded</Type>
      <SequenceNumber>10000</SequenceNumber>
      <Url>~remoteAppUrl/AnnouncementsReceiver.svc</Url>
    </Receiver>
  </Receivers>
</Elements>
```

Remote event receivers implement the *IRemoteEventService* interface. This interface consists of two methods: *ProcessEvent* and *ProcessOneWayEvent*. You use the *ProcessEvent* method to handle synchronous events, and the *ProcessOneWayEvent* method to handle asynchronous events. The new web project comes with template code that implements the *IRemoteEventService* interface and uses the *TokenHelper* class to retrieve a CSOM *ClientContext* for calling back into SharePoint. Listing 4-18 shows the implementation code for handling the events defined in Listing 4-17.

LISTING 4-18 Event handling code

```csharp
public class AnnouncementsReceiver : IRemoteEventService
{
    public SPRemoteEventResult ProcessEvent(RemoteEventProperties properties)
    {
        SPRemoteEventResult result = new SPRemoteEventResult();
        switch (properties.EventType)
        {
            case RemoteEventType.ItemAdding:
                result.ChangedItemProperties = new Dictionary<String, object>();
                result.ChangedItemProperties.Add("Body", "New Text");
                break;
```

```
            case RemoteEventType.ItemDeleting:
                result.ErrorMessage = "Items cannot be deleted from this list";
                result.Status = SPRemoteEventServiceStatus.CancelWithError;
                break;
        }
        return result;
    }
    public void ProcessOneWayEvent(RemoteEventProperties properties)
    {
        HttpRequestMessageProperty requestproperty =
        (HttpRequestMessageProperty)OperationContext.Current.
        IncomingMessageProperties[HttpRequestMessageProperty.Name];
        string contexttokenstring = requestproperty.Headers["x-sp-accesstoken"];
        if (contexttokenstring != null)
        {
            SharePointContextToken contexttoken =
            TokenHelper.ReadAndValidateContextToken(
            contexttokenstring, requestproper-ty.Headers[
              HttpRequestHeader.Host]);
            Uri sharepointurl = new Uri(properties.ItemEventProperties.WebUrl);
            string accesstoken = TokenHelper.GetAccessToken(
            contexttoken, sharepointurl.Authority).AccessToken;
            using (ClientContext clientcontext =
            TokenHelper.GetClientContextWithAccessToken(
            sharepointurl.ToString(), accesstoken))
            {
                if (properties.EventType == RemoteEventType.ItemAdded)
                {
                    List list =
                    clientcontext.Web.Lists.GetByTitle(
                    properties.ItemEventProperties.ListTitle);
                    clientcontext.Load(list);
                    ListItem item =

                    list.GetItemById(properties.ItemEventProperties.ListItemId);
                    clientcontext.Load(item);
                    clientcontext.ExecuteQuery();
                    item["Body"] += "New Text";
                    item.Update();
                    clientcontext.ExecuteQuery();
                }
            }
        }
    }
}
```

Using the search REST API

SharePoint 2013 provides a RESTful endpoint that you can use to retrieve search results and query suggestions. When coupled with the REST app patterns presented throughout the book, you can easily create sophisticated search-based apps. Table 4-1 describes the available search endpoints.

TABLE 4-1 Search REST endpoints

Endpoint	Description
http://[host]/[site]/_api/search/query	Runs search queries by using HTTP *GET*
http://[host]/[site]/_api/search/postquery	Runs search queries by using HTTP *POST* to overcome URL length limitations
http://[host]/[site]/_api/search/suggest	Retrieves query suggestions by using HTTP *GET*

To use the search REST API, an app must make a permission request, and that request must be granted during app installation. The required permission request is formatted similarly to any other permission request and is available in Visual Studio by using the designer associated with the app manifest. The following code shows the underlying XML that forms the requested permission:

```
<AppPermissionRequests>
  <AppPermissionRequest Scope="http://sharepoint/search"
    Right="QueryAsUserIgnoreAppPrincipal" />
</AppPermissionRequests>
```

The simplest way to run a query against the REST API is to pass a keyword query. You do this by setting the value of the *querytext* parameter in the RESTful URI. You can use this approach for either the *query* or *suggest* endpoints. The *querytext* can be any legal keyword query language (KQL) construction, including managed properties and operators. The following code shows two examples of returning search results with keyword queries:

```
http://wingtip.com/_api/search/query?querytext='SharePoint'
http://wingtip.com/_api/search/query?querytext='Title:SharePoint'
```

The real power of the REST API lies in all of the available query parameters that can be used. These parameters reflect many of the properties historically available through the *KeywordQuery* class. By using these parameters, you can control the columns returns, sorting, paging, and relevance model to name just a few. Table 4-2 lists some of the key query parameters. For a complete list, readers should refer to the SharePoint 2013 SDK.

TABLE 4-2 Query parameters

Parameter	Description	Sample
selectproperties	Specifies the managed properties to return	http://wingtip.com/_api/search/query?querytext='SharePoint' &selectproperties='Title,Path'
sortlist	Specifies the managed properties by which to sort the results	http://wingtip.com/_api/search/query?querytext='SharePoint' &sortlist='Title:ascending'
startrow	Zero-based index of first result to return	http://wingtip.com/_api/search/query?querytext='SharePoint' &startrow=10
rowsperpage	Specifies the number of results per page	http://wingtip.com/_api/search/query?querytext='SharePoint' &startrow=10&rowsperpage=10
rowlimit	Specifies the maximum number of records to return	http://wingtip.com/_api/search/query?querytext='SharePoint' &rowlimit=100
sourceid	Specifies the ID of the result source against which the query should run	http://wingtip.com/_api/search/query?querytext= 'LastName:B*' &sourceid='B09A7990-05EA-4AF9-81EF-EDFAB16C4E31'

Because access to the search engine is available through the REST API, building search-based apps is just a simple matter of creating a library that forms the appropriate URI and parses out the results. Once the results are returned, you can use the MVVM pattern described earlier to render the results. Figure 4-10 shows an app that creates an employee directory by using an A–Z toolbar that runs queries against the people result source. Listing 4-19 shows partial code from the app that creates the RESTful URI.

FIGURE 4-10 You can create Apps that utilize search functionality to find people, documents, and list items.

LISTING 4-19 People search

```
load = function (query) {
    $.ajax(
            {
                url: _spPageContextInfo.webAbsoluteUrl
                    + "/_api/search/query?querytext='LastName:"
                    + query
                    + "*'&selectproperties='LastName,FirstName,JobTitle,
                                            WorkEmail,WorkPhone'"
                    + "&sourceid='B09A7990-05EA-4AF9-81EF-EDFAB16C4E31'"
                    + "&sortlist='LastName:ascending'",
                method: "GET",
                headers: {
                    "accept": "application/xml",
                },
                success: onSuccess,
                error: onError
            }
        );
}
```

Using app-level External Content Types

External Content Types (ECT) are used in Business Connectivity Services (BCS) for connecting Share-Point with external data sources such as databases and web services. In SharePoint 2010, ECTs were defined at the farm level and installed in the Business Data Connectivity service application. Once installed in the service application, ECTs could be used as the basis for defining an External List. External Lists look a lot like standard SharePoint lists; however, External Lists are backed by an external data source. This section assumes that you are familiar with the general concepts surrounding ECTs and have built an External List in SharePoint 2010.

SharePoint 2013 introduces a new type of ECT that you can define against an Open Data Protocol (OData) source and contained within an app. Defining an ECT within an app is powerful because it allows for the creation of External Lists within an app that are not dependent on access to the Business Data Connectivity service application in the SharePoint farm. This means that you can contain ECTs within apps, install them with an associated app, and remove them when the app is removed. Figure 4-11 shows the high-level architecture supporting app-level ECTs.

FIGURE 4-11 App-level External Content Types are made possible through the use of the *FileBackedMetadataCatalog* and a custom BDC Metadata model.

An app can only contain a single BDC Metadata Model file defining ECTs. The model itself can contain many ECT definitions, but the app can only support one model. Microsoft Visual Studio 2012 makes it easy to add app-level ECTs that are based on OData endpoints by providing a simple dialog box that requests the data source endpoint. In the Visual Studio Solution Explorer, right-click the app project, and then in the settings menu that opens, click Add, and then click Content Types for an External Data Source. Visual Studio starts the SharePoint Customization Wizard which prompts you for the OData service URL. Figure 4-12 shows the wizard with the publically available Northwind source specified.

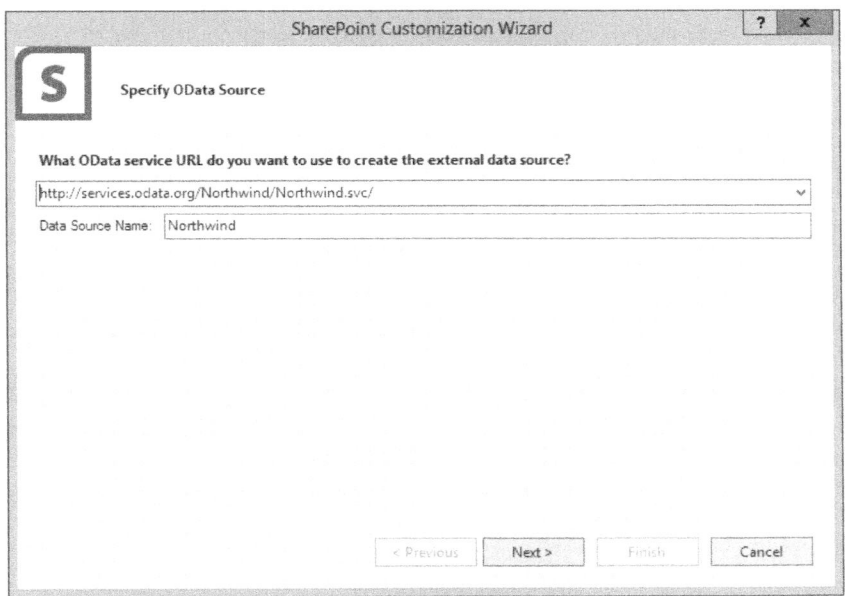

FIGURE 4-12 Visual Studio 2012 provides a wizard for connecting to OData sources.

On the next wizard page, you are prompted to select the entities to expose. Visual Studio creates a model that includes ECTs defined for each entity you select. You can also elect to have Visual Studio create an External List based on the entities. Figure 4-13 shows the options.

When the wizard completes, Visual Studio creates the BDC Metadata Model and the External List definition. You can view and edit both the model and the list definition as necessary in the app project. When the app is deployed, the associated BDC Metadata Model is stored in a document library within the app. At that time, an instance of the *FileBackedMetadataCatalog* class is spun up and the model is loaded into it. The *FileBackedMetadataCatalog* class is part of the BCS API, and it acts as an in-memory catalog for ECTs. This is like having a Business Data Connectivity service application dedicated to the app, which is then used to generate the External List instance.

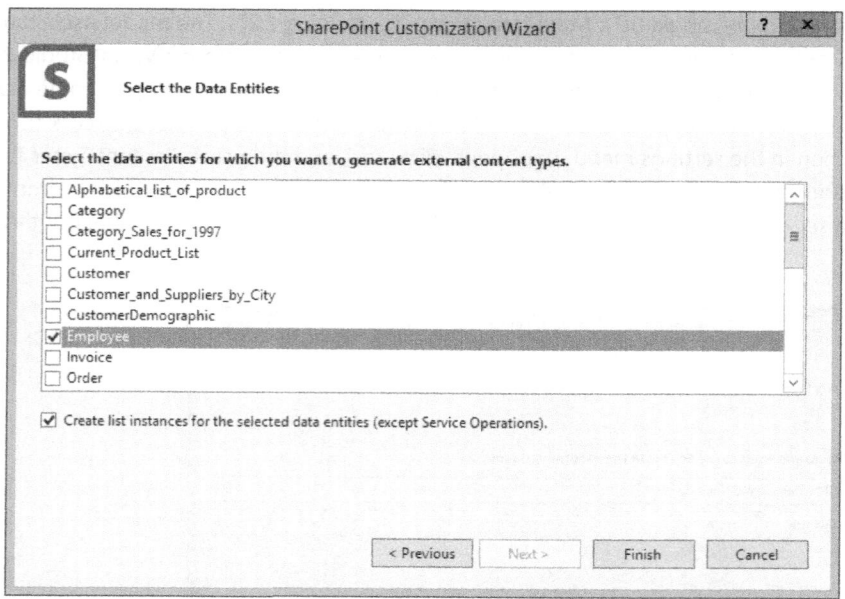

FIGURE 4-13 Visual Studio 2012 provides a wizard for easily creating external Content Types from OData sources.

Although Visual Studio automatically creates the BDC Metadata Model and External List instance, it does not provide any mechanism for displaying the External List. To display the data, you can either use the REST API to access the list or you can define an XSLT list view web part inside the <Module> element that deploys the *Default.aspx* page. Both of these techniques work for standard lists and External Lists.

Using the social feed

SharePoint 2013 offers some nice improvements in the social networking arena, and chief among them is the *social feed*. The social feed contains all of the activity around a user in the form of a list. These activities can be either user-generated posts or system-generated events such as notification of a change in your profile. Figure 4-14 shows a view of the social feed on a user's public page.

Reading and writing to the social feed is a capability that makes it possible for your apps to participate in the community within an organization. SharePoint 2013 makes this possible by providing CSOM and REST interfaces to the social feed. These interfaces make it possible to interact with user profile properties, posts, and replies. Figure 4-15 shows a sample MVC4 app displaying a user post from the social feed.

FIGURE 4-14 The Social capabilities of SharePoint are centered on the newsfeed.

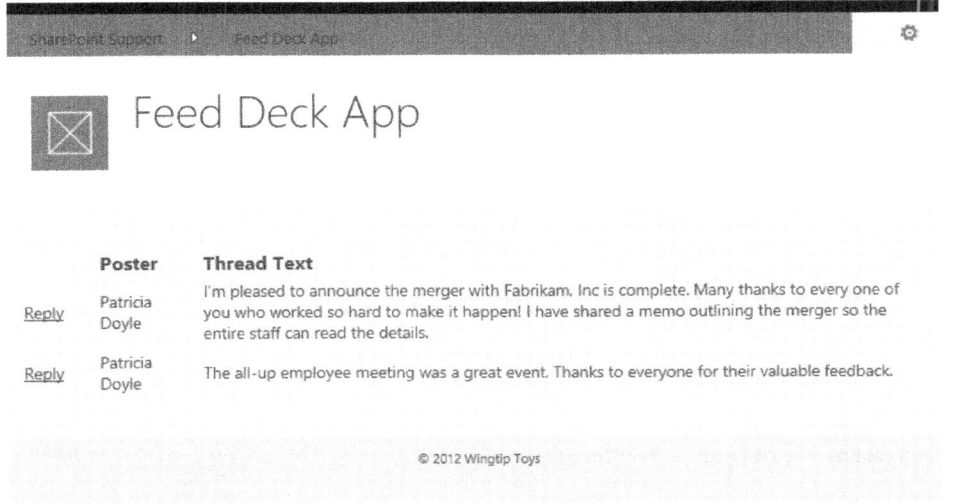

FIGURE 4-15 Using the Social API, you can utilize feed data and profile information in apps.

To get started by using C# and CSOM against the social feed, you need to set a reference to the *Microsoft.SharePoint.Client.UserProfiles.dll* assembly, which is located in the ISAPI folder. This assembly gives you access to the *SocialFeedManager* and the *PeopleManager* classes with which you can read and write to the social feed and user profiles, respectively. Listing 4-20 presents a method from the MVC4 app that reads the social feed for a given user account.

LISTING 4-20 Reading the social feed

```
public ActionResult ShowThreads(string SPHostUrl, string Account)
{
    using (ClientContext ctx = new ClientContext(SPHostUrl))
    {

        //Get display name from the user's profile
        PeopleManager peopleManager = new PeopleManager(ctx);
        PersonProperties personProps = peopleManager.GetPropertiesFor(Account);
        ctx.Load(personProps, o => o.DisplayName, o => o.AccountName);
        ctx.ExecuteQuery();

        // Get feed for the person
        SocialFeedManager socialFeedManager = new SocialFeedManager(ctx);
        ctx.Load(socialFeedManager);

        SocialFeedOptions feedOptions = new SocialFeedOptions();
        ClientResult<SocialFeed> feed =
            socialFeedManager.GetFeed(SocialFeedType.Everyone, feedOptions);
                ctx.ExecuteQuery();

        //Collect all the posts
        List<FeedThread> feedThreads = new List<FeedThread>();

        for (int i = 0; i < feed.Value.Threads.Length; i++)
        {
            SocialThread thread = feed.Value.Threads[i];
            FeedThread feedThread = new FeedThread();
            feedThread.Id = i;
            feedThread.Poster = personProps.DisplayName;
            feedThread.ThreadId = thread.Id;
            feedThread.ThreadText = thread.RootPost.Text;
            feedThreads.Add(feedThread);
        }
        //Send posts to view
        ViewBag.FeedThreads = feedThreads;
    }
    return View();
}
```

The code in Listing 4-17 receives the target account as a query string parameter. The *People Manager* is then used to look up the display name for the account in the user's profile. After that, the *SocialFeedManager* is used to look up the user's posts for display. The *SocialFeedType* is set to

Everyone to retrieve the posts, but can be set to any of the following values to produce different views of the social feed: *Personal, News, Timeline, Likes,* or *Everyone.*

Each displayed post in the app has an associated thread identifier, which is the unique ID used to reference the thread in the social feed. Using the thread identifier, the app can allow users to reply to any of the presented threads. Listing 4-21 shows the code from the MVC4 app that posts a reply.

LISTING 4-21 Replying to a post

```
public ActionResult Reply(string SPHostUrl, string ThreadId, string ReplyText)
    {
        using (ClientContext ctx = new ClientContext(SPHostUrl))
        {
            SocialFeedManager socialFeedManager = new SocialFeedManager(ctx);
            ctx.Load(socialFeedManager);

            SocialPostCreationData postCreationData =
                new SocialPostCreationData();
            postCreationData.ContentText = ReplyText;
            socialFeedManager.CreatePost(ThreadId, postCreationData);
            ctx.ExecuteQuery();
        }

        return View();
    }
```

Conclusion

The SharePoint 2013 app model requires developers to adopt new patterns for app development. If the app is primarily developed by using JavaScript and REST, an MVVM pattern is recommended; if it is primarily developed by using C# and CSOM, an MVC pattern is recommended. Within these new app patterns, SharePoint developers can take advantage of advanced capabilities and features such as cross-domain call support and API support for major SharePoint workloads, including search, Business Connectivity Services, and social networking.

Index

Symbols

$Deferred method, 144
$expand operator, in RESTful operations, 80
$ symbol, jQuery selector syntax using, 55
$top, in RESTful operations, 81
&amp, combining parameters together using, 27
(hash) sign, jQuery selector syntax using, 55

A

access tokens, 116, 122–125, 135
access tokens, Windows Azure ACS creating, 112
ACS, Windows Azure
   about, 112
   creating access tokens, 122
   creating context tokens, 116–118
   keeping configuration data for app principals in
      sync, 113
   OAuth authentication and, 102, 121, 122
Active Directory accounts, 96
Active Server Pages (ASPX), 146–148
Add() function, 48
Add New Item command, 22
administrator permissions, installing apps requiring, 37
ajax method, jQuery, 82–83, 139
&amp, combining parameters together using, 27
anonymous functions, 48–49
<App> element, 41–42
app catalog site
   publishing apps to, 35
   using Create App Catalog page to configure user
      access permissions to, 36
app code isolation, understanding, 8–9
app designs, table of, 45

app distribution, for adding pages and lists to app web
      during installation, 29
app event handlers, 161–162
   debugging, 43
   declaring, 161
app events, architecture of, 41–43
app host domain, 114
app hosting models. *See also* autohosted apps;
      See also provider-hosted apps; *See*
      also SharePoint-hosted apps
   creating app web in, 30
   Publish command with, 10–14
   understanding, 10–14
   using app events in, 41
   using client web part in implementing app part,
      22–23
app installation scopes, understanding, 7
App Installation Service, locating timer job definition
      named, 39
AppInstalled event, 42
app launcher, 38
app launcher, about, 8
app-level external content types, 166–168
app lifecycle events, trapping, 41–44
App Management Service
   creating instance of, 6
   in SharePoint farm supporting apps, 5–6
app manifest
   about, 14–17
   changing metadata in, 40
   configuring to support internal app
      authentication, 100
   editing in Visual Studio 2012, 16–17
   permissions requests inside, 108
   Permissions tab of designer, 110
   requirements when developing apps for use in
      Office 365 as, 118–119

B

backward compatibility, support for creating classic-mode web application using, 97
BDC Metadata Model file, defining ECTs, 167
binding events, 57
bindings, declarative, 139–140
building MVVM apps, 137–146
Business Connectivity Services (BCS), 166
button on ribbon, defining, 25

C

CAB files, for adding pages and lists to app web during installation, 29
CAML (Collaborative Application Markup Language) queries, 66–67, 75
Cascading Style Sheets (CSS), selector syntax and, 56
CDN (Content Delivery Network), 55
Central Administration
    creating app catalog site in, 35
    creating instance of App Management Service using, 6
    locating timer job definition at, 39
.cer file, creating, 131–132
chrome control, 153–156
classic-mode web applications, support for creating, 97
class structure, for encapsulating CRUD operations against REST API, 88–89
client app, 113
ClientContext class, 60, 162
ClientContextRuntime class, 60–61
client ID, 102, 114
ClientId attribute, 118–119
ClientId entries, 148, 150
ClientRequestException error, 62
client secret (app secret), 114
ClientSecret entries, 148, 150
client-side code, running on browser, 8–9
Client-Side Object Model (CSOM)
    about, 45, 58–59
    app authentication using, 98, 99–100, 103–104
    architecture, 59
    challenges of web forms pattern, 146–148
    contexts, 59–60
    developing apps using MVC4 framework, 148–152

JavaScript
    about, 69–71
    CRUD operations using, 73–77
    returning collections, 70–71, 71–73
managed
    about, 61
    creating lists using, 65–66
    handling errors, 62–65
    returning collections of items, 61–62
    returning list items, 66–67
    update operations, 67
    working with document, 67–68
RESTful endpoints in APIs through, 78
retrieving ClientContext, 162
using against social feed, 168–170
Client.svc endpoint, 69, 70, 78
Client.svc service, 59, 61
ClientWebPart elements, 22
client web part, implementing app part using, 22
client web parts
    about, 22–23
    adding to SharePoint app project new, 22
    vs. app parts, 22
    vs. standard web parts, 22–23
closures, 49
cloud-based model, ix
cloud-hosted apps
    app principal for, 113
    app start page linking back to host web in, 21
    creating app web in, 30
    programming TokenHelper class, 119–122
    requirements when developing apps for use in Office 365 as, 118–119
    upgrading, 40
    using internal authentication, 100–101
    vs. SharePoint-hosted apps, 8–9
    web forms and, 148
cloud-hosted service Windows Azure ACS as, 112
Collaborative Application Markup Language (CAML) queries, 66–67, 75
collections of items, returning, 61–62
contact data library, 140
contacts ViewModel, 141–142
<Content> element, XML within, 22
Content Delivery Network (CDN), 55
content owners, 113
content server, 113
contexts, 59–60
context tokens, 116–118, 121–122

Office 365
app catalog site in, 35
app principal for cloud-hosted apps in, 113
app web hosting domain, 20
creating app service applications using, 6
installing and configuring apps within tenancy of, 7, 38
market for, ix
SharePoint app model working within, 5
supporting autohosted apps, 13
supporting OAuth authentication in, 102
tenancy, 112, 114–115, 117, 120
understanding flow of app authentication in, 116–118
Windows Azure ACS and, 112
Office Store, publishing apps to, 34–35
onGetUserNameFail function, 70
onGetUserNameSuccess function, 70
on-premises farms
autohosted apps and, 13
configuring OAuth support for, 112
creating app catalog site in, 36–37
creating app service applications for, 6
default tenancy in, 5
installing and configuring apps using tenancy scope, 7
Office 365 working within, 5
supporting external authentication, 102
upgrading to newer versions of SharePoint, 2
using S2S authorization by establishing trust with provider-hosted apps, 102
Open Data Protocol (OData), 77
defining ECT against, 166–168
query operators, 80–81
$order operator, in RESTful operations, 80

P

packaging apps, 29–34
Page_Load event, 87–88
paging items, in RESTful operations, 81
PATCH method, 91–92
PATCH operations, 86
PeopleManager class, 170–171
permission grants, 157
permission requests, 107
permissions
acquiring on fly using authorization code, 126–128

managing app, 104–111
permission types, 110
postMessage API, 156
POST operations, 89–90
PowerShell
creating app catalog site in, 35
creating instance of Site Subscriptions Settings Service using, 6
PowerShell script
creating x.509 certificates with public/private key pair, 131–132
registering trusted security-token issuer, 132
ProcessEvent method, 43–44, 162
ProcessOneWayEvent method, 42, 162
promise pattern, 143–146
<Properties> element, 41–42
PropertyOrFieldNotInitializedException error, 62
prototype pattern, 53–54
prototypes, 50
provider-hosted apps. *See also* app hosting models
about, 10
creating app web in, 30
debugging, 17
installed in SharePoint tenancy, 10–11
installing, 11
ongoing maintenance of, 11
Publish command with, 18
setting start page URL for, 17
using chrome control, 153
using S2S authorization by establishing trust with on-premises farms, 102
using S2S trusts for developing, 134–135
provider-hosted apps, using app events in, 41
public/private key pair
creating x.509 certificates with, 131–132
S2S trusts based on, 129
Publish command, with autohosted apps, 18
publishing apps
about, 34
displaying, 37
to app catalog site, 35
to Office Store, 34–35
PUT operations, 86

Q

query parameters, for REST API, 164
querystring parameter, 170
querytext parameter, 164

About the Authors

 **SCOT HILLIER** is an independent consultant and Microsoft SharePoint Most Valuable Professional, focused on creating solutions for Information Workers with SharePoint, Microsoft Office, and related Microsoft .NET technologies. He is the author/coauthor of 15 books and DVDs on Microsoft technologies, including *Inside Microsoft SharePoint 2010*. Scot splits his time between consulting on SharePoint projects, speaking at SharePoint events such as Tech Ed, and delivering training for SharePoint Developers. Scot is a former United States Navy submarine officer and graduate of the Virginia Military Institute. He can be reached at *scot@shillier.com*.

 **TED PATTISON** is an author, instructor and owner of Critical Path Training (*www.CriticalPathTraining.com*), a company dedicated to education on SharePoint technologies. Ted has worked with Microsoft's Developer Platform Evangelism group and the SharePoint Product team to research and author SharePoint developer training material early in the alpha phase of the product lifecycle for SharePoint 2007, SharePoint 2010, and SharePoint 2013. He is also the coauthor of *Inside Microsoft SharePoint 2010*.

What do you think of this book?

We want to hear from you!

To participate in a brief online survey, please visit:

microsoft.com/learning/booksurvey

Tell us how well this book meets your needs—what works effectively, and what we can do better. Your feedback will help us continually improve our books and learning resources for you.

Thank you in advance for your input!

Critical Path Training is your fastest way up the SharePoint 2010 learning curve.

Listen to what our customers have to say:

"

[The Great SharePoint Adventure] was the best course I've ever taken. Ted [Pattison] did an excellent job of presenting the information, and the demos were extremely useful.

John, British Columbia

Andrew [Connell] is a rock star. Easily the best instructor I've had for a technical training class. He knows SharePoint, keeps it entertaining, and doesn't forget how it's done in the real world. Top notch.

Tim, Michigan

Maurice Prather is the best Microsoft trainer I have ever had at any conference, seminar, or paid training.

Tim, Dallas

Asif [Rehmani] is a wonderful instructor. He paced the class well and used lots of real world examples to apply the materials. I also appreciated him suggesting outside vendors for sharepoint products; it's nice to hear from the people who really know these vendors!

Heidi, Florida

Matt McDermott was as entertaining as he was educational. Phenomenal instructor. Timing of the course was perfect and was a good pace all week. Plenty of time for labs. I would recommend this course to all SharePoint IT Professionals.

Daniel, Florida "

Get training directly from the instructors who wrote this book. Critical Path Training offers hands-on training, online training, private onsite classes and courseware licensing.

| Ted Pattison | Andrew Connell | Scot Hillier | Maurice Prather | Asif Rehmani | Matt McDermott | David Mann | John Holliday |

www.CriticalPathTraining.com

@criticalpath

Lightning Source UK Ltd.
Milton Keynes UK
UKOW06f0541050913

216524UK00006B/29/P

9 780735 674981